Feeding Your Baby the Healthiest Foods

FROM BREAST MILK TO TABLE FOODS

Louise Lambert-Lagacé

Fitzhenry & Whiteside

Fitzhenry & Whiteside Limited
195 Allstate Parkway
Markham, Ontario   L3R 4T8

www.fitzhenry.ca   godwit@fitzhenry.ca

Fitzhenry & Whiteside acknowledges with thanks the Canada Council for the Arts, the
Government of Canada through its Book Publishing Industry Development Program,
and the Ontario Arts Council for their support of our publishing program.

National Library of Canada Cataloguing in Publication

Lambert-Lagacé, Louise, 1941-
Feeding your baby the healthiest foods : from breast milk to table
foods / Louise Lambert-Lagacé. — 2nd ed.

Includes bibliographical references and index.
ISBN 1-55005-109-1

1. Infants—Nutrition. I. Title.

RJ216.L353 2004   649'.3   C2003-906808-0

Some of the material in this book first appeared in the author's Feeding Your Baby
in the Nineties published by Stoddart Publishing Co. Limited in 1992.
The advice provided in this book is based on the author's research and experience
as a registered nutritionist. Readers are advised to consult a medical doctor
about their individual concerns.

This book contains references to certain names that are registered trademarks (™).
These names are listed on page 294.

Cover design : Kinetics Design & Illustration
Text design : Tannice Goddard

06 05 04 03   3 4 5 6
Printed and bound in Canada

To Pascale and Janique,
two wonderful mothers who have shared
with me their questions and concerns.

Contents

Introduction

 $\mathcal{F}$ eeding your baby the healthiest foods is an art based on choosing tasty, enticing foods and understanding something about nutrition. It is a daily exercise in imagination, respect, and understanding. Imagination is needed to think up new food ideas; respect and understanding are needed when your baby shows likes and dislikes that may not correspond with your menu plans. Feeding your baby enhances your baby's growth and development while giving you a sense of pride and joy.

I first practised this art with my three daughters and have since perfected it through more than 30 years of work as a consulting dietitian. When I wrote the first edition of *Feeding Your Baby* back in 1974, my three daughters were at school and I was beginning my career as a dietitian. I was also a broadcaster then and received questions on infant nutrition every single week. My producer encouraged me to write a book on the topic, but I had limited experience and little scientific data to back my content. I nonetheless accepted the challenge and realized the topic was quite important, after selling 100,000 copies of the book in the first six years.

Since then, *Feeding Your Baby* has been revised four times. I am now enjoying grandmotherhood and am interested more than ever in child nutrition. I have revisited every section of the book with my daughters and many parents who have consulted me on infant nutrition issues at my nutrition clinic in Montreal. Scientific research in this area has been abundant during the past 20 years; new information on breast milk, solid food, colic, and food allergies is emerging from many and various sources. Food products for babies change every season, it seems, and your questions have changed greatly over the years.

One thing has not altered, however, and that is your concern for your baby. My objective — to help you out with the best information available — has also remained the same. To do this, I have surveyed parents, nurses, and doctors in the field. My research assistants have visited food shops and drugstores and taken note of the latest foods, supplements, and formulas available.

As a result, this book is different from the previous editions. It presents the same approach concerning the importance of breast milk and the slow introduction of solids, but it provides much more information on several aspects of breastfeeding, including the weaning process and the return to work. It introduces many examples of true-life situations (boxed stories), which serve as comforting examples of how challenges can be met.

You will also find a postnatal menu, which you can use whether you breastfeed or not, with tips on how best to nourish yourself after childbirth; suggestions for vitamin supplements (which one to give and when); recommendations for preventing or curing colic, constipation, diarrhea, or even food allergies; and a whole new chapter on infant cereals, telling you which one to offer, depending on what type of milk you give your baby. There is also up-to-date information on what is happening to commercial baby foods and tips on how to prepare your own food purees — with easy instructions and many new recipes. You will even learn how to cope with a fussy 15-month-old and his new eating behaviour and learn that it has nothing to do with the way you fed your baby during the first 12 months.

Always remember that the art of feeding your baby the healthiest foods is a daily exercise to practice a day at a time. The process will improve with time and with your baby's enjoyment of good food. It will help your baby build good eating habits for many years to come.

Every answer or recommendation provided in this book is considered a general guideline that applies to a majority of babies. But never forget that there are always exceptions to general rules and that your baby may be an exception, on occasions.

If your baby is not responding in the way you expect, you may need to experiment with new ideas or consult a nutritionist. If your baby has strong negative or allergic reactions, you may also need to consult a nutritionist or a physician.

Feeding your baby the healthiest foods and seeing your baby develop good eating habits can bring you a sense of great joy and satisfaction. I hope the suggestions in this book will help you and your baby gain much enjoyment from this challenging but rewarding time.

Louise Lambert-Lagacé

ONE

Good Nutrition Means Healthier Babies

"Anyone who has observed infants for any period of time can testify to the intense activity occurring in and around their mouths — the primary site for learning in the first few months of life."
— JULIE MENNELLA, 1998

Good nutrition is the result of a careful feeding program based on top-quality foods given in adequate quantities to ensure maximum development and growth — according to your infant's own genetic potential. It entails many hours of tender loving care. It respects the infant's nutritional needs, appetite, digestive capacities, likes, and dislikes. It nurtures a positive attitude toward eating. It uses a very basic tool: the best food available!

This is surely the ideal program for every parent and a logical first step toward lifelong healthy eating. But perfect guidelines written in books are not always possible to follow in real-life situations. I believe in compromise and do not consider an alternative solution as a failure. After all, parents try their best to be perfect, but nobody's perfect all the time.

The keys to good nutrition in the first years of life are numerous and varied. Some may affect your own way of eating, some provide short-term solutions to specific problems, but most are long-term eating strategies. None of the basic principles is really difficult to apply, and all work toward a healthier baby.

The basic nutrition guidelines presented in this book are in line with the most recent position of the Canadian Paediatric Society, Dietitians of Canada, and Health Canada. They also take into account current worldwide research on infant nutrition.

Good Nutrition Makes Common Sense

Feeding your baby the best food available at the right time does not mean you have to follow complicated scientific procedures. Classic studies done by Dr. Clara M. Davis in the late twenties and early thirties confirmed that newly weaned infants could rightly choose their own foods in the quantities they desired from a fairly wide range of natural foods — unmixed, unaltered, and unseasoned. One of the experiments lasted six to twelve months and involved three hospital ized infants who did very well when offered only "foods that supplied in abundance all the nutritional elements known to be required for good health and sound growth." These included "high-quality proteins, fresh fruit and vegetables, eggs, milk, and whole-grain cereals." Such an experiment could not be replicated in a home setting because very few parents would agree to offer a daily selection of 33 different foods! But the message remains loud and clear: Feed your baby the best food in its most natural state, respect his or her appetite at all times, and optimum growth and development will follow.

Good Nutrition Makes Quite a Difference

When choosing breast milk as your baby's first food, you are not only providing exceptional nutrients and useful antibodies — you may also be enhancing the cognitive development of your child, says Dr. James Anderson from the University of Kentucky, who has done a meta-analysis of 20 studies on the topic. Breast milk also has the capacity to reduce infections and allergic reactions during the first years of life. Good nutrition implies slow introduction of solid foods, which allows your infant to swallow more efficiently and digest more easily. The slow introduction of whole cow's milk can also decrease the risk of dehydration and anaemia.

Good Nutrition Does Not Mean Dieting

There are more obese children today than 20 years ago, but in 90 percent of all cases, a heavy baby at birth does not become a fat baby at 12 months, and a fat one-year-old does not necessarily become an obese adult. However, in families where the father or mother or both have severe weight problems it is advisable to monitor the rate of weight gain quite closely between 12 months and school age and to make proper adjustments when weight gain is excessive during pre-school years.

Research on rapidly multiplying fat cells has been done mainly on animals. Very few experiments have been carried out on humans. What we do know is that there are several periods of intense fat-cell multiplication during childhood and adolescence and that this multi-plication is greatest during the first 12 months. We also know that susceptible infants can become overweight while eating no more calories than normal-weight infants. The problem is not a simple one, but irreversible obesity at one year is a myth, whereas normal weight at the end of adolescence is a sure route to maintaining normal weight in the long term.

Before 12 months of age, there are no scientific reasons to limit the food intake of a fat baby. Possible side effects of such restriction include nutritional deficiencies, reduced spontaneous physical activity, lowered body temperature, and reduced resistance to infections. There is even a danger in offering skim milk during the first year of life. The best way to control overweight during that period is to avoid forcing a child to eat and to encourage regular, physical, fun activities. This practice also translates into more parent-child interaction, which is very desirable. Other mild measures to prevent overweight can be taken during the second year of life, although these will usually affect the living and eating habits of the whole household.

Good Nutrition Prevents Iron Deficiency Anaemia

Too many infants still suffer from iron deficiency during the first two years of life. Anaemia is no small problem; it not only affects your baby's appetite and level of energy but can also decrease resistance to infection and, in severe cases, lead to cognitive deficits that are not always reversible. Breastfeeding for at least six months, supplementing with iron when needed, or offering an iron-fortified formula at birth are the best preventive measures to avoid such a serious deficiency.

Good Nutrition Prevents or Cures Gastrointestinal Problems

When constipation becomes a problem once solid foods are introduced, offering more fluids between feedings and adding a small amount of insoluble fibre can help produce softer stools. When severe diarrhea occurs, proper refeeding can prevent dehydration and hasten recovery.

Good Nutrition Prevents Dental Problems

By avoiding the use of a pacifier covered with honey or another sweet substance and by not giving a bottle of juice, milk, or sugared water at bedtime, the tragic problem of rampant caries is less likely to occur. (*Rampant caries* refers to the "destruction" of the front teeth as a result of long, lasting contact of the teeth with sugary substances.)

By rationing, if not avoiding, the consumption of sweets, particularly between meals, and by showing your child at an early age how to brush her teeth regularly, dental caries will be greatly reduced.

Good Nutrition Is Also a Question of Love

M.F.K. Fisher, one of the greatest food writers of our times, was asked why she wrote about food and eating and drinking. She replied: "It seems to me that our three basic needs for food, security and love are so mixed and mingled and entwined that we cannot think of one without the others. So it happens that when I write of hunger, I am really writing about love and the hunger for it, and warmth and the love of it, and the hunger for it, and then the warmth and richness and fine reality of hunger satisfied . . . all in one."

Feeding your baby the healthiest foods is your way of loving and caring and responding to your baby's basic needs.

Good Nutrition during Infancy Is a Step in the Right Direction

This list of benefits is by no means exhaustive. But, sorry to say, you cannot count on good nutrition during the first 12 months to provide lifelong protection from major diseases. Sound eating practices make a difference during the first years of life but need to be maintained for many years to ensure long-term health benefits.

Good nutrition is not only an effective tool to prevent disease. It is also a health investment strategy for tapping into the top-quality energy found in good-tasting and healthy foods.

Good nutrition is a must for a healthy infancy.

TWO

Sharing Food, Sharing Values

Good nutrition is the result of a careful feeding program based on top-quality foods given in adequate quantities to ensure maximum development and growth — according to your infant's own genetic potential. Such a feeding program becomes the cornerstone on which to build your child's long-lasting eating habits. Good nutrition is so closely connected to healthful foods that children need to be raised in the spirit of this connection.

Good eating habits are not developed in the classroom or in the gymnasium. They go back to our first eating experiences and become implanted in our memory for the rest of our lives. Remember for one moment the flavours you really enjoy, the meals you dream of, the foods you always want to avoid, the foods you detest. Can you really separate these eating habits from your early years?

Children Learn about Food in Many Different Ways

Children learn to enjoy food around the kitchen table, in a family setting, in a particular environment. They associate foods with certain rituals, with special celebrations, with happy moments. They will easily adopt foods their parents consider healthy if they are exposed to these foods and stimulated to taste them. Exposure and stimulation are key ingredients in establishing good eating habits.

Children are born imitators. They love to imitate their parents, their siblings, and older children. Studies have shown that the nutrient content of their diet can be influenced by their parents' eating habits. In the Framingham children's study (a long-term study carried out in New England), it was found that if both parents ate large amounts of saturated fats, their children were five times more likely to eat large amounts of such fats, compared with children in families where parents did not consume such a high-fat diet.

Children Thrive on Positive Reinforcement

By giving children verbal praise or other forms of recognition and approval when they eat the right food the right way, you reinforce healthy eating behaviour. But when you pay a lot of attention to undesirable behaviours such as food refusal or poor table manners, the child can subsequently use the problem behaviour to get your attention.

Children also thrive on stimulation. Children in families with greater stimulation are characterized by better psychomotor development and better language skills, as well as better nutritional status. On the other side of the coin, children of mothers who are discontented, nervous, and unhappy with their role of mother and homemaker have poorer diets and lack the full benefits of good nutrition.

Food Can Become a Solution to Every Problem

Fed when hungry, infants are physically satisfied. Cuddled in your arms while breastfed or formula-fed, they are emotionally satisfied. For all babies, physical and emotional satisfaction become associated with meals and with maternal affection. The child responds to two distinct needs — hunger and affection — but these needs can eventually be confused by the baby if you are not careful.

Babies who are fed whenever they cry or are overfed to make them sleep longer cannot tell the difference after a few weeks between the need to eat and other needs. Food becomes the way to satisfy all needs: the need for attention, the need for affection, the need for diversion.

Based on many years of research, Dr. Hilde Bruch, a renowned psychiatrist now retired from Baylor College of Medicine in Texas, stresses the need to properly train the hunger mechanism so that it develops appropriately. Babies are not necessarily born as either big or small eaters. They learn to be hungry when it is time. They learn to know when to stop. They can easily unlearn very early in life.

Infants who are forced to finish a bottle do not learn to control their appetite. Babies who nurse for more than 40 minutes do not learn to control their appetite. Children who are forced to clean their plate are not learning how to control their appetite. They are only learning to obey. You can help your baby from the very first weeks of life to recognize his or her body needs and to satisfy them appropriately.

It Takes Two to Develop a Normal Appetite

You and your baby both have a role to play in the normal development of your baby's hunger mechanism.

At birth, your newborn baby is not totally dependent. He can express his needs and desires within the first few hours of life:

- He can cry, cough, swallow, and vomit.
- He can smell and hear.
- He can distinguish between touch and pain.
- He can turn his head in the direction his cheek is touched.
- He can twist and kick his feet.

You can help your baby develop by responding to his actions and reacting correctly to his messages, thus allowing him to become aware of his potential to communicate his feelings and limits. If you feed your baby to appease all his cries or to console and comfort him, you are not interpreting your baby's messages correctly. But if you offer food in reply to a real cry of hunger, you contribute to the proper development of your baby's hunger mechanism. The right reaction at the right moment is one of the key factors influencing your baby's eating behaviour.

If your baby refuses to drink the last drop of formula, why insist? Your baby is trying to tell you his limit: he has had enough. If you respond to his message of satiety, you are helping him develop his own sense of satiety. If not, you are passing along the message of acceptable overeating.

If your baby refuses meat or vegetables when you start introducing solid foods, let him have his way, but do not necessarily give up on that particular food. Offer it with another meat or vegetable and see how he reacts. His acceptance of new foods can develop quite gradually and require all your patience and understanding. Forcing him to swallow green beans, for instance, is showing a lack of respect for his message of distaste. After all, we all have our own whims. We like some vegetables and hate some!

When your baby loses his appetite, never force him to eat. His health is not in danger. Appetites normally vary throughout the first years of life, and usually an appetite drop coincides with a period of decreased growth rate. If you understand and react correctly to the messages your baby sends you at every meal, you enable him to participate actively in the feeding process.

Healthy Foods Can Become Fun Foods

If you have bypassed healthy foods all your life for many good reasons, you don't find as much pleasure in tasting fresh poached fish or dark, leafy vegetables or plain, creamy yogourt. Children who are raised on these foods do not have this problem. But healthy foods do not seem to be on everyone's menu. A recent survey has shown that french fries have become the favourite vegetable of American youth and that they make up a third of their usual vegetable intake. Another survey has indicated that 12 percent of preschoolers are drinking 9 ounces or more of soft drinks every day and that 25 percent of teenagers are drinking more than 26 ounces of soft drinks each day.

If you enjoy and serve wholesome and tasty foods, however, you will have no difficulty selling these good foods to your child.

– If you regularly serve vegetables of all colours and shapes, raw or cooked, your child will accept them much more easily.
– If you express special appreciation for spring's first asparagus, summer's fresh string beans, and autumn's bounty of squash and eggplant, you are helping your child develop a positive attitude toward these foods.
– If you regularly prepare fish and shellfish of all kinds, your child will not resist seafood experiences and will easily go beyond frozen fish sticks or breaded fish cakes.
– If you use fresh fruit in season for daily desserts, your child won't feel miserable without a cake, a pie, or a dozen cookies to end a meal.
– If you prepare meals without meat as a normal occurrence, your child will welcome a great variety of vegetarian dishes.

You don't need to preach nutrition. Always remember that a child can appreciate the taste of a freshly squeezed orange without knowing its vitamin C content; she can enjoy broiled liver without knowing its richness in iron. Your goal is to have a happy, healthy eater, not a junior nutritionist!

> *The other day at the supermarket, I overheard a young boy in front of the vegetable counter telling his friend that he really enjoyed spinach until his mother told him it was good for him. I will always remember this!*

Food Alone Is Not Enough

Total environment plays a vital role in the proper development of even a houseplant. Water and light are not the only factors that make it thrive. Total environment also affects your child's growth and development and can go beyond feeding the right kinds and amounts of foods. Affection from loving family members needs to supplement the daily menu and is essential to the most favourable environment.

The association between food and the socio-affective environment has been the subject of considerable research in Latin America, in studies looking for ways to minimize the effects of malnutrition on young children. One of these studies looked at weight gain and the health status of two groups of infants living in the same village in Guatemala. One group received supplementary foods for the first six months, while the control group did not. The supplemented babies came from larger, poorer, and less educated families. They gained less weight and were sick more often during the six-month period than the non-supplemented babies. The extra food did not compensate for the lack of human interaction these babies endured in their disadvantaged environment. This extreme example shows the valuable contribution of attention and affection to the total nourishment of a baby.

Eating Rituals Are Important

Among several rituals that affect family bonds, eating meals together was rated among the most important in a survey published in the nineties. Rituals mean security, and rituals feed the soul; families shape our soul.

Taking time to eat is an important value to pass on. Sharing meals with others is more than swallowing the proper amounts of protein, fat, and carbohydrates. Meals become social events that provide much more enjoyment than eating alone. Even with different timetables, sharing meals with your child at least a couple of times a week should be a priority — to provide precious doses of family interaction.

Food represents nurture, consolation, constancy, survival, ethnic solidarity, and ties with the past.

Food rituals are shaped over the years and become a thread of warmth and love.

THREE

Why Choose Breast Milk?

You've heard about the exceptional qualities of breast milk, but scientists around the world continue to discover new nutrients and antibodies in mother's milk that provide either nutritional, emotional, immune, or anti-allergenic benefits. Recent research has even discussed the impact of breastfeeding on the infant's mental development.

For all these reasons, Health Canada, in conjunction with the Canadian Paediatric Society and Dietitians of Canada, declared in 1998 that *"breastfeeding is the optimal method of feeding infants and that breastmilk is recommended for all infants with very few exceptions."** The advantages of extended breastfeeding are indeed indisputable and include nutritional, immunological, and psychologi-

---

* From the document *Nutrition for Healthy Term Infants*, page 22.

cal benefits to both infant and mother, notes the American Dietetic Association in their most recent position statement.

Before making a final decision about what kind of milk to feed your baby, learn more about the many benefits of breastfeeding.

Breastfeeding Makes Life Easier

Breastfeeding can make your life easier because breast milk is always ready to serve, does not require any preparation, travels well, is always at the right temperature, does not contain any additives or preservatives, and stays fresh day in and day out without refrigeration. No other food on earth is as convenient.

Breastfeeding allows you to save time and money. There is no need to buy infant formula, bottles, or nipples, no need to wash or sterilize bottles and nipples. You can feed your baby anywhere, anytime. You can even travel with your baby and always have the healthiest food on hand.

Breast Milk Is Much More Than Just a Food

Numerous nutrients and antibodies have been identified in breast milk, but one cannot forget that breast milk is much more than just a food. A newborn infant needs warmth, affection, nutrition, and protection against infection. She can satisfy all these needs with breast milk. Breastfeeding involves body contact, closeness, intimacy. It generates warmth that flows from the breast to the infant's mouth and vice versa. It provides exceptional bonding. Many years ago, Dr. Marshall Klaus and Dr. John Kennel did a very careful study of initial parent-child interactions. They were struck by the high incidence of abandoned and abused children and by the failure of children to thrive during the first years of life after separation from one or both parents occurred during the first months of life. And they identified a common cause for these sad situations. They found a link between a higher frequency of these problems and the lack of mother-infant physical contact during the first days of life.

Breastfeeding also benefits you. The hormones that stimulate the milk flow called the *letdown reflex* help contract your uterus back to its pre-conception size, enhances your maternal instinct, and increases your physical attachment to your baby. As you become more and more confident in your power to provide good nourishment to your baby, breastfeeding becomes a source of pride, a boost to your self-esteem.

Breast milk is much more than just a food — for you and for your baby.

During the past few years, I had the wonderful opportunity of following the growth of my three grandchildren and seeing them double their birth weight with breast milk exclusively. I was overwhelmed. It helped me understand how proud and confident a mother can become by being the unique food provider for many months.

Breast Milk Opens Up the Flavour World

Research done at the Monell Chemical Senses Center in Philadelphia indicates that human milk is rich in flavours and directly reflects the foods and spices (garlic, mint, vanilla, carrot) eaten by the mother. An infant is capable of detecting sensory changes in breast milk and will alter her sucking behaviour when the milk is flavoured; she will suck for longer periods when the milk has a taste of either garlic or vanilla.

The flavour world of a breastfed infant is potentially much richer than previously thought. Breast milk gives your baby an opportunity to learn about the flavour of foods long before solids are introduced.

Breast Milk Is Adapted to the Needs of the Newborn

Life just after birth is not that easy for a baby. After a nine-month stay in a warm environment, being fed on demand 24 hours a day, a newborn is faced with having to breathe, maintain an adequate body temperature, eat, digest, and eliminate while also trying to avoid infections. The main components of breast milk are marvellously adapted to meet most of his needs.

During the first few days after birth, breast milk is yellowish. At this time, it is called *colostrum* and has fewer calories and less fat but more protein, vitamins, and minerals than mature milk. It even has a different composition if your baby is premature, and it gradually changes over the course of a few weeks. It is also rich in antibodies. No formula can provide all the benefits of this "initiation drink."

During the second week of life, breast milk is called *transition milk.* It contains less protein and more fat and lactose than the colostrum, and its caloric content is slowly increasing to suit the infant's needs.

Breast Milk Is Most Useful for Infants with Special Needs

The most common special needs are those of infants born prematurely. The unique nutritional qualities of breast milk, including a suitable composition of proteins and fatty acids, allow for better digestion. They also accommodate themselves to the feeding tolerance as well as the gradual maturation of the premature infant's digestive and neurological systems. The higher requirements for certain nutrients, including protein, calcium, phosphorus, and zinc are met if the infant weighs 2,000 grams (4 lb. 3 oz.) or more. If the infant weighs less than 2,000 grams, a supplement must be provided, but it will never replace breast milk.

Breast milk has also been used with great benefit for infants with cleft palate, inborn errors of metabolism such as phenylketonuria, cystic fibrosis, and Down's syndrome.

Mature Breast Milk Has Unique Nutritional Qualities

Three to four weeks after birth, the composition of mature breast milk stabilizes, but it still varies during the day, even during a feeding, providing more water at the beginning of a feeding and more fat at the end. *If your baby is more thirsty than hungry*, he will take a small amount of milk from each breast. If *he is hungry more than thirsty*, he will feed longer at the first breast until he gets the rich milk at the end of the drink. The major components have definite characteristics.

The *protein* content in breast milk is much easier to digest than proteins in cow's milk or even other infant formulas. Once in the stomach, these proteins coagulate into easily digested, miniature particles that are absorbed easily by infants, unlike the harder and larger protein particles found in cow's milk.

The *cholesterol* content of breast milk is remarkably stable, even if you eliminate all cholesterol and saturated fats from your own diet. Cholesterol is considered an essential ingredient for a baby's growth and development. Investigators indicate that animals fed high levels of cholesterol early in life are better able to cope with cholesterol later in life, and they maintain lower cholesterol levels. No infant formulas have as yet been supplemented with cholesterol.

Lactose, the natural carbohydrate present in milk, is much more abundant in human milk than in any other milk, and for very good reasons. Once it is transformed into galactose, a simple sugar, it actively participates in the development of the central nervous system and greatly enhances the absorption of calcium in breast milk.

Other *complex carbohydrates* in breast milk called glycoconjugates can inhibit pathogens and are now considered a source of protection for breastfed infants.

Breast Milk Contains Fat That Enhances Visual and Brain Development

This is a long and fascinating story.

Your baby's brain gains approximately 750 grams (1 lb. 10 oz.) during her first year of life. In fact, the nerve tissues of the human brain and the eye develop very rapidly during the last trimester of pregnancy and early postnatal months. These tissues require important amounts of fat, but not just any kind of fat, to ensure proper growth of the central nervous system and good visual acuity. The fat that can do the job comes from the two essential fatty acids — linoleic acid and alpha-linolenic acid (also called the omega 6 and omega 3 fatty acids) — found in vegetable and fish oils. To become functional in the infant's brain, these dietary fats need to be processed and stretched into long-chain fatty acids called AA and DHA. This stretching process goes on smoothly except during the first few months of life because of the infant's limited ability to carry on such a process. In other words, a baby needs a direct supply of these important fats called AA and DHA. Luckily, the foetus benefits from a maternal transfer of AA and DHA during the last three months of pregnancy, and the infant receives a fair amount in breast milk.

Preterm babies and formula-fed babies do not receive this adequate supply of AA and DHA and could have less than optimal brain and eye development as a result. Since the early nineties, scientists have become aware of this situation and have reviewed it quite extensively. Their conclusion is that breast milk provides optimal amounts of AA and DHA. Breastfed infants, term and preterm, also have more of these fatty acids in their red blood cells and better visual acuity during the first months of life when compared to formula-fed infants. Among formula-fed infants, other research has even shown that a supplement of these fats added to a formula during the first four months of life could make a difference in problem-solving scores at age ten months. No commercial formula has yet been supplemented with such fats. Only breast milk can provide your baby with these important fatty acids at a critical period in the development of the central nervous system and the retina.

Breast Milk Has an Appropriate Dose of Minerals

Iron in breast milk was once perceived as insufficient for the infant. However, research has shown that the type of iron found in breast milk, even if present in small amounts, is absorbed by the infant very well because of active interaction with other components. Surveys have repeatedly found that breastfed babies rarely show signs of iron deficiency anaemia compared with babies fed cow's milk or non-fortified infant formulas. The Canadian Paediatric Society confirmed the effectiveness of iron in human milk and stated that this iron is adequate for a full-term, normal-weight baby until the age of six months or until solid foods are introduced.

Calcium and *phosphorus* are found in smaller quantities in human milk than in cow's milk, but these amounts are more respectful of the infant's immature renal system (kidneys) and at the same time sufficient to ensure growth and development of the bones and teeth.

Breast milk contains three times less *sodium* and *potassium* than cow's milk. These amounts are much better suited to the baby's needs and immature renal system.

Zinc is present in large quantities in the colostrum secreted by the breasts during the first days after birth. It enhances the baby's overall immunity during the first critical week. Then it slowly decreases in quantity as the colostrum matures into breast milk. This zinc is better adapted to the infant's needs than the zinc added to infant formulas.

Selenium is also present in small amounts if your intake of this nutrient is adequate. Some experts suggest that it should be added to infant formulas to prevent any possible deficiencies. (Selenium is found mostly in fish, seafood, and liver. Meats, eggs, and whole grains also contain some.)

Breast Milk Provides Sufficient Vitamins — Except Vitamin D

Vitamin C content varies slightly, for the mammary glands are equipped to process some and so supply the infant with adequate quantities. The content may increase if your diet is plentiful in fruit and vegetables that are rich in vitamin C.

The *vitamin A* content of colostrum is twice the amount found in mature breast milk, but the supply remains adequate throughout infancy.

Vitamins of the B complex are present in sufficient amounts, especially when you are well nourished. Levels respond to dietary adjustments and to supplementation. Mothers who take vitamin B supplements automatically increase the vitamin B content of their milk.

Vitamin D varies slightly and is not influenced by your intake. Whether you take a supplement or not, the vitamin D found in breast milk does not always provide effective protection against rickets, especially if you avoided fortified milk or followed a strict vegetarian diet during pregnancy or if you have dark skin or, lastly, if your baby is seldom exposed to sunshine.

Breast Milk Supplies Plenty of Water

Even in warm weather, breast milk supplies an adequate amount of water. A breastfed baby does not require any extra fluid. If he is thirsty, he will feed more often, for shorter periods, and will get plenty of water.

Breast Milk Protects against Infections

During the first few months of life, a baby does not have the built-in resistance to face the outside world, a highly contaminated environment. Her defence mechanisms, or immunological system, are only partially completed. That explains why one infant in ten suffers from an infection during delivery or in the early months of life.

It is well known that breast milk protects babies all over the world from all kinds of infections. It lowers the incidence of diarrhea in North America as well as in the Third World. Studies provide evidence that even in countries such as ours, breastfeeding protects against gastrointestinal and respiratory infections. Babies breastfed for three months or more have significantly fewer gastrointestinal and respiratory illnesses during the first year of life compared to formula-fed infants. The conclusion of a study conducted in Manitoba in a Native community showed that formula-fed infants were hospitalized with infectious diseases ten times more often and spent ten times more days in the hospital during the first years of life, compared to the fully breastfed infants.

Another study shows that infants breastfed exclusively for a minimum of four months have fewer episodes of ear infections during the first year of life. When supplemented with formula before four months, the breastfed infants were more likely to develop an ear infection. Exclusive breastfeeding in this case seemed to make the difference and really protect the infant.

It has also been shown that if breastfed infants suffer from respiratory illness or otitis (ear infection), they are not as sick as formula-fed infants and do not become dehydrated.

It is more evident than ever that breast milk can protect against several types of infections.

Breast Milk Supplies Plenty of Antibodies

Breast milk provides an abundant quantity of protective agents during the critical first months, especially through the colostrum secreted during the first days after delivery.

All classes of *immunoglobulins* are present in breast milk and remain active as long as you breastfeed, but the doses are definitely higher just after birth then generally drop by the third week of life. One of these immunoglobulins, called "sIg A," is not affected by the normal acidic environment of the stomach; it remains intact until it reaches the intestinal tract and lines the intestinal wall with an antiseptic material. This helps the baby react against such pathogens as the polio virus and bacteria that could enter the body through the stomach.

The *bifidus factor* is 40 times more abundant in the colostrum than in mature milk. This factor promotes the development of an intestinal flora that can effectively limit the multiplication of undesirable bacteria. There is a striking difference between the flora of a breastfed baby and that of a formula-fed infant — and this surely explains the very low incidence of intestinal infections among the first group. It is interesting to note that the bifidus factor resists freezing temperatures as well as very high temperatures.

The *glycoconjugates* present in breast milk can also inhibit pathogens. Many complex carbohydrates, such as glycoconjugates and oligosaccharides, are now considered to be major sources of protection for breastfed infants.

Lactoferrin is another protective agent that provides a strong defence against bacteria. It has also been shown to inhibit the growth of Candida albicans, a fungus that can cause gastrointestinal trouble.

Breast Milk Protects against Allergies

Breast milk is a powerful tool to help decrease the incidence of infantile allergies. Just after birth, the baby has a limited capacity to deal with allergenic substances. The intestinal wall is more permeable in these early months, so that allergenic foods can leak into the system more easily, causing all kinds of problems, from eczema to asthma.

Allergies are frequently reported during infancy, affecting from 2 to 10 percent of infants. Many studies published since the eighties have confirmed the anti-allergenic powers of breast milk — especially in infants with a family history of allergies (i.e., when a parent, brother, or sister already has an allergy problem). (See Chapter 6, Breastfeeding Is Not Always Easy, for a discussion of colic in breast-fed infants and Chapter 17, Frequent Problems — and Solutions, for measures to take to avoid food allergies.)

Food antigens are transferred from the mother's diet to the breast milk, but very few exclusively breastfed infants develop allergic responses.

Breast Milk Is Adapted to Each Species

Breast milk is adapted to each species, and its main ingredients vary, depending on the needs of each species. Protein content, for example, varies according to each mammal's growth rate. The higher the protein content of the milk, the faster the species grows. A horse doubles its birth weight in 60 days and drinks a milk with 2 percent protein. A rabbit doubles its weight in six days and drinks a milk with 12 percent protein. A calf doubles its weight in 50 days and drinks a milk with 3.4 percent protein. A human baby doubles its weight in approximately 150 days and receives a milk with one percent protein.

The protein and mineral content of the milk has an impact on the number of feedings needed in 24 hours. The denser the milk, the longer the interval between each feeding. Mice produce one of the most diluted milks of all species and spend 80 percent of their time feeding their young. Rabbits produce a very dense milk and feed their young only once a day. Humans produce a less concentrated milk and need to feed their babies several times a day.

The fat content of the various milks is related to the size of the animal and to the environmental temperature of its natural habitat. The larger the animal and the colder the environment, the higher the fat content of the milk. Elephant's milk contains 20 percent fat, seal's milk 43 percent, and that of the blue whale, 50 percent fat.

The carbohydrate content of milk varies according to the rate of brain development after birth. Accordingly, human milk contains more carbohydrate, in the form of lactose, than any other milk.

Nature has thought of everything. The kangaroo, which often suckles two young of different ages at the same time, produces two types of milk; the younger animal drinks a more concentrated milk from one nipple, and when the older one nurses from another nipple, it receives a more diluted milk, suited to its needs. The Hokkaido monkey gives birth in the spring and nurses its young all summer. In the autumn, the mother lets the baby forage for himself and replenishes her own stores. But when snow appears and food is scarce, the young monkey resumes his intake of mother's milk for another season.

By choosing to breastfeed, you are providing your baby with the healthiest food on the market.

FOUR

You May Think You Can't Breastfeed . . .

*Y*ou may not be certain how to manage breastfeeding. You may also feel you have a number of valid reasons not to breastfeed. But before giving up on the idea altogether, evaluate the situation once more. The obstacles may be no more than a challenge.

Your Health Does Not Allow You to Breastfeed?

According to health experts in Canada, the consensus is loud and clear: very few illnesses can stop a mother from breastfeeding. Those that do present an obstacle include her having untreated active tuberculosis or a diagnosis of HIV positive, or her child having a rare case of galactosemia. Fortunately, these problems are infrequent. In fact, 99 percent of mothers can breastfeed because in all other circumstances, even if you have a serious medical condition or need to take regular medication, you can choose to breastfeed.

You Are Unable to Breastfeed Just after Birth

You may have had a Caesarian or a long labour and are unable to breastfeed immediately after birth. You may have been so tired and stressed that nothing seemed to happen when you first tried breast-feeding — although the ideal situation is to initiate breastfeeding within half an hour after birth. Don't feel discouraged and don't give up: 35 percent of mothers experience delayed onset of lactation, even up to more than 72 hours after birth. If your baby does not get enough breast milk during the first 24 hours and has to receive formula feedings during your stay in the hospital, you can still breastfeed adequately once you are back home.

Michelle, 37, had an unscheduled C-section after 33 hours of labour. She could not breastfeed her baby just after birth and succeeded only a few times in the hospital. But finally, a few days after the birth, when she was back at home, she began good milk production. She continued to breastfeed for more than five months, enjoying the close contact with her healthy baby.

You Have Inverted or Flat Nipples

The most effective antidote to this is the use of breast shells (plastic or glass). You put them over the nipple and areola inside your bras-siere for six to eight weeks (or longer) after delivery. You may need a larger bra to accommodate the shells. These shells, available through La Leche League International, provide an even, gentle, and constant pressure over the areola, causing the nipple gradually to evert. Continue wearing the shells (Woolwich shields) at all times between feedings until lactation is well established.

Sandra, 35, wanted to breastfeed but did not really prepare herself during pregnancy. She gave birth easily but realized immediately after birth that her baby could not latch onto her breast because she had flat nipples. She tried but could not breastfeed during her stay at the hospital. Three days after birth, in her home alone with her baby, she finally succeeded and kept on breastfeeding for many months.

To make things easier in the case of flat nipples, pump your milk a few hours after birth to stimulate milk production (see Chapter 9, Working and Breastfeeding, pages 80–82), stretch your nipples, or start wearing the Woolwich shields as soon as possible.

You Have Had Breast Surgery

If you have had surgery to remove a benign cyst or to increase the size of your breasts, you can still breastfeed successfully in most cases as long as the nipples were not removed. Check with the lactation clinic in your area.

You Have Small Breasts

You may have small breasts and wonder if you can adequately breastfeed. Good news! There is no relationship between breast size and the volume of milk produced. In fact, larger breasts hide more fat but not necessarily more milk stores. During pregnancy, the mammary gland network in each breast increases as a result of hormonal changes, and the local milk "factories" are responsible for milk production, quite independent of breast size. Confidence in your power to breastfeed seems to have a much greater impact on milk volume than the size of your breasts.

You Do Not Want to Damage Your Breasts

The size of your breasts has increased during pregnancy and will increase even more during breastfeeding. Your breasts may lose some muscle tone, especially if they are large to begin with or if your skin lacks elasticity. But if you support them well day and night with a brassiere, there will be a minimum of damage.

You Are Worried about Your Weight

You meet women who breastfeed and cannot lose any weight, but you've heard that breastfeeding helps women lose weight more rapidly after a pregnancy. What's the latest? Research and clinical observations show that most women keep some of the excess weight gained during pregnancy but lose it gradually during the first year, whatever type of milk feeding they choose. In fact, two out of three women will still have an extra 2.3 kilograms (5 lb.) 12 months after birth — a very small excess. The more weight you gain during pregnancy, the more you lose during the first six weeks, whether you breastfeed or not.

A study done in Louisiana followed a group of mothers for six months after birth. Caloric intakes and weights were compared among totally breastfeeding mothers, partially breastfeeding mothers, and mothers who gave infant formula. Breastfeeding mothers ate 2,000 calories per day, lost slowly in the first three months, but came to a total loss of eight kilograms (18 lb.) at six months. Mothers who gave formula ate 500 calories less each day and lost a comparable eight kilograms (18 lb.) at six months. Mothers who alternated between breast milk and formula ate 2,000 calories per day and lost seven kilograms (16 lb.) at six months. As you can see, breastfeeding allows weight loss at a reasonable pace, but to maintain adequate milk production, you cannot lose too quickly.

If you want to lose some weight without affecting your milk supply, avoid any strict diet leading to rapid weight loss. Remember that pollutants accumulated throughout your lifetime are stored in your fat tissues, and the faster you lose, the greater the quantity of pollutants you release from the fat and secrete in your milk. Even more important, if you dramatically reduce your daily caloric intake, you can jeopardize your milk supply by reducing your capacity to produce enough.

Barbara, 29, gained 25 kg (55 lb.) during her pregnancy and gave birth to a healthy baby weighing 4 kg (about 9 lb.). She lost weight gradually during the first 6 months and lost the rest when she returned to work, still breastfeeding her baby until the age of 11 months.

There's no need to rush to lose weight. Your pre-pregnancy weight will come back if you maintain a healthy diet and exercise on a regular basis.

You've Been a Junk Food/Fast Food Eater for Years

You may feel your diet will not allow you to properly supply your baby with top-quality milk. Don't worry. The nutritional qualities of breast milk are somewhat independent of your daily intake of nutrients. In Third World countries, mothers who eat little food, sometimes of poor nutritional value, succeed in producing breast milk that is rich in protein, fat, carbohydrates, and immunological substances for at least three months. This kind of milk saves millions of lives throughout the world. Your milk is sure to be good enough. And it is never too late to improve your diet and increase your intake of vitamin-rich fruit and vegetables and good whole-grain cereals! It's easier than you think.

You Are Worried about Losing Your Freedom

Becoming a parent means redefining your concept of freedom — finding ways to reconcile your needs while not jeopardizing your baby's. Providing tender loving care to a newborn requires quite a few hours a day, but this new role can become very gratifying. Whatever type of milk you choose to give your baby, your freedom will be limited for some months. If you choose to breastfeed, you can plan free time for yourself once your milk production is well established. Toward the fourth or fifth week, express your milk with a pump or manually, let the father or a friend give baby a bottle, and enjoy the freedom!

Your Baby Is Premature

Prematurity has increased slightly in recent years. Nearly 7 percent of Canadian babies are born before the 37th week of gestation. However, prematurity is not an obstacle to breastfeeding, according to Health Canada. On the contrary, your milk represents the best food and provides invaluable benefits for your premature infant. It is different from breast milk produced for a term infant and it is well adapted to the nutritional needs of a smaller infant. It contains elements that are not found in any commercial formula.

If your baby is too small and cannot suck adequately, you can pump your milk, and the medical team will pass it on to your baby through a very thin tube. Pumping your milk on a regular basis will help you increase your supply and allow you to breastfeed your baby more easily once the sucking reflex has improved and once you and your baby leave the hospital.

The neonatal team at a children's hospital in the Montreal area strongly encourages mothers of premature babies to express their milk for their babies. Even if a mother can supply only 5 mL (or

1 tsp.) of breast milk, the nursing staff will give the baby this amount of invaluable milk. The nurses at this hospital often succeed in convincing mothers who, at first, did not want to breastfeed but who came to realize the important contribution their milk could make. In many cases, these small infants remain in the hospital for a certain number of weeks; mothers are invited to come to the hospital to pump their milk in a reserved area or to deliver frozen breast milk to the hospital on a regular basis.

Two paediatricians from the Institute of Maternal and Child Health in Colombia developed what they called the Kangaroo method in the late seventies and thus saved many lives of premature infants with very low birth weights. This method consists of having the mother keep her infant on her chest under her clothes, directly on her skin, 24 hours a day. It allows warm contact and easy access to the breast, for frequent feedings. Compared to sophisticated incubators, this simple, low-tech method showed a significant reduction in the morbidity and mortality of these fragile babies and improved mother-child bonding. I had the opportunity to meet a group of Kangaroo mothers in Guatemala a few years ago. I was overwhelmed by the impact of this approach on the infants' growth and on the mothers' pride.

Providing breast milk or breastfeeding your premature baby can make a great difference in your baby's health and your sense of well-being.

You Are Expecting Twins

The birth rate of twins has increased to 2.1 percent of all births in Canada. Breastfeeding twins, even triplets, can be done and is done by many mothers. The more frequently the infants suckle, the more milk you can produce. The experience is worthwhile, but nursing two babies simultaneously presents positioning problems. Seek some advice from a lactation consultant* or a self-help group in your area to help you find the right position. If you decide to feed one baby at a time, use a soother to calm one baby while breastfeeding the other or have the father feed the second baby with previously expressed breast milk that has been kept in the refrigerator in a sterile bottle.

Marsha, 41, gave birth to twin boys and already had two little girls at home. Food allergies were present in the family, and she was well aware that breast milk could retard such problems. At the beginning, she tried to breastfeed the two babies at once but did not feel comfortable. She then chose to breastfeed one baby at a time. At night, she would breastfeed in bed on her side, and slept until the baby had finished. Then she changed sides to breastfeed the other. She alternated breasts for each baby's drink. The first weeks were somewhat hectic, but she managed to breast-feed both boys for seven months.

To be able to cope with such an exceptional demand, mothers must eat sufficiently, rest as much as possible, and forget the rest of the world!

Your Baby Has Jaundice

Jaundice is not a rare problem among newborns: 50 percent of healthy, full-term infants and 80 percent of premature babies develop it. The type of jaundice that can occur during the first days after birth is easily taken care of by frequent breast milk feedings and exposure to sunlight. Frequent feedings allow the baby to receive more colostrum, which acts as a laxative and helps eliminate the first stool;

* A lactation consultant is a health-care professional who focuses on providing education and management to prevent and solve breastfeeding problems and to encourage a social environment that effectively supports the breastfeeding mother-child pair. For more information, contact Jacki Glover, president of the Canadian Lactation Consultant Association (e-mail: jacki@glover.org).

as a result, it lowers the bilirubin levels — the orange-coloured pigments that travel in the blood and cause jaundice.

A baby with jaundice should be under observation, and levels of bilirubin should be checked. Some health-care professionals suggest giving water instead of breast milk, but this is seldom helpful — to the contrary.

Even if your baby needs a session of phototherapy to decrease bilirubin levels, continue to breastfeed on demand.

Jonathan was born at term and weighed 4 kg (about 9 lb.). A few hours after birth, he developed jaundice because of a blood incompatibility; his mother has O positive, while he has AB. The nurse recommended that the mother stop breastfeeding, even if the mother wanted to continue. After leaving the hospital, the baby fed very little and eliminated no stool, and his skin turned even yellower than before. He was readmitted to the hospital, and after a 12-hour session of phototherapy while being breastfed by his mother, the bilirubin decreased to acceptable levels. Jonathan left the hospital and continued to breastfeed.

Feeding frequently on demand is the best method to lower the bilirubin levels when jaundice occurs during the first week of life.

You Have Had a Caesarian

This surgery causes pain and discomfort but does not affect your milk production, so you can still breastfeed. You can produce as much milk as if you had had a regular delivery, but you need a bit more time to recover before beginning a breastfeeding routine. Breastfeeding may even stimulate the uterus to contract and return to its normal size sooner.

Ask for local anaesthesia during a Caesarian, if it is possible, so that your baby can develop a good sucking reflex sooner after birth.

Do not hesitate to take medication against pain, but make sure it is not contraindicated for breastfeeding. Plan to have your baby live-in if possible, and ask the father to take care of baby while you rest. Slowly find the best position to breastfeed, and ask for all the help you can get.

You Are Worried about Becoming Exhausted Quickly

This can easily happen if you don't take good care of yourself before and after delivery. You can build up your resistance during the last month of pregnancy by getting enough sleep, eating winning foods, and forgetting about doing a lot of work in or outside your home. Nobody denies that giving birth, initiating breastfeeding, and coping with day and night schedules represent big challenges. All the same, the first week can be euphoria, even if your baby requires many feedings and loads of attention. By the second week, when your baby improves her feeding and sleeping schedule, don't hesitate to take naps whenever you feel like it, snack on healthy foods as often as needed, and listen to inspiring music to maintain your physical and emotional strength.

You Have Postpartum Blues

The weeks following your baby's birth are considered to be a critical time for the onset of mood disorders. Maternity blues occur quite frequently and are thought to be caused by the rapid, post-pregnancy decline in levels of hormones that have direct and indirect effects on the central nervous system. The postpartum blues last only a few days in most cases, but they affect mothers who breastfeed as well as mothers who formula-feed.

Do not hesitate to seek help if you continue to feel depressed for more than a few weeks, but don't give up breastfeeding.

You Are Taking Medication

Most prescription drugs and over-the-counter drugs pass into breast milk in very small quantities, but even antibiotics are allowable if you breastfeed and you really need to take them. Nonetheless, always check with your doctor or your pharmacist for possible side effects before you take anything, especially during the first months, whether it is cough syrup, Aspirin, suppositories, inhalers, or special therapeutic creams. You never know.

> *After Janice had given birth to a 4 kg (9 lb.) boy, the doctor gave her a prescription for two Tylenol with codeine every four hours to minimize the pain following a difficult labour. But she received no advice as to possible side effects. At three days of age, her baby was not crying for milk or soiling his diaper and he slept like an angel. All the same, something wasn't normal. The baby was taken to the hospital and found to be slightly dehydrated. He had lost 280 g (about 10 oz.) since birth. The baby was too weak to suck, so Janice had to express a small amount of milk and give the baby a few teaspoons. She also stopped taking the medication. Within six hours, she was able to resume normal breastfeeding, and the infant slowly came back to a normal routine.*

The American Academy of Pediatrics suggests that when you are considering drug therapy while breastfeeding, you should ask your doctor the following questions:

- Is the drug really necessary?
- Is the drug being used in the safest dose?
- Does the drug present a hazard to the infant, and if so, what should be done to monitor infant vital signs, symptoms, and blood levels?
- Can the infant's exposure to the drug be minimized if you take

the drug after feeding or just before the infant has a lengthy sleep period?

Once you've received adequate answers, you are in a better position to make a decision and monitor any possible reaction in your infant.

You Smoke

Smoking is definitely not a healthy habit, but it is not a formal contraindication to breastfeeding if done within acceptable limits. Research has shown that smoking more than ten cigarettes a day can reduce your milk production, affect the letdown reflex, and increase your baby's irritability. It has also been shown to limit weight gain after four or five weeks.

Here are some guidelines to reach these acceptable limits:

- Cut down the number of cigarettes you smoke a day, especially if you normally smoke more than ten a day.
- Smoke after you feed or one hour before, but never during feeding.
- Avoid smoking in the baby's room or in the house, to reduce your baby's exposure to a minimum.
- But breastfeed!

*Very few problems can seriously limit
your capacity to breastfeed.*

FIVE

Breastfeeding 101

*M*others have breastfed for many thousands of years, and learning to breastfeed seems unnecessary in traditional societies. In our world, however, we have lost the touch for a few generations and need to be reinitiated into this natural way of feeding our babies. These days, mothers also often live far from their own parents and extended family. If this is your situation, you will have no experienced family members to answer your everyday questions or to help you manage. This chapter will give you some answers and some useful tips on how to succeed in this exceptional endeavour.

Recruit Allies

Make sure your partner understands your decision. His help and support are essential ingredients in your success. If the rest of your family or your in-laws do not approve, try to ignore their wise-cracks, and build an alternative network of people who can support you. If you have difficulties in the first few weeks, talk to a lactation consultant. Do not wait until a problem becomes serious.

Get Ready during Pregnancy If You Can

Getting ready may mean buying an answering machine or subscrib-ing to a message centre so that phone calls will not bother you while you are feeding the baby. Getting ready will also mean buying a brassiere that is adjustable and useable for both pregnancy and lactation. This will give you good support. Once in a while during pregnancy, open the flaps in the front of the brassiere and expose the nipple and the areola under the clothing to experience a gentle, soft abrasion of the surface. Swedish mothers attribute the absence of sore nipples to the fact that they expose their breasts to sunshine and wear loose clothing routinely throughout their young adult life. This is an efficient and inexpensive way of conditioning your breasts before delivery, as long as you avoid sunburn, of course!

Getting ready means having a supply of ready-made dinners, snacks, and suppers in the freezer so you need not worry about preparing meals during the first weeks after delivery.

Getting ready means having parents and friends agree to share some of your housekeeping responsibilities: shopping, entertaining an older child, helping out with homework, walking the dog.

Getting ready means finding a cozy spot in the house for nursing.

If you still have not made your final decision, let me dispel a few other worries you may have.

Choose a Baby-Friendly Hospital If You Can

The hospital where you choose to give birth can really help you during the first 24 to 48 hours of breastfeeding. The health-care staff of a Baby-Friendly hospital helps you initiate breastfeeding within half an hour of birth, shows you how to breastfeed or to maintain lactation if you are separated from your baby, gives the infant no food or drink other than breast milk unless medically indicated, encourages rooming-in 24 hours a day, encourages breastfeeding on demand, etc. Such a hospital is not that easy to find. Some maternity wards are plastered with posters on breastfeeding babies but the absence or non-implementation of a breastfeeding policy in the vast majority of hospitals in Canada often causes frustration and problems during this critical period.

In 1989, the WHO (World Health Organization) and UNICEF developed guidelines for maternity services in order to provide the ideal environment for breastfeeding mothers. These guidelines, summarized in ten steps (see chart on page 41) have been adopted and implemented in 15,000 hospitals around the world. All hospitals in Norway and Sweden are Baby Friendly. In Canada, there is only one UNICEF-designated Baby-Friendly hospital as of July 1999: the Brome-Missisquoi-Perkins Hospital in Cowansville, in the province of Quebec. It took four years of collaborative work to obtain this accreditation: doctors, administrators, nurses, mothers, local health services, and government worked at it and succeeded.

If you want a Baby-Friendly hospital in *your* area, you can make it happen by becoming involved at the community level and working toward the adoption of the ten steps. For help in starting this worthwhile project, contact the Breastfeeding Committee for Canada (BCC).*

Nurse on Demand

Visit your local hospital before delivery to see if you can room-in

---

* Address inquiries to the BCC's national coordinator, Marilyn Sanders, Box 65114, Toronto, ON, M4K 3Z2; fax: (416) 465-8265; e-mail: bfc@istar.ca

Ten Steps to Successful Breastfeeding*

Every facility providing maternity services and care for newborn infants should:

1. Have a written breastfeeding policy that is routinely communicated to all health care staff.
2. Train all health care staff in skills necessary to implement this policy.
3. Inform all pregnant women about the benefits and management of breastfeeding.
4. Help mothers initiate breastfeeding within a half-hour of birth.
5. Show mothers how to breastfeed, and how to maintain lactation even if they are separated from their infants.
6. Give newborn infants no food or drink other than breast milk, unless *medically* indicated.
7. Practise rooming-in — allow mothers and infants to remain together — 24 hours a day.
8. Encourage breastfeeding on demand.
9. Give no artificial teats or pacifiers (also called dummies or soothers) to breastfeeding infants.
10. Foster the establishment of breastfeeding support groups and refer mothers to them on discharge from the hospital or clinic.

with your baby. After delivering, you can decide if you want your baby in your room at all times, depending on your strength and the support available from the nursing staff.

The first few days are days of learning and adjustment. Nursing

* *Source:* Protecting, Promoting and Supporting Breast-feeding: The Special Role of Maternity Services, A Joint WHO/UNICEF Statement. Published by the World Health Organization, 1211 Geneva 27, Switzerland.

on demand as often as every couple of hours is important to initiate a good milk supply. Very frequent feedings during the first 24 hours not only stimulate the production and secretion of milk but provide your baby with plenty of fluids that can help prevent jaundice, a common problem among newborns. Frequent feedings also allow you to respond to your baby's unique needs for warmth and affection.

Breastfeed As Soon As Possible

Begin breastfeeding within the first hour after birth. During that very special hour, your baby is usually wide awake, actively discovering his new environment and responding to your messages. His sucking reflex is particularly strong. He then falls into a deep sleep and does not cry intensely until the third day. Early sucking triggers breast-milk production, and a number of studies have associated successful breastfeeding with this initial feeding in the first hour of the infant's life.

If you did not succeed during the critical first hour, do not give up!

Suzanne, 34, gave birth quite easily but could not breastfeed during the critical first hour. After many unsuccessful trials, she succeeded the third day after delivery and continued for more than six months.

Find a Comfortable Nursing Position

Make sure the nipple is well back in the baby's mouth, with the gums, hard palate, and tongue pressing on the areola. Good positioning is a key to effective breastfeeding.

Let Your Baby Be the Leader

Offer both breasts at each feeding. When your baby becomes disinterested in the first breast, change to the second breast until she becomes disinterested once more. Never interrupt your baby for a burp when she is actively sucking. Wait until she pauses so that she can reject swallowed bubbles.

Give yourself a few weeks to feel comfortable with your baby and to come to a satisfactory schedule. The entire breastfeeding process is the result of many daily interactions between you and your baby.

Avoid Giving Your Baby Other Fluids

Avoid giving your baby formula or sweetened water between feedings. This only decreases your baby's appetite and can easily disrupt your milk production. Breast milk provides all the fluids your baby needs, even in warm weather — and extra fluids can decrease breast-milk intake.

Diane, 35, gave birth during the summer. After a few weeks, she realized her baby was always refusing to feed after she came out of the pool. She then noticed that the baby did not like to suck cold nipples. So, after swimming, she warmed up her nipples with a warmed face cloth, and the baby regained his appetite.

Don't Worry If Your Letdown Reflex Is Slow

The letdown reflex is a physiological reaction that causes the release of milk from the breast. Sucking stimulates the hormonal system, which then triggers the flow of milk. But if your milk flow does not come readily when your baby begins to suck, don't worry. The letdown reflex evolves over time and may take a few weeks to become consistent.

Once the initial tenderness of the breasts decreases and you and your baby become more experienced, the letdown reflex will occur much sooner after the baby starts sucking. Note that this reflex is very sensitive to your mood, and can be inhibited if you are in a rush, tense, embarrassed, or preoccupied. Before you develop the perfect breastfeeding strategy, try applying some heat on the breasts ten minutes before feeding time by taking a bath or a shower or applying a heating pad or hot, wet towel to your breasts.

You Think You Cannot Produce Enough Milk

All mothers are concerned about not producing enough milk. To reassure yourself, count wet diapers. If your baby wets at least six diapers a day, he is drinking enough milk.

If you need to increase your milk supply, just breastfeed more often and that will increase your milk production.

Your baby can show signs of increased hunger during the second week of life, at about five or six weeks, and at about three months. Increasing the number of feedings will allow you to meet his demands.

During the first three months, never reduce the number of feedings to less than six times in 24 hours. If, some days, you need to breastfeed more often, this is your way of responding to your baby's needs.

Your Baby's Growth Is a Good Indicator

Do not worry if your baby loses some weight during the first week of life, as this is quite normal. After that, your baby's growth is the most reliable way of assessing the adequacy of your milk supply. Ideally, a breastfed baby gains one kilogram (2.2 lb.) per month over the first three months and half a kilogram (1.1 lb.) per month during the following three months.

This is an average weight gain. Your baby can exceed or go slower than this curve and still be getting sufficient milk.

Visit your doctor five to six days after the birth to make sure your baby's growth is all right.

Table I		
Normal Weight Gain during the First Six Months		
at birth	3.2 kg	7 lb.
at 1 month	4.1 kg	9 lb.
at 2 months	5 kg	11 lb.
at 3 months	5.9 kg	13 lb.
at 4 months	6.4 kg	14 lb.
at 5 months	6.8 kg	15 lb.
at 6 months	7.3 kg	16 lb.

Growth Failure versus Slow Weight Gain

There is an important difference between growth failure and slow weight gain.

A baby who cries constantly or is apathetic, has dark urine, very few stools, drinks little at every feed, and drinks less than six times in 24 hours can be underfed and dehydrated. This is not normal and means that medical supervision is required.

If, on the other hand, your baby wets six diapers a day; has pale, diluted urine; has frequent stools; and drinks at least six times for 15 to 20 minutes, she may have slower weight gain, but you need not worry.

You Want to Express Your Milk

You can develop your skills in expressing milk as early as during the first week, in order to help avoid breast engorgement. You can hand-express your milk or use a manual or electric pump. Use any pump recommended by your local breastfeeding support group (La Leche or other), but avoid any that function with a pear.

To express your milk, use the technique described in Chapter 9, Working and Breastfeeding, pages 80–82. On your first attempt, you can take up to 45 minutes to obtain a small amount of milk, but with experience, you will become able to pump larger amounts in 30 or 20 minutes.

You Want to Skip a Feeding Once in a While

You can skip a feeding once your milk production is well established, at around the fifth or sixth week. To do this, however, you need to express your milk and store it adequately in sterile bottles (see pages 82–83). Your absence makes it easier for your baby to accept a bottle. Before having someone bottle-feed your baby (the baby's father or grandmother or the babysitter), provide them with good instructions and leave the house so that your baby will not feel your presence close by.

Take a Full Month to Recuperate and Adapt

Be realistic. Plan your life around breastfeeding. Avoid or eliminate any stress; it is your worst enemy. Don't try to be superwoman and maintain a busy schedule, a clean house, and social activities while breastfeeding day and night. Learn to cut corners and let people know you are doing this. Forget the rest of the world.

After four to six weeks, life becomes easier. And there's no formula to prepare, no milk to reheat, no bottles to clean, and no need to travel with bottles. You can go out with your baby everywhere. You just need to find quiet spots to breastfeed peacefully. Some women choose to breastfeed in the parking lot, in their own car, with no one watching.

Learning to breastfeed goes hand in hand
with learning to nurture your baby.

SIX

Breastfeeding Is Not Always Easy

It is not that easy to breastfeed at the beginning. It's a real challenge. "You should not only mention the good sides of the story," one of my daughters pointed out when she began breastfeeding. "You should prepare mothers for difficult moments during the first few days." My daughter is right. She had a few problems in the first few weeks and saw many of her friends give up after two or three weeks, once the worst was over. Too many mothers resign too soon and never know the benefits of the breastfeeding experience. To avoid this trap, seek out advice from experienced mothers or self-help groups when you need support.

You Have Cracked or Sore Nipples

In a case like this, the pain is strong but it doesn't last. It hurts you but it does not affect your baby's health. Nonetheless, you must find a solution promptly. If your nipple is cracked, it may bleed, and your baby can swallow a few drops of blood that end up in the diaper. It is not serious for the baby, but you need to treat your nipples to relieve the pain. Readjust your position (see page 42). Before you feed, soften the wound with a warm, wet towel. If your breast is firm and swollen, express a small amount of milk before you breastfeed.

Brownish blood found in a diaper comes from cracked nipples and is not a sign that the baby is in danger. The breast milk itself presents no risk either.

Nurse your baby often, on demand, and make sure the baby sucks properly and swallows. Once the breast is drained, do not let your baby suck; use a pacifier instead.

Never use soap on your breasts when you wash them; rinse with water and dry carefully. After a feeding, dry the nipples in fresh air and make sure they are dry before replacing the bra flaps.

To enhance the healing process, let a few drops of breast milk dry on the nipple. You can also use a few drops of flaxseed oil or the contents of a vitamin E supplement capsule, or even put a used, cooled teabag on the nipple for five to ten minutes after a feeding.

Nicole was in tears. It was three in the morning and she was suffering from painful cracked nipples. Her five-day-old baby had blood in her diaper. Nicole had no stored breast milk and did not know what to do. Finally, she took a hot shower and a Tylenol to relax, expressed some milk to relieve her swollen breasts, and slowly resumed breastfeeding. This was the best thing she could have done. The next day she resumed breastfeeding and applied breast milk on her nipples after each feeding. The pain was bearable.

You Have Hard and Swollen Breasts

Engorgement may be the problem if your breasts feel hot, hard, and tender, with painful swelling. This can happen when more milk is produced than the infant actually drinks or when feedings are too far apart. Reconsider your feeding schedule and have your baby feed more often on demand, from both breasts. Express excess milk after a feeding or prior to a feeding to relieve pressure. Take a warm shower or apply a hot, wet towel on the breasts to start the milk flow.

At the end of a feeding, gently massage your breasts to help recirculate the milk flow or express any leftover milk. If needed, apply a bag of ice or frozen peas 15 to 20 minutes after a feeding.

You Are Very Tired and Have a Fever

Mastitis can start like an engorgement but will progress into an infection accompanied by a fever. Your breasts will feel warm, and some areas will become reddish and very tender. This is a signal that you need more rest while increasing the number of feedings, to decongest your breasts. If your baby does not suck enough, hand- or pump-express to relieve the pressure. You can put ice chips on your nipple five minutes before feeding to decrease the pain.

If the pain is acute, however, take an acetaminophen like Tylenol (an analgesic less likely to cause gastrointestinal problems) 20 minutes before nursing. An antibiotic prescription might be necessary.

Your Baby Has Colic

Colic occurs in approximately 13 percent of infants, and breastfed babies are as vulnerable to it as formula-fed babies. It usually begins during the second or third week and normally disappears before the fourth month.

These are the symptoms. The infant has sudden attacks of pain, a distended and tense abdomen, drawn-up legs, arched back, pushed-out belly, clenched hands, and flushed face. Symptoms often become worse after 4 p.m. Babies can cry and scream for hours. The cause is not easy to track down: it can be related to poor burping technique, under- or overfeeding, air swallowing, or food intolerance caused by your own diet.

The following techniques may help control colic:

– Make sure your baby is in the correct position while breastfeeding, to limit air swallowing.
– Feed on demand.
– Make sure the first breast is completely emptied before switching to the second, so that your baby receives an adequate amount of fat and energy. A lack of fat can cause symptoms of hunger, with crying and fussiness.
– Overfeeding or an overactive milk ejection may cause symptoms like colic.
– Gulping of milk may lead to excess ingestion of lactose from the foremilk (the milk secreted in the first minutes of a feeding), and this may lead to abdominal pain.
– Don't hesitate to rock and cuddle your baby more often.
– Sometimes your baby will respond better if comforted by another person, such as the father or grandmother.

If all this doesn't work, try eliminating from your diet allergenic foods such as milk products or other protein food, for at least seven days. If you notice a difference, reintroduce milk products a few days later to challenge the baby's reaction. If the elimination of milk products or protein food appears to be the solution, change your menu, but make sure it is nutritionally adequate. (See menus, Chapter 8, Postnatal Menus for All Mothers, pages 70–76.)

During the past 25 years, I have received numerous calls from mothers with colicky babies. I always start by suggesting the non-food approach. I then go on to the elimination of milk products, which has often given good results. I have noticed that after having eliminated all milk products and seeing results, it is not always necessary to maintain a complete elimination. Babies seem to tolerate a small intake well.

Sometimes, other foods rich in protein, such as beef, soy, and chicken, are the offending ones. In this case, a rotation diet can be the solution.

I now realize that colicky babies react to protein-rich foods that were eaten regularly and in great quantity during pregnancy but that they will tolerate other protein-rich foods. Their reaction is not a true allergic reaction, but an intolerance that will disappear well before the age of 12 months.

You Have Not Found a Solution

Even if you try your best, problems can persist. You may have consulted the best people in your network, and their proposed solutions haven't worked. You may be ambivalent but still have come to the conclusion that you need to quit breastfeeding. This decision is very hard to make and even harder to live with, but you may feel that your survival depends on it. Comfort yourself by knowing that you have not failed as a mother. You simply have been unable to fulfill your breastfeeding goal. But even if you have breastfed for only a couple of weeks, your baby will have gained unique immunity and you will have lived through a unique and fulfilling experience.

Breastfeeding can be a challenge!

SEVEN

Improving Your Menu for Better Breastfeeding

Your baby requires food 24 hours a day. You are hungrier and thirstier than usual, which is normal. Your nutritional needs are at an all-time high, even if your body uses some of your fat stores to produce breast milk. If you do not want to be drained by the experience, you can improve your menu.

To maintain a decent and healthy diet, there is no need for exceptional foods, exotic fruit, constant snacks, or complicated recipes. You don't have to eat tons of food to produce sufficient milk. You should simply eat a generous menu and forget strict rules.

Stock a Few Things before Giving Birth

If you planned this exceptional period during pregnancy, you will already have some homemade or store-bought frozen meals and snacks in the freezer: meat loaves, broccoli or spinach quiches, macaroni and cheese, spaghetti sauce, cooked chicken or turkey, pizza bases, different whole-grain breads, muffins, and date squares, for instance.

If you did not think about stocking up before delivery, it is never too late to buy such dishes at the supermarket or from your favourite caterer. You can even suggest this type of gift from your friends or colleagues.

Store emergency foods such as almonds, sunflower and sesame seeds, cheese, canned kidney beans or chickpeas, roasted soynuts, evaporated milk, canned salmon, silken tofu, shrimp or tuna, peanut butter, applesauce, and so on, for instant snacks or light meals.

With such provisions, you can survive for at least a week with little or no cooking, simply by adding to your shopping list a few items such as milk, yogourt, vegetables, and fruits in season.

Winning Foods, from Morning till Night

Choose foods that are user friendly — simple to prepare! Never forget that you are in your recuperating month, adapting to your new life.

Choose top-quality foods, filled with nutrients in every mouthful.

Increase your energy level and your overall resistance by eating more often — at least every three hours. Think in terms of at least three meals and three snacks per day. Eating more often helps increase your metabolic rate, helps you burn calories more efficiently, and facilitates weight loss when needed. Make sure you include at every meal:

- One or more foods rich in protein such as meat, poultry, fish, seafood, legumes, milk, cheese, soy, and yogourt.
- At least a few vegetables and fruit in the form of salad, juice, or fresh fruit.

– One or more servings of whole-grain products such as whole-wheat bread, brown rice, and whole-wheat pasta.

Have a healthy snack as often as needed, day or night, and especially when you are tired or have not eaten for more than three hours.

For these snacks, foods rich in protein — such as a glass of milk or soy drink or a bowl of yogourt — are also very helpful.

Fibre-rich foods such as fresh fruit, dried fruit and nuts, roasted soynuts, or bran-rich muffins are not to be neglected either if you want regular bowel movements.

Forget Your Cooking Skills and Ask for Help

Forget about stews, pies, and fancy meals. Forget about the ultra-clean kitchen. Set aside having guests over for meals and concentrate on the essential: maintaining a good level of energy and making sure that you have a well-fed baby.

Ask your mother, a friend, or the baby's father to buy the groceries once you have made the list. Recruit helpers for feeding tasks. No one can refuse to peel a few vegetables, prepare a yogourt dip, or make a dozen muffins for the week.

Dare to ask a friend or an aunt to offer you as a gift one of your favourite meals — such as a lasagne, a shepherd's pie, or a tuna casserole. Depending on the response, you may want to request the same favour from other friends or work colleagues. The worst that can happen is that you may need to reciprocate some day!

You Can Return Slowly to Your Pre-Pregnancy Weight

You know that you need to eat more food when you breastfeed and you know that a weight-reducing diet can negatively affect your milk supply. At the same time, you feel frustrated carrying along some of the extra pounds you stored during pregnancy. You are not alone living this dilemma, and you can do something about it.

To make those extra pounds melt away slowly, the first rule is to eat a healthy menu similar to the one presented on page 63. You should make no changes the first month. This allows your milk production to become well established. Four weeks after delivery, the majority of new mothers weigh between 5.5 and 7 kilograms (12 to 15 lb.) more than before pregnancy.

After this period, continue to eat the same quantities of foods rich in protein and the same quantities of fruit, vegetables, and whole grains but modify your menu slightly. Choose 1 percent milk instead of 2 percent, forget butter on your bread, substitute muffins with whole-grain pitas, oatmeal cookies with larger servings of brown rice, and cheese with yogourt. Cook with less oil than usual.

This moderate cut in your fat intake can lead to a loss of 500 grams (1 lb.) per week without counting any calories and without jeopardizing your milk supply. Research done with 20 breastfeeding mothers at the paediatric clinic of the University of Iowa showed that this approach can lead to good results.

You can also return to regular physical activity and lose some weight that way, without jeopardizing your breastfeeding experience.

However, your main objective remains your baby's growth and constant weight gain. If this stops happening, go back to your original menu.

Lynn came to see me while she was breastfeeding. Her baby was three months old. She felt great but wanted to lose some weight. Her doctor had encouraged her to eat well over 2,500 calories per day to produce enough milk. She had gained a fair amount of weight during pregnancy and was still gaining instead of losing. While looking over her menu, I found a lot of extras: sweets, desserts, fried foods, and second helpings, which were not needed for her health or for milk production.

I suggested that she cut out some of these extras (cookies, pies, fried foods) but recommended that she keep all the essentials: good-quality protein at every meal, sufficient low-fat dairy products, generous servings of fruit and vegetables, and basic whole-grain products.

With this approach, she was able to lose one pound per week, and she continued to breastfeed for many months.

Drink Fluids Moderately

Interesting research carried out over seven days with 19 breastfeeding mothers measured how adding fluids affected the volume of milk the mothers produced. The results showed that a 25 percent increase in fluid intake did not increase the volume of breast milk produced. In other words, you don't need to force yourself to drink in excessive quantities to ensure that you have a good milk supply.

Remember to drink enough water to quench your thirst. A daily intake of approximately eight glasses of water, juice, or other non-alcoholic drinks seems adequate.

How about Coffee?

The caffeine found in coffee, tea, chocolate, many cola-based drinks, and certain drugs (see the Caffeine Chart at the end of this chapter) is a recognized stimulant. Caffeine absorption by the breastfed infant varies between 0.06 and 1.5 percent of the maternal dose. High caffeine intake (nine to ten cups a day) is reported to pass into the infant's blood.

It is difficult for a baby to eliminate caffeine, and the stimulant causes restless behaviour, especially when large quantities of caffeine-rich foods and beverages are consumed.

If your baby is calm and sleeps well, don't worry. However, if you would like to see your baby sleep more hours, try cutting down your intake to a minimum of one or two cups of coffee per day or switch to decaf or caffeine-free alternatives, such as herb teas, cereal-based hot beverages, or simply hot water (heated in the microwave for 1 minute and 30 seconds).

How about Alcohol?

Alcohol is rapidly transferred to breast milk. Even 30 minutes after a drink, alcohol modifies the odour of breast milk and negatively affects your baby's appetite. The baby sucks rapidly at the beginning but will usually drink less milk than usual; some studies have reported a 25 percent reduction.

Alcohol will have a stronger effect on a younger and smaller infant than on a heavy four-month-old, and it also has a greater impact if you drink before your periods come back.

The relaxing effect of alcohol does not last long, and after a few glasses, it inhibits your letdown reflex. Contrary to popular belief, it does not prolong your baby's sleep; in fact, your baby will fall asleep more often but for shorter periods of time.

To avoid upsetting your baby, when you have one drink, postpone nursing for at least one hour. It takes more than one hour to metabolize the ten grams of alcohol contained in one glass of white wine or one light beer. This delay does not completely eliminate the alcohol, but it decreases the concentration in your breast milk.

When you plan to attend a party and feel like having a few drinks, enjoy yourself — but express your milk a few days before and store it adequately. After the party, feed your baby with the bottle of stored breast milk, and to limit engorgement, express your milk but discard it.

You can also choose to enjoy diluted drinks like spritzers (half white wine and half soda) or you can splurge on virgin spritzers: half grape juice and half sparkling water.

The Fat You Eat Goes into Your Breast Milk

The kind of fat you have eaten for years affects the kind of fat present in your breast milk. If you have never indulged much in fried foods, chips, cookies, or margarine, you can rest assured, and if you were a fast food junkie or a cookie monster, it is not too late to improve your diet and the content of your breast milk. Just modify your fat intake and put more emphasis on the good fats found in different vegetable oils, fish, and seafood — and avoid fried foods.

You can easily incorporate 15 to 30 millilitres (1 to 2 tablespoons) of a cold-pressed oil into your daily menu, using, alternately, sunflower oil, canola, and olive oil. Use these oils in salad dressings or on steamed vegetables. If you want to use them in cooking, do so on low heat and avoid frying at all times.

Avoid hydrogenated fats as much as possible by cutting out chips, fried foods, and most margarines; these fats pass into the breast milk and are far from being healthy.

Breast Milk Is Not Pollutant Free

Like all foods, even the most nutritious ones, breast milk is not pollutant free.

Many undesirable substances such as DDT, PCBs, dioxins, and chemicals from pesticides are present in our environment and in our food supply. They accumulate in our bodies without our knowledge and can pass into our breast milk. They are usually stored in our fat tissue, which means that rapid weight loss can trigger the process of more pollutants sneaking out of our fat stores and leaking into breast milk.

The amounts of DDT in breast milk have significantly decreased since 1960, when DDT was banned in North America. The PCBs used in paints, inks, and transformers that have been banned in Canada since 1977 are still present in our tissues (they are stored in all animal fat tissues). Fish from contaminated waters such as those of the Great Lakes are among the main food sources of PCBs today. The concentrations of pollutants in breast milk are still significant, but they present no risk, since your baby's exposure will last only a few months and not a lifetime.

Pollution tends to travel toward the two magnetic poles, which means that the most contaminated breast milk in the world is produced by Inuit mothers who feed on large quantities of fish from the polluted waters of the Arctic. Even in these extreme cases, breast milk offers Inuit infants much more benefit than risk.

Pesticides are present in our food supply but accumulate more readily in foods of animal origin. In fact, meat, poultry, fish, butter, and milk products contain more pesticides than beans, peas, lentils, fruit, and root vegetables. This explains why breast milk from vegan or strict vegetarian mothers has less pesticide residue than that of other mothers.

You cannot ignore the problem, but pollutants should not hinder your lactation experience. The amount of environmental contaminants present in breast milk does not warrant restricting your baby's breastfeeding.

You can also do certain things to decrease the amounts of contaminants in your breast milk.

To Cut Down the Pollutants

Avoid fresh-water fish, especially from contaminated areas. Check with your local health unit. Choose a variety of ocean fish and seafood such as cod, sole, halibut, crab, and haddock or "farmed" fish, such as trout and salmon. Eat smaller and younger fish; they contain fewer pesticides.

Avoid fish oils (cod liver or halibut oil).

Choose leaner cuts of meat and trim away fat. Eat chicken without the skin even if you cook it with the skin on.

Choose low-fat cheeses when possible.

Avoid crash diets that mobilize pollutants in your fat tissue and cause them to secrete through your breast milk.

Choose organic, whole-grain cereals, leaf vegetables, fruit, and cold-pressed oils when possible. If organic choices are not available, peel the fruit and wash the leafy vegetables thoroughly.

What Are the Problem Foods?

In theory, there are no problem foods, but in practice all the foods you eat change the taste of breast milk. Strong-flavoured vegetables such as onions and garlic and those of the cabbage family do affect the taste, but few babies object. Research has even shown that babies appreciate the taste of garlic. They nurse for longer periods and take in larger quantities of breast milk when it has a garlicky flavour. Before you eliminate good but strong-flavoured foods from your menu, check your baby's reaction and act accordingly.

A ten-day-old breastfed baby had no problem until he started refusing his mother's milk. He would suck actively for two minutes and then turn away from the breast. After consulting a lactation specialist and verifying her breastfeeding position, the mother realized she had eaten many peppermint candies in the previous few days. A few hours after the mother stopped eating the candies, the baby resumed normal breastfeeding.

If your baby suddenly changes his breastfeeding behaviour or refuses to drink after a few minutes for no apparent reason, check your menu and make the proper adjustments.

Highly spiced or salty foods change the taste of breast milk but do not really belong on your list of winning foods.

Fried foods, sweets, and rich desserts can give you *and* your baby digestive problems; you seldom gain anything by eating such foods.

The Question of Allergies

If your baby has colic and has not responded to any of the strategies described in the previous chapter (pages 49–51), she may be temporarily intolerant of the milk products on your menu. Avoid all of them for at least three days and adjust your menu accordingly. (See "A Daily Menu without Milk Products" at the end of this chapter.)

If you see no improvement, try eliminating another protein-rich food such as beef or chicken and note any change.

If you have a family history of food allergies and your baby has shown a few reactions, you may wish to avoid these foods during the breastfeeding period: eggs, nuts and peanuts, fish and seafood.

What about Medication?

Pay close attention to medication because all drugs reach your breast milk and your infant rapidly. Most have little effect on the infant, but some should be avoided, so you should consult your physician before starting any special drug therapy. Always use the safest oral analgesic — one that is easy on the gastrointestinal system, such as an acetaminophen like Tylenol. Reduce the infant's exposure by taking the medication just after a feeding or just before your baby's lengthiest sleep period.

Oral contraceptives taken in low doses do not present a problem once the milk supply is well established, but some concerns remain over the long-term effects of such steroids excreted in breast milk. Any time after birth, alternative contraceptive methods are recommended, such as the use of a condom with or without foam.

Pay close attention to your baby's behaviour. Any significant change can signify a reaction to the medication you are taking. If your baby has no energy, sleeps all the time, does not drink well, or wets only a few diapers a day, he may be having a reaction and he should be taken to the doctor at once.

The Question of Vitamin Supplements

Vitamin and mineral supplements during lactation can be beneficial. Continue with the multivitamin and mineral supplement you were taking during pregnancy. Your nutritional needs are high at this time, and key nutrients are missing in many women's diets during lactation.

If you need to eliminate all milk products from your menu, replace regular milk with a fortified soy milk beverage, or else take 1,000 milligrams of calcium each day.

If you are lacto-ovo vegetarian and you regularly eat a wide variety of winning foods, there is no need to worry.

If you are a strict vegetarian and eat no food of animal origin, make sure you drink four glasses of fortified soy milk beverage each day for a good supply of protein, calcium, zinc, and vitamin D. Add 15 to 30 millilitres (1 to 2 tablespoons) of blackstrap molasses to your menu, for extra iron. Nibble on nuts and seeds for calories. To ensure your baby's normal growth and development, make sure you get sufficient vitamin B_{12} every day by drinking the fortified soy milk beverage or by taking a supplement because that vitamin is not available in plant foods.

Plan to have, each day, in food or supplements:

1.5 mcg vitamin B_{12}
1,000 mg calcium
5 mcg (200 International Units) of vitamin D

> *When you improve your menu,*
> *you enhance your milk production capacities,*
> *and you will have a better level of energy.*

Your Daily Menu

should include

– at least 6 servings of whole-grain products

One serving equals:

one slice of whole-grain bread

or one bowl of whole-grain cereal, hot or cold

or 200 mL (3/4 cup) cooked brown rice

or 250 mL (1 cup) cooked whole-grain pasta

– at least 6 servings of fruit and vegetables

A few times a week, give priority to dark-green leafy vegetables and fruit and vegetables that are rich in vitamin C and beta-carotene.

One serving equals:

125 mL (1/2 cup) cooked vegetables or fruit

or 250 mL (1 cup) raw vegetables

or 125 mL (1/2 cup) fruit or vegetable juice

or 1 medium-sized fresh fruit

– approximately 4 servings of milk products

One serving equals:

250 mL (1 cup) whole, 2%, 1%, or skim milk

or 45 g (1 1/2 oz.) ripened cheese

or 200 mL (3/4 cup) yogourt

– approximately 2 servings of foods rich in protein

One serving equals:

90 g (3 oz.) meat, poultry, or fish*

or 25 mL (1 cup) cooked beans

or 115 g (4 oz.) tofu

or 2 eggs

---

* Avoid sporting fish or other fish from polluted lakes, such as pike and wall-eye. Choose farmed fish such as trout and salmon. Choose ocean fish and seafood: haddock, halibut, cod, turbot, sole, lobster, shrimp, scallops.

A Daily Menu
without Milk Products

(Provides all the nutrients you need, including calcium.)

– at least 6 servings of whole-grain products

– at least 6 servings of fruit and vegetables
Include a daily serving of broccoli or kale
because of their richness in calcium.

– at least 750 mL (24 fl. oz.) of soy beverage
fortified with calcium and vitamin D
Use this beverage in cereal, soups, sauces, or creamy desserts.

– approximately 2 servings of foods rich in protein
This will depend on your and your baby's tolerance.
Include meat, poultry, or fish or substitutes,
including a daily serving of tofu or legumes
or canned fish (eat the bones).

– at least 30 mL (2 tbsp.) a day of sesame seeds
These could be whole or ground, and served on cereal,
soups, or cooked vegetables —
or as a dip for fresh fruit.

Note: If you do not succeed in eating sufficient amounts of calcium-rich foods such as sesame seeds, broccoli, kale, or fortified soy beverage, take supplements that give you 1,000 mg of calcium per day.

Table 2
Caffeine Chart

Beverages	*Caffeine*	Chocolate	*Caffeine*
	mg in 200 mL		mg
	(7 fl. oz.)	Bar 28 g (1 oz.)	5–20
Soft Drinks		Baking 28 g (1 oz.)	45
Regular	23–42	Cocoa/hot 200 mL	
Diet	21–35	(7 fl. oz.)	8–14
Caffeine-free	.08	Syrup 30 mL	
		(2 tbsp.)	10–17
Coffee			
Instant	82–94	**Medications**	*Caffeine*
Percolated	130–166		mg per tablet
Drip	182–204	*Non-prescription*	
Flavoured	58–122	Aspirin compounds,	
Decaffeinated	6–10	Bromo-Seltzer	32
		Cope, Midol	32
Bagged Tea		Excedrin, Anacin	32–60
Black, 5 min. brew	56–72	Dristan, Sinarest	30
Black, 1 min. brew	30–48	NoDoz	100
		Vivarin	200
Loose Tea		Pramaline,	
Black, 5 min. brew	58	Dexatrim	140–200
Black, 3 min. brew	50	Coricidin	32
Green, 5 min. brew	30		
Iced Tea	12–26	*Prescription*	
		APCs (aspirin,	
		phenacetin, caffeine)	32
		Darvon compound	32
		Migral	50

EIGHT

Postnatal Menus for All Mothers

*Y*ou have fed and nurtured your baby for nine months. Your body has transferred key nutrients to the foetus. You have given birth and have not yet fully recovered. Your sleeping hours have shrunk. Your schedule is upset and domestic help is non-existent. Do take care of yourself if you want to survive and live happily through these first months of motherhood.

Treat yourself to a healthy menu, whether you are breastfeeding or not. Food cannot substitute for lost sleeping hours, but it can help restore your strength during the first critical weeks.

To feel good without gaining another ounce, make better food choices. Look at the seven daily menus suggested in this chapter. Seek help. Ask your partner or a good friend to do the grocery shopping. Buy prepared foods from your favourite caterer or even frozen entrees at the supermarket. The bottom line is to reduce your cooking activities and to increase your resting hours. The objective is to boost your energy.

If you are breastfeeding, increase the amounts of food as suggested on pages 70–76, depending on your appetite, and add as many snacks as you need.

If you are not breastfeeding, eat well but forget the snacks. Choose low-fat dairy products and reduce your fat intake in order to regain your pre-pregnancy weight more rapidly.

If you are vegetarian, eat protein-rich foods at every meal and as snacks. Include tofu or legumes once a day or many times a week to obtain sufficient iron and magnesium.

If you have eliminated milk products, consult page 64 for a suggested menu.

In any case, *if you want to reduce your meat intake* for other reasons, make sure you include other iron-rich foods on your menu and don't forget to add a vitamin C–rich fruit or vegetable at every meal (see page 216) to improve iron absorption.

A Shopping List

To prepare a meal plan similar to the one suggested in this chapter, use the following as a reminder list in order to include all important food groups. You don't really need to have a different breakfast every morning. Just choose the one you prefer. Always include enough protein to support your energy level for three or four hours.

Buy enough snack foods to last for the week. It is better to stock more in case you are not able to go out shopping with your young baby.

Don't forget to buy plenty of fresh vegetables. Eat them raw or cooked. Buy ready-to-eat carrots or salad greens or even small salads that are already prepared — but without the dressing.

Choose fibre- and mineral-rich cereal products:

- rolled oats or muesli
- shredded wheat cereal or another whole grain cereal
- mixed muffins (bran, carrot, raisin bran, apple, and oatmeal)
- whole-wheat pasta
- brown rice
- whole-grain pita breads
- whole-grain bread
- whole-wheat pizza crust

Buy protein-rich foods for approximately 14 meals:

- canned salmon or tuna
- canned red kidney beans or chickpeas
- deboned chicken breasts
- minced lean beef or calf's liver
- frozen fish fillets (or a frozen fish meal, to reheat at the last minute)
- natural peanut or almond butter
- fresh eggs
- spaghetti sauce in a jar or from a caterer
- hummus (chickpea puree with sesame) or tofu

Do not forget calcium-rich milk products:

- ricotta cheese
- yogourt, plain or fruit flavoured
- fruit yogourt yops, a few
- mozzarella or cheddar cheese
- 2%, 1%, or skim milk

Colour your menus with vitamin-rich fruit and vegetables:

- alfalfa sprouts
- oranges
- grapefruit
- bananas
- clementines when in season, at least a dozen
- cantaloupe
- kiwi fruit
- fresh or thawed strawberries
- fresh pineapple
- applesauce
- ready-to-eat cabbage and carrots
- regular carrots
- ready-to-serve mixed greens
- frozen spinach
- green or red pepper
- tomatoes, fresh or canned
- ready-to-eat vegetables: broccoli, cauliflower, green onions, lettuce
- zucchini

Have fun with snack foods and extras:

- dried fruit: raisins, prunes, dates, or figs
- almonds or mixed, unsalted nuts
- sunflower or sesame seeds
- molasses (blackstrap), to add iron to your meals
- engevita or torula yeast, to add B vitamins to *power milk* (See recipe at the end of the chapter.)

Take better care of yourself and improve your daily eating habits. This is the ideal moment to do so.

DAY 1

With Meat, Fish, or Poultry *Lacto-ovo Vegetarian*

BREAKFAST

grapefruit (1/2)	grapefruit (1/2)
banana muffin with	banana muffin with
ricotta cheese	ricotta cheese
milk or café au lait	milk or café au lait

LUNCH

raw carrot sticks	raw carrot sticks
chunky lentil soup	chunky lentil soup
whole-wheat bread (2	whole-wheat bread (2
slices)	slices)
plain yogourt with fresh	plain yogourt with fresh
or thawed strawberries	or thawed strawberries

DINNER

baked chicken breast	baked pasta, broccoli,
herbed brown rice	and cheese casserole
steamed broccoli	whole-wheat pita bread
whole-wheat pita bread	salad greens
fresh pineapple slices	fresh pineapple slices
herbal tea	herbal tea

If you are breastfeeding, *If you are breastfeeding,*
eat plenty of snacks: *eat plenty of snacks:*
fruit and milk *fruit and milk*
yogourt *yogourt*
sunflower seeds *sunflower seeds*

DAY 2

With Meat, Fish, or Poultry	Lacto-ovo Vegetarian

BREAKFAST

orange juice	orange juice
oatmeal with raisins and milk	oatmeal with raisins and milk
whole-wheat bread, toasted	whole-wheat bread, toasted
milk or café au lait	milk or café au lait

LUNCH

red pepper rings	red pepper rings
grilled salmon sandwich or pita bread stuffed with salmon	grilled English muffin spread with peanut butter or cheese
banana	banana
glass of milk	glass of milk

DINNER

brown rice and chicken casserole	brown rice and lentil casserole
steamed zucchini and carrots	steamed zucchini and carrots
gingerbread muffin and orange yogourt	gingerbread muffin and orange yogourt
herbal tea	herbal tea

If you are breastfeeding, eat plenty of snacks:
bran muffin
yogourt or milk
power milk (p. 77)

If you are breastfeeding, eat plenty of snacks:
bran muffin
yogourt or milk
power milk (p. 77)

DAY 3

With Meat, Fish, or Poultry	Lacto-ovo Vegetarian

BREAKFAST

quartered orange	quartered orange
muesli-type cereal with milk	muesli-type cereal with milk
whole-wheat bread, toasted (2 slices)	whole-wheat bread, toasted (2 slices)
milk or café au lait	milk or café au lait

LUNCH

salad of cooked and raw vegetables	salad of cooked and raw vegetables
cheese cubes and nuts	cheese cubes and nuts
whole-wheat bread or bran muffin	whole-wheat bread or bran muffin
fresh cantaloupe	fresh cantaloupe
milk	milk

DINNER

broiled hamburger	red kidney beans with herbs and brown rice
coleslaw with apples	coleslaw with apples
whole-wheat bread	whole-wheat bread
fresh fruit salad	fresh fruit salad
herbal tea	herbal tea

If you are breastfeeding, eat plenty of snacks: milk and dried fruit yogourt carrot muffin

If you are breastfeeding, eat plenty of snacks: milk and dried fruit yogourt carrot muffin

DAY 4

With Meat, Fish, or Poultry	Lacto-ovo Vegetarian

BREAKFAST

grapefruit	grapefruit
shredded wheat with	shredded wheat with
milk, garnished with	milk, garnished with
nuts and wheat germ	nuts and wheat germ
whole-wheat bread,	whole-wheat bread,
toasted	toasted
milk or café au lait	milk or café au lait

LUNCH

vegetable juice	vegetable juice
chopped egg sandwich	chopped egg sandwich
with alfalfa on whole-	with alfalfa on whole-
wheat bread	wheat bread
fresh kiwi	fresh kiwi
milk	milk

DINNER

oven-poached fish fillet	whole-wheat macaroni &
sliced tomato	cheese
steamed broccoli	sliced tomato
whole-wheat bread	salad greens
banana with yogourt	banana with yogourt
herbal tea	herbal tea

If you are breastfeeding,   *If you are breastfeeding,*
eat plenty of snacks: *eat plenty of snacks:*
power milk (p. 77)   *power milk (p. 77)*
apple and cheese   *apple and cheese*
dried fruit and nuts   *dried fruit and nuts*

DAY 5

With Meat, Fish, or Poultry   *Lacto-ovo Vegetarian*

BREAKFAST

orange juice	orange juice
1 egg (soft-boiled or poached)	1 egg (soft-boiled or poached)
whole-wheat bread, toasted (2 slices)	whole-wheat bread, toasted (2 slices)
milk or café au lait	milk or café au lait

LUNCH

minute minestrone soup with kidney beans	minute minestrone soup with kidney beans
whole-wheat bread (2 slices)	whole-wheat bread (2 slices)
yogourt with fresh mandarin oranges	yogourt with fresh mandarin oranges
milk	milk

DINNER

tomato juice	tomato juice
seafood pizza	vegetarian pizza with cheese
garden green salad	garden green salad
applesauce	applesauce
herbal tea	herbal tea

If you are breastfeeding, eat plenty of snacks: apple and peanut butter yogourt power milk (p. 77)

If you are breastfeeding, eat plenty of snacks: apple and peanut butter yogourt power milk (p. 77)

DAY 6

With Meat, Fish, or Poultry   *Lacto-ovo Vegetarian*

BREAKFAST

orange and grapefruit juice	orange and grapefruit juice
shredded wheat	shredded wheat
sprinkled with nuts,	sprinkled with nuts,
raisins, and milk	raisins, and milk
whole-wheat bread,	whole-wheat bread,
toasted, or bran muffin	toasted, or bran muffin
milk or café au lait	milk or café au lait

LUNCH

green pepper rings	green pepper rings
grilled cheese sandwich	grilled cheese sandwich
with tomato	with tomato
fresh pear	fresh pear
milk	milk

DINNER

pasta primavera with	pasta primavera with
shrimp	lentils and sunflower seeds
whole-wheat bread	whole-wheat bread
lettuce-and-spinach salad	lettuce-and-spinach salad
yogourt and strawberries	yogourt and strawberries
herbal tea	herbal tea

If you are breastfeeding,   *If you are breastfeeding,*
eat plenty of snacks: *eat plenty of snacks:*
fruit juice and yogourt   *fruit juice and yogourt*
    yop (p. 77)   *yop (p. 77)*
milk   *milk*
almonds and figs   *almonds and figs*

DAY 7

With Meat, Fish, or Poultry   *Lacto-ovo Vegetarian*

BREAKFAST

quartered orange	quartered orange
bran muffin	bran muffin
milk or café au lait	milk or café au lait

LUNCH

vegetable juice	grated carrot salad
tuna and brown rice	split pea & barley soup
salad	whole-wheat bread
whole-wheat bread	fresh cantaloupe
fresh cantaloupe	milk
milk	

DINNER

stir-fried chicken with	stir-fried tofu with
vegetables	vegetables
Chinese cabbage salad	Chinese cabbage salad
whole-wheat bread	whole-wheat bread
tangerine	tangerine
oatmeal cookie	oatmeal cookie
herbal tea	herbal tea

If you are breastfeeding, eat   *If you are breastfeeding, eat*
plenty of snacks: *plenty of snacks:*
power milk (p. 77)   *power milk (p. 77)*
yogourt   *yogourt*
bran muffin   *bran muffin*

Instant Healthy Snacks

—◆—

Power Milk

250 mL (1 cup) skim or 1% milk (or fortified soy beverage if you prefer)
15 mL (1 tbsp.) engevita or torula yeast*
10 mL (2 tsp.) wheat bran
10 mL (2 tsp.) honey or maple syrup

In a large glass, mix all ingredients and serve cold.

If you want to make a larger quantity for future snacks, use a litre of milk and multiply all other quantities by 4. Mix well and keep in a pitcher in the refrigerator.

This power milk keeps for 2 to 3 days in the refrigerator. Mix well before serving.

Nutritional Value
250 mL (1 cup) contains much more protein, B vitamins, iron, and magnesium than a plain glass of milk or fortified soy beverage.

Fruit Juice and Yogourt Yop

250 mL (1 cup) plain yogourt, 2% or 1%
30 mL (2 tbsp.) frozen fruit juice

Choose orange juice, grape juice, or any frozen fruit juice.
In a large glass, mix both ingredients and serve cold.

Nutritional Value
250 mL (1 cup) supplies 14 g of protein.
If prepared with frozen orange juice, 250 mL (1 cup) also provides 50 mg of vitamin C.

---

* Engevita and torula yeast can be purchased in a natural food store.

NINE

Working and Breastfeeding

If you are planning your return to work in a few weeks or months, you will have a hard time accepting the separation from your baby and may wish to continue breastfeeding. Many mothers have done it; in fact, among breastfeeding mothers who go back to work, six out of ten continue to breastfeed at least four months after their return.

Breastfeeding while coping with an employment schedule is a challenge, but the experience is well worth it. It provides more intimacy with your baby and can offset the separation to a degree.

Mary had to return to work four months after Paula's birth. She wanted to continue to breastfeed because she knew that a breast-fed baby had better resistance to infections. She wanted to supply these additional antibodies with her breast milk. She organized herself to combine both tasks, and succeeded.

Carefully Plan Your Return to Work

Use your last weeks of maternity leave to get ready physically and mentally. Finalize your arrangements with the babysitter or the day-care. Your greatest challenge will be to maintain your energy level. Always go for the easiest solution. Learn to cut corners. Rest as often as possible and make sure that you get enough sleep. Do the essentials and leave out the frills.

Choose the Feeding Strategy Most Convenient for You

Exclusive breastfeeding implies that you give your baby breast milk exclusively, at the breast or in a bottle. You can continue to breastfeed your baby, morning and night on demand, and provide bottles filled with your milk for other feedings. Depending on his age, your baby may need two to three bottles or more during the work day.

Suzanne is a teacher. When she returned to work in September, her baby was nine months old. She continued to breastfeed in the morning; the babysitter gave the infant a bottle of breast milk at noon, and Suzanne breastfed after school and at night. During weekends, she breastfed normally on demand. To maintain her milk supply, Suzanne expressed her milk during lunch break in the teacher's room and stored it until classes were over. She transported the breast milk in an insulated lunch bag and kept it in the freezer or the refrigerator, depending on when she wanted to use it.

Mixed feeding implies that you breastfeed in the morning, when you come back from work, and at night. The rest of the time, the babysitter feeds the baby with iron-fortified formula.

Minimum breastfeeding consists of breastfeeding only once or twice per day, in the morning and/or at bedtime. The other feedings consist of iron-fortified formula given by you or the babysitter.

The best strategy is the most convenient one for you. Adapt your breastfeeding schedule to your type of work and your lifestyle. You should feel comfortable with your choice.

Plan a Schedule That Includes Breastfeeding As Often As You Wish

To continue breastfeeding in the most convenient way, choose the option that is most convenient:

- The babysitter can bring the baby to your workplace.
- You can have lunch at home.
- You can go to the daycare centre during lunch, if it is close by.
- You can work part time.
- You can work from your home.
- You can express your milk at work and bottle-feed your baby with it later — or you can offer milk in a glass or in a cup with a special spout, available in stores that sell baby bottles.

Spend at least one rehearsal day going over your strategy with the daycare centre or the babysitter, so that you feel secure when you return to work. Once you start working, give your ideal strategy a try and see how it works. Don't hesitate to adjust as you go along.

Learn to Express Your Milk

Before you go back to work, develop your ability to express your milk with a pump or manually. Some mothers prefer to do it by hand. Even if, at your first trial, it feels like an impossible task, do not despair; hand-expressing your milk is the easiest method. Nonetheless, if this is not convenient, try a pump, either manual or electric.

The La Leche League and other support groups can recommend a variety of pumps. Start with a manual pump, which is less expensive. If it does not suit you, you can then rent an electric pump through your local health centre and keep it in a safe corner of your office.

Many mothers do not like to express their milk because it makes them feel like a milk cow. They have a hard time relaxing and wait impatiently for the letdown reflex. If they think about their baby or sit in front of their baby's photo, they often rediscover the pleasure of having their baby close by, and they succeed in expressing their milk.

Expressing your milk can initially require as long as 45 minutes for both breasts, but with practice, the whole operation can take 20 to 30 minutes. You learn as if it were a new sport and become better with practice.

Jenny was breastfeeding with the greatest of ease, but could not pump any significant amount of milk even when using all the tricks of the trade. She realized that in the early mornings, when she breastfed her baby on one breast, she could ask the father to pump the second breast. With this method, a good quantity of milk was expressed — because her breasts were already filled with milk.

To express your milk at work, wear clothes that are loose and easily opened in front. Find a quiet spot. Express your milk into a clean bottle, rinsed with boiling water. Avoid glass containers because some nutrients present in breast milk tend to cling to glass. If necessary, transfer your milk to a clean thermos or a double plastic bag for baby bottles. Keep the thermos or bag in your lunch bag, cooled by an ice pack. Do not forget to write the date on the container.

Julie thought the ritual was very complicated at the beginning, but once she incorporated it into her daily routine, she found it quite easy and enjoyed the benefits of breastfeeding her baby for three more months than originally scheduled.

Store Breast Milk with Care

To provide breast milk for all your baby's feedings, develop your ability to express milk and start building a supply a few weeks before returning to work. Store breast milk in sanitized plastic bottles or the disposable plastic bags used in baby bottles. With these bags, use two because they break easily. Fresh breast milk will keep:

- 6 to 10 hours at room temperature,
- 5 to 8 days in the refrigerator,
- 3 to 4 months in the freezer compartment of your refrigerator,
- more than six months in a deep freezer.

Frozen breast milk can be kept thawed for 1 hour at room temperature and for 24 hours in the refrigerator.

Samantha, 31, returned to work when her baby was six months old. Every lunch hour, she expressed the equivalent of a bottle of breast milk. She kept the milk in a cooled lunch bag, then transferred it to the babysitter for the next day's feeding. One day, she forgot to take an ice pack to work and could not find a refrigerator, so she discarded her milk.

After she heard that breast milk could be kept at room temperature for a couple of hours, she did not discard another drop.

If your baby is between the ages of three and six months, express approximately 90 millilitres (3 oz.) per bottle. Do not store more than needed in one bottle (to avoid wasting your breast milk). If your baby is older than six months, increase the quantity according to his or her appetite. When your baby is hungrier, the babysitter can give a second bottle when needed. This is better than throwing out leftover breast milk at every feeding.

Tell the Babysitter Breast Milk Looks Different

Breast milk does not look like cow's milk; it is not homogenized, so the fat does separate. Its shade can vary from blue to yellow to brown. This is normal. If it has been well stored, there is no reason to worry about its appearance.

Acquaint Your Baby with a Bottle

Your baby will be accustomed to feeding on your breast and so may refuse to drink from a bottle at first — especially if you wait too long to introduce it. Introduce a bottle of breast milk during the second month or even before, so this mode of feeding is accepted by the baby and you will be able to skip a feeding once in a while. For the first feeding from a bottle, ask the father or the babysitter to feed the baby from the bottle. Then leave the house so your infant does not expect a feeding from *you*.

Gradually continue to accustom your baby to the bottle and to your absence during the following weeks. If your baby refuses the bottle, recheck the nipple, its shape, the hole, and the aftertaste. Try another nipple if necessary.

Be patient but persevere. Your breastfed baby is not the only one who has resisted bottle feeding. Do not wait until the day before you return to work. This will make things easier for you and your baby.

Sylvia introduced the first bottle when her baby was four weeks old and persevered until the eighth week before she accepted it.

To Reheat Breast Milk

Give clear instructions never to reheat breast milk in the microwave or in boiling water. This is not necessary. Just have the babysitter put the bottle or bag filled with breast milk in a bowl of warm water or under hot, running water. Then your sitter should shake the bottle or bag well, check the temperature by putting a few drops on the wrist, and serve.

Plan a Breastfeeding Break after Work

Once you step back into the house, devote your first 45 minutes to your baby. Make sure your baby is not fed for two hours before you come home so that when you arrive, you can avoid having engorged breasts and a baby who is not hungry.

Find the coziest spot and breastfeed your baby in peace. Unplug the phone if necessary, and if possible, recruit help for other domestic chores — including the preparation of the night meal. The father is surely the best candidate for that job!

Stay Healthy

To fulfill this special mandate, treat yourself to a very healthy diet, never skip a meal, and get rest as often as possible. Ask your babysitter or the father to buy the groceries and to prepare the evening meal, whenever possible. Continue to take a multivitamin and mineral supplement to protect your nutrient stores. Revisit the menus in Chapter 8, Postnatal Menus for All Mothers , and fill up on winning foods every day.

A Success Story

When the work environment provides support, it can make your life much easier. A few years ago, a community hospital made a commitment to promoting breastfeeding among its employees. The administration rented an electric pump and made arrangements for nursing mothers to pump their milk in an appropriate and accessible location during working hours. This simple program was shown to be effective in helping working mothers continue nursing after their return to work.

Your success in breastfeeding while at work depends
a lot on your ability to recruit help around you. Expressing
your milk becomes easier as you go along. Good luck!

TEN

Other Milks — Before and after Six Months

*E*ven if breast milk is impossible to copy and offers more nutrition than any infant formula, you can decide not to breastfeed your baby for many good reasons, or you may have breastfed a few weeks or months and wish to offer your baby the most appropriate substitute.

Alternatives to breast milk have been used for centuries, but because of unsatisfactory sanitation practices, they were never available on a large scale. Safe infant formulas are a product of the twentieth century and are now being offered to more than 75 percent of Canadian babies at one point during their infancy. Commercially prepared infant formulas have become the second-best choice, the most suitable alternative to breast milk during the first six to nine months of life. Other milks such as ordinary cow's milk (whole or partially or totally skimmed), evaporated milk, and goat's milk are not recommended for a newborn baby.

Infant formulas are essentially designed to fulfill the infant's nutritional needs and constantly undergo modifications to mimic breast milk better. They change as often as once or twice a year, based on the most recent research on breast milk. At least 20 different formulas are on the market. Before you choose the appropriate formula for your baby, let us go over the main formula categories and their components.

Before Six Months

Milk-based Infant Formulas

- Bonamil, fortified with iron
- Enfalac, without iron or fortified with iron
- Good Start, fortified with iron
- Similac, without iron or fortified with iron
- Similac Advance
- SMA, without iron or fortified with iron
- Unilac, without iron or fortified with iron

Iron-fortified, milk-based formulas are recommended for term babies, born healthy, who are partially breastfed or not breastfed at all — as an alternative to breast milk until six to nine months of age.

These formulas are prepared from cow's milk that has been diluted and processed so that the concentrations and proportions of its nutrients are similar to those found in breast milk.

The *protein* found in Bonamil, Similac, and Unilac resembles cow's milk protein, with 82 percent casein and 18 percent lactoserum. The protein found in Enfalac and SMA imitates breast milk, with 40 percent casein and 60 percent lactoserum. Good Start contains only lactoserum. Despite these differences and later modifications, the protein in infant formulas is more allergenic than in breast milk and has no anti-infectious properties.

The main source of *carbohydrate* in these formulas is lactose, the same type of carbohydrate found in breast milk. Good Start also contains a small amount of maltodextrin.

The *fat* content is generally a blend of different oils, such as palm olein, soy, coconut, safflower, and sunflower. At present, the blend is regularly modified to mimic the fat composition of breast milk and supply the right proportion of the two essential fatty acids — linoleic and alpha-linolenic acid. No formula contains AA and DHA (see pages 19–20).

The *mineral* content imitates that of breast milk.

The *iron* content varies, depending on the formula. Health authorities in Canada recommend an iron-fortified formula for all healthy, term, non-breastfed babies, in order to decrease the incidence of anaemia among young infants. The iron-fortified formula helps prevent iron deficiencies that can lead to long-term damage in a child's neurological development.

Studies show that infants fed iron-fortified formulas are not more constipated and do not have more gastrointestinal problems than infants fed non-fortified formulas — but they do have darker, greener stools.

All milk-based infant formulas are fortified with iron but come in a non-fortified version as well. Read the label to make sure you are buying the one you want.

The *vitamin* content of formulas tends to imitate the content of breast milk, with the exception of vitamin D, which is added in sufficient amounts (10 micrograms (400 IU) per litre) to prevent rickets (see Chapter 11, Vitamin and Mineral Supplements, pages 103–6).

You can purchase these formulas in drugstores or grocery stores. Some can be bought in three different forms:

– *a liquid concentrate:* Simply add water equal to the amount of formula. Use tap water or bottled spring water. In all cases, boil at least two minutes and let cool. This concentrate provides greater stability of nutrients than those in powdered or granulated concentrate.

– *a powdered or granulated concentrate:* Follow the instructions on the container, using the exact measures of powder and water indicated. One study showed that several problems can occur when this type of formula is mixed: difficulty in reading the instructions, incomplete information on the label, difficulty measuring the powder, the powder becoming sticky.

– *a ready-to-serve formula:* No dilution is required. This type is more expensive but can be practical when you are travelling with your baby.

Always look for expiry dates on the package, and do not use the formula beyond that date.

The composition of infant formulas changes on a regular basis, in order to better imitate breast milk. When a substance or a nutrient is identified in breast milk and proven to be very useful for the infant's health, manufacturers eventually find ways of incorporating it into their formulas. At present, the important fats found in breast milk, called AA and DHA (see Chapter 3, Why Choose Breast Milk?, pages 19–20), are not yet added, but they may be in the near future.

Soy-based Infant Formulas

- Alsoy
- Enfalac ProSobee Soy
- Isomil
- Nursoy

These soy-based infant formulas are recommended for babies from strict vegetarian families, babies who cannot tolerate cow's milk protein or lactose, and babies who are partially breastfed or are not breastfed at all.

All soy-based formulas are fortified with iron but contain no lactose.

Prepared with soy and adapted to the nutritional needs of newborns, these formulas are consumed by 20 percent of infants in Canada. They are not to be confused with a wide range of soy milk beverages such as So Nice, So Good, Vitasoy, and Edensoy, which are not modified to suit the nutritional needs of infants.

Infants allergic to cow's milk protein can also react to soy in 30 percent of cases. In fact, soy-based formulas are not hypoallergenic at all, and they should not be used as such.

The *protein* in soy-based formulas comes from soy flour, which is isolated and then fortified with a small amount of L-methionine, an essential amino acid found in breast milk. This improves the quality of the plant-based protein.

The *carbohydrate* content varies among the different brands. Isomil and Nursoy have no lactose but a blend of sucrose and glucose polymers, a corn by-product that is easier for the baby to absorb. Enfalac ProSobee Soy has only glucose polymers, while Alsoy has a blend of sucrose and corn maltodextrins.

An infant who is intolerant to lactose following a severe attack of diarrhea or because of a rare metabolic disease call galactosemia can tolerate and assimilate the other sugars present in soy-based formulas or in other lactose-free formulas such as Similac LF or Enfalac Prosobee Soy without lactose.

The *fat* content is a blend of different oils, such as soy, safflower, coconut, sunflower, and palm olein. The blend is constantly re-adjusted to respond to the latest research.

The *vitamin and mineral* content imitates that of breast milk. All soy-based infant formulas are fortified with iron.

You can purchase these formulas in drugstores in liquid concentrate or powdered form.

Hypoallergenic, or Therapeutic, Infant Formulas

- Alimentum
- Enfalac Nutramigen
- Enfalac Pregestimil

These infant formulas, also called therapeutic, are prepared to meet the particular needs of very sensitive infants who cannot tolerate either cow's milk or soy protein and who are partially breastfed or not breastfed at all.

The first formula to be developed in this category dates back to the 1940s and answers the special needs of very sensitive babies. In order to reduce the infant's exposure to whole protein, cow's milk protein in such formulas is predigested, filtered, and purified in a lab until it becomes a casein hydrolysate. This type of protein is easier to digest and absorb, and it is considered less allergenic.

That explains why the American Academy of Pediatrics classifies these formulas as hypoallergenic and useful in many cases of allergies and colic. Such highly processed formulas are recommended for infants with a family history of allergy, who have demonstrated symptoms of allergies.

These formulas contain no lactose but they include every vitamin and mineral needed for proper growth during the first year of life; they are all fortified with iron. They are available in drugstores in ready-to-feed, or powdered form.

Emily was breastfed for at least six months but had severe colic whenever her mother ate milk products or soy or beef protein. Her family history revealed numerous cases of food allergies. When she was weaned, she was fed a hypoallergenic formula for many months, well into the second year of her life. But eventually, she was able to eat milk and soy products without any allergic reaction.

An infant who is not breastfed, who is allergic to cow's milk, and whose parents have food allergies will benefit from this type of formula and may have to remain on such a formula for many months until his immune system has matured.

Formulas for Premature Babies

- Enfalac for preemies
- Enfalac Special for preemies
- Simila Special Care, without iron or fortified with iron
- SMA Preemie

These formulas are indicated when a premature baby is not breastfed or is partially breastfed and weighs less than 2 kilograms (4 1/2 lb.).

They contain more calories than regular formulas, as well as carbohydrates and fats that are easier to digest and assimilate. These formulas are available in hospitals.

Evaporated Whole Milk, Cow or Goat

Evaporated whole cow's or goat's milk is not recommended as an alternative to breast milk or infant formula for newborn infants.

This type of milk contains too much protein and does not suit the nutritional needs of infants, even when diluted and sweetened. It is particularly deficient in iron and essential fatty acids. Compared with whole cow's milk, however, it is easier to digest because the protein has been heat-treated.

If you cannot breastfeed and cannot afford to buy milk- or soy-based infant formula, this type of milk is considered a third choice once it is properly diluted and given with the appropriate supplements.

If you do buy evaporated whole milk, choose a type that has been fortified with vitamins C and D. In the case of evaporated goat's milk, look for a kind that is fortified with vitamins C and D and folic acid.

For babies younger than six months, it is important to dilute evaporated milk. This decreases the renal solute load and makes things easier on the infant's kidney system — by reducing the amount of protein and sodium. Dilute the milk with water that has been boiled at least two minutes and then cooled. Add white sugar or dextrose (available at drugstores) to increase the caloric content. Do not use honey or corn syrup before 12 months of age. (See the Dilution Chart at the end of this chapter.)

When your baby is three months old, add an iron supplement to his or her diet, to prevent anaemia. Each day, give your baby iron in the form of drops (0.5 millilitres of Fer-In-Sol) in a small amount of water or in a formula bottle. Continue giving this iron supplement until 12 months of age.

After four months, a supplement of essential fatty acids is needed. Add 5 millilitres (1 teaspoon) of sunflower or canola oil per day to the formula and eventually to the infant cereal you give to your baby.

A recent survey done on infant feeding practices by the U.S. Food and Drug Administration revealed that 33 percent of mothers of newborns mixed formula with warm tap water and up to 48 percent heated bottles in the microwave. Some mothers even left prepared formula at room temperature for more than two hours. Such mistakes can lead to adverse health consequences such as diarrhea and should be avoided.

How to Prepare Formula

For the first four months, sterilize the infant's feeding equipment.

The *water* used in the preparation of the formula can be tap water or well water that meets safety standards or commercially bottled water (with the exceptions of carbonated and mineral water). However, none of these waters is sterile, and you must use pathogen-free water for infants under four months of age. To do so, the *water should be brought to a rolling boil for at least two minutes.* Boiled water can be stored for two or three days in the refrigerator, in a sterilized and tightly closed container.

1. Wash all equipment (bottles, nipples, caps, tongs, measuring cup, opener) and sterilize and boil for at least two minutes.
2. Boil the water you will use to dilute the powder or the concentrate for at least two minutes. Let it cool in a sterile, closed container.
3. Rinse the top of the can with boiling water; shake vigorously; open with a sterilized opener.
4. If using a ready-to-serve formula, pour it into the sterilized bottles.
5. If using the powdered form, pour cooled water into a large, sterilized pitcher, and add the proper amount of formula, according to the directions on the label. Stir gently.
6. If using the concentrate, pour cooled water into the bottles and add the proper amount of formula to each bottle.
7. Use the sterilized tongs to apply caps and nipples.
8. Refrigerate immediately, for use within 24 hours. Shake to mix the formula as needed.
9. Once open, a can of ready-to-serve or concentrate should be emptied into a sterilized pitcher, covered, and refrigerated. Any unused portion should be discarded after 48 hours.

When and How Much to Feed Your Baby

A baby's appetite varies as much as an adult's. So you are playing a guessing game as you try to predict exactly how much formula to pour into each bottle. There are nonetheless a few guidelines to help you out.

During the first few weeks, a baby is often hungry but does not consume large quantities at once. In general, the nutritional needs of infants are met with approximately 60 to 90 millilitres (2 to 3 oz.) of formula per 450 grams (1 lb.) of weight, per day (see chart below).

There is no upper limit before the age of four to five months, and there is no urgency to introduce solid foods, even if your baby requires more milk.

However, never force a baby into finishing a bottle even if he falls asleep during a feeding. Give him the chance to tell you he has had enough to eat.

The following chart gives you examples of what quantities of formula you might offer to your baby. Do not consider any of these suggestions as rigid rules. Always be flexible and adjust quantities according to your baby's hunger signals!

Table 3
How Much Formula to Offer

Baby's Weight	Baby's Daily Needs	Amount in Bottle	Number of Feedings/Day
3.2 kg (7 lb.)	420–630 mL (14–21 fl. oz.)	100–120 mL (3.4–4 fl. oz.)	5 to 7
4.5 kg (10 lb.)	600–900 mL (20–30 fl. oz.)	150–180 mL (5–6 fl. oz.)	5 to 7

How Many Feedings per Day?

The first week after birth, you may need to feed your baby up to ten times a day and even more often. During the second and third weeks, six to eight feedings can be sufficient.

If your baby weighs less than 2.7 kilograms (6 lb.), feed him every three hours (approximately seven to eight times a day). A formula-fed baby is hungry less often than a breastfed baby, but your baby will nonetheless have growth spurts and will require more formula some days.

As your baby's weight increases, her need for night feeding decreases and she can be satisfied with five feedings a day.

Serve Cold or Lukewarm?
Serving temperature can vary. Some babies prefer cold milk during the summer and lukewarm milk in the winter. If your baby prefers it warm, place the bottle under hot running water for a few minutes. *Avoid heating the formula in the microwave* because microwave heat is not evenly distributed, so you will risk burning your baby with small quantities of very hot milk. Many such cases have been reported.

Try always to offer milk at approximately the same temperature for your baby's security and comfort.

Storing the Formula
Keep the bottle of unused infant formula in the refrigerator for no more than 24 hours. *Never leave it at room temperature.* This will cause bacteria to develop rapidly and will lead to gastrointestinal infections and diarrhea.

After Six Months

Breast milk is still the best milk to offer your baby after six months. If you are still partially breastfeeding or have already replaced breast milk with infant formula, you have the following choices.

Transition Formulas

- Enfalac Next Step
- Follow-up

- Follow-up Soy
- Similac Advance 2

These formulas were developed and used in Europe for a long time, but they arrived in Canada only a few years ago. They are adjusted to the nutritional needs of six-month-old babies who still cannot drink regular cow's milk. They contain slightly more protein, carbohydrates, and calcium than formulas for newborns, and they have less fat. They are particularly rich in iron, to satisfy the needs of a baby who still eats a very limited amount of solid food. They facilitate the transition between breast milk or infant formula and regular cow's milk.

After Nine Months

Infant formulas try to mimic breast milk and are more or less adapted to the newborn's needs. Other milks, such as whole cow's milk and whole goat's milk, are not adapted and not recommended before your baby reaches the age of nine months.

Pasteurized Whole Cow's Milk, 3.25% BF
Whole cow's milk can be introduced into the infant's diet between the ages of 9 and 12 months.

Whole cow's milk, containing 3.25% butterfat (BF), is not adjusted to the infant's nutritional needs and digestive capabilities. It contains too much protein and too many minerals for the infant's renal system (kidneys) to handle. It has too few of the essential fatty acids (linoleic and alpha-linolenic), and it has insufficient lactose, zinc, vitamin C, and niacin. It is harder to digest and has been associated with blood loss in the stool. It is very poor in iron and so increases the risk of iron deficiency.

Once your baby is nine months old and eating approximately 200 mL (3/4 cup) of solid foods every day (including a daily intake of iron-fortified infant cereal), he can switch to pasteurized whole cow's milk. His daily intake of iron-rich foods can then counterbalance the impact of the cow's milk.

Pasteurized Whole Goat's Milk, 3.25% BF
Whole goat's milk can be introduced into the infant's diet between the ages of 9 and 12 months.

For reasons very similar to the ones just described for whole cow's milk, whole goat's milk is not adapted to the infant's needs during the early months and should not be introduced before the age of nine months. To be useful, it must be fortified with vitamin D and folic acid. (Folic acid fortification has been allowed in Canada since 1998 and is indicated on the label.) Whole goat's milk is considered to be easier to digest but it is not necessarily a hypoallergenic alternative if your baby is allergic to cow's milk.

Once your baby is nine months old and eating approximately 200 mL (3/4 cup) of solid foods every day, you can introduce this milk. Always look for goat's milk that is fortified with vitamin D and folic acid.

After 18 Months

Partially Skimmed Milk
During the first two years, 2%, 1%, and skim milk are inappropriate milk choices, but they can be introduced after 24 months if the rest of the family drinks this type of milk.

Skim milk contains too much protein and too many minerals for the baby's immature renal system and too few calories for growth and development. It is deficient in essential fatty acids and can limit the normal development of the central nervous system. The limitations of 2% and 1% milk are very similar.

In the seventies, when it seemed that every North American wanted to prevent cardiovascular diseases, many babies were fed skim milk before six months. Scientists found that four-month-old babies fed skim milk drank larger volumes of milk and ate more solids to compensate the lack of calories in the milk. They were still gaining some weight but losing a fair amount of fat tissue. They survived the very low fat diet but their resistance was lowered and they had less ability to combat infection.

Introducing such milks too early only leads to overconsumption of food and can increase other long-term risks.

After 18 months, 2% milk may be an acceptable alternative if the child is eating a variety of foods and growing at an acceptable rate.

Soy Beverages or Drinks

- Vitasoy
- So Nice
- So Good
- Edensoy
- Soy Dream

Soy beverages or drinks that are fortified with calcium and vitamin D can be introduced into the baby's diet after 24 months, but not before.

These are not recommended for babies under two years of age because they do not supply enough calories and do not always have adequate protein to support normal growth during the first 24 months. If you do use these, make sure they are fortified with calcium and vitamin D.

**The right milk at the right time
allows you to satisfy your baby's nutritional needs.**

Table 4

The Right Milk at the Right Time

At Birth

(in order of preference)

• breast milk

• iron-fortified infant formula

Between 6 and 9 Months

(in order of preference)

• breast milk

• transition formula

Between 9 and 12 Months

(in order of preference)

• breast milk

• transition formula

• whole cow's or goat's milk (once your baby is eating
200 mL (3/4 cup) of solid foods per day, including iron-fortified cereal)

12 to 24 Months

(in order of preference)

• breast milk, if desired

• whole cow's or goat's milk

Table 5

Dilution Chart for Evaporated Cow's or Goat's Milk

Age (Months)	Evaporated Milk	Boiled Water, Cooled	White Sugar or Dextrose	Total Volume
1 to 2	300 mL (10 oz.)	600 mL) (20 oz.)	45 mL (3 tbsp.)	900 mL (30 oz.)
6	480 mL (16 oz.)	480 mL (16 oz.)	none	960 mL (32 oz.)

ELEVEN

Vitamin and Mineral Supplements

In recent years, it has become an acceptable and widespread health routine to take extra vitamins and minerals. More than 50 percent of North American adults swallow supplements every day. Very few among them have a precise idea of what they really need or what is really missing from their daily diet. Many use these supplements in large doses to prevent illness or retard aging.

In the case of infants, the need for supplements is more clearly defined.

Babies Are Born with Stored Nutrients

If you have eaten adequately during your pregnancy and if you have given birth to a normal-weight term baby, your baby will be well equipped with nutrient stores — especially vitamin D and iron.

If you have neglected your diet during pregnancy or if your baby was born prematurely with a low birth weight, you will need to build up your baby's nutrient stores.

The Role of Supplements

During the first years of life, supplements may be needed to fill nutritional gaps. Dosages will not exceed nutritional needs as delineated for infants in *Nutrition Recommendations for Canadians* (1990). The supplements required also depend on your eating habits while you breastfeed and on the type of milk you give your baby.

During the second year of life, your baby may need a supplement, depending on what she will not or cannot eat.

But be careful. Choose the right supplement and give the proper dose. A baby's body mass is relatively small, and excessive quantities of supplements can be more dangerous than they are for adults.

Vitamins and Minerals That Can Be Missing

Babies need at least nine different vitamins and six different minerals for normal growth and development — as well as good-quality protein, essential fatty acids, and adequate carbohydrates. They have a very limited menu but must receive all these nutrients during this extremely rapid growth period.

The type of milk you give your baby will determine the type of supplement she needs. The nutrients that are most often deficient are vitamin D, iron, and vitamin B_{12}.

Vitamin D
Unlike any other vitamins, vitamin D is not present in significant amounts in foods except in fish oils. It is naturally produced in the skin upon exposure to sunlight. It then helps the body absorb calcium and allows for good bone growth.

When vitamin D is deficient, babies develop rickets — that is, they have bowed legs and knock-knees that become apparent when they begin to walk. Their teeth are less well formed and they decay earlier. Thirty years ago, rickets was not rare in Canada. Fortifying milk with vitamin D since then has almost eliminated the problem. The condition has not been completely eradicated, however. In northern Manitoba, 48 cases of rickets were reported among breast-fed babies born between 1972 and 1984.

Three factors influence the vitamin D status of an infant: vitamin D status at birth, vitamin D intake, and exposure to sunlight.

- If, during pregnancy, you did not consume any milk, had little exposure to sunlight, and did not take a vitamin D supplement, you may be deficient in vitamin D yourself, and your baby will have limited stores of vitamin D.
- Even if you breastfeed your baby, your breast milk will not supply him with sufficient vitamin D. Very few breastfed babies develop rickets, but the risk exists and can lead to serious problems.
- If your baby is born at the end of summer, exposure to sunlight will be limited. If your baby's skin is dark, sun exposure has a smaller impact on the formation of vitamin D because dark skins do not let the sun's rays penetrate as easily.

Sunlight or Supplement?
If your baby is breastfed and was born in the spring, expose him to sunlight regularly, so he can get his vitamin D. Plan your baby's sunbaths from April to September, before 10 a.m. or after 2 p.m., for a period varying between 5 and 30 minutes per day. Babies with darker skin need to sunbathe longer than those with lighter skin. There is no need for a baby to tan to obtain sufficient vitamin D, but do not use a sunscreen. This prevents the penetration of UV rays through the skin and blocks vitamin D synthesis. Sunbathing needs to be done before the fall, since after September, sunrays at Canadian

latitudes do not stimulate the formation of vitamin D.

If your baby is breastfed and was born in late August, give him a vitamin D supplement from the beginning of September to the end of March that provides 10 micrograms (400 IU) per day, beginning during the second week of life and continuing until the age of 24 months. The chart below shows *total* daily amounts (not supplements) recommended for infants in Canada.

Table 6

Vitamin D: Daily Recommended Amounts for Infants in Canada

10 micrograms (400 IU)	0 to 4 months
10 micrograms (400 IU)	5 to 11 months
10 micrograms (400 IU)	12 to 24 months

If you live in northern latitudes (above 53°N), the recommendation goes up to 20 micrograms (800 IU) per day.

Vitamin D Supplements Available
(See the chart, Baby Supplements, on page 114.)

- *D-Vi-Sol or D-Ovit, in drop form*
- *Tri-Vi-Sol or Triovit, in drop form*
- *Tender Age A, D, C, in liquid form*

Other Situations

- If you are giving your baby milk- or soy-based infant formula, she is receiving adequate amounts of vitamin D. This vitamin is also added to evaporated milk and cow's milk. Babies fed such formulas do not need a vitamin D supplement.
- Once your breastfed baby is weaned to an infant formula or to cow's milk, there is no need for a vitamin D supplement.
- If your breastfed baby is weaned to a regular soy beverage (even if

not recommended), choose one that is fortified with vitamin D and calcium.

Vitamin D from sunlight, food, or a supplement is essential to prevent rickets, but a serious calcium deficiency can also contribute to this illness, as recently reported in The New England Journal of Medicine. *A weaned baby needs the right amount of milk and sunlight — in others words, he needs adequate calcium, as well as vitamin D, to build strong bones.*

Iron

Iron deficiency is the most frequent nutritional deficiency among North American babies before the age of two. Research done in Vancouver a few years ago on iron status and the feeding practices of 434 healthy babies found that 7 percent of infants were iron deficient at nine months and 24 percent had low iron stores. Some of these infants were being breastfed; others were being bottle-fed with cow's milk or low-iron infant formulas. Iron-fortified cereals had been introduced to 95 percent of the surveyed babies by the time they were six months old. This would seem to show that it is vital to provide enough iron very early in your baby's life.

Iron is needed to carry oxygen around in the blood. It plays an important role in a child's psychomotor development during the first 12 months of life. Iron deficiency leads to mild anaemia that can go unnoticed, and then to more severe symptoms of pallor, loss of appetite, decreased tolerance for exercise, irritability, decreased resistance to infection, and impaired behaviour. It usually develops at the end of the first year because of an accumulated lack of iron during preceding months. Some cases of severe anaemia can lead to cognitive deficits and cannot always be corrected.

Variable Iron Stores at Birth

Iron is part of the nutritional heritage that a baby receives at birth.

This heritage depends on the mother's health and nutritional status and on the length of pregnancy. A term baby of normal weight who received a placental transfusion before the cord was cut will usually have good iron stores for at least four months. A premature baby born at seven or eight months will generally have used all his iron stores by the age of two months.

Jennifer was born prematurely after eight months of pregnancy and weighed 2.5 kg (5 lb. 5 oz.). She did not receive all the iron she could have absorbed during the ninth month of pregnancy. If she were totally breastfed, she would need additional iron at about two months.

Pamela was a term baby and weighed 3.5 kg (7 lb. 7 oz.) at birth. If she were formula-fed with an iron-fortified formula until nine months, she would not need any iron supplement during the first year of life.

Type of Milk Determines Iron Needs

- If your baby was born at term and is totally breastfed, there is no need for an iron supplement before the age of four to six months. Breast milk contains little iron but it is exceptionally well absorbed.
- If your baby was born prematurely or weighed less than 2.5 kilograms (5.5 lb.) and is totally breastfed, he should receive an iron supplement at two months of age. Choose a supplement in the form of ferrous sulfate, which is easy to absorb, and do not give him more than 15 milligrams per day.
- If your baby is fed with an iron-fortified infant formula, whether milk- or soy-based, there is no need for an iron supplement. One litre (34 fl. oz.) of a formula like this provides between 7 and 12 milligrams of iron, in the form of ferrous sulfate. During the past 25 years, this type of formula has succeeded in significantly decreasing the incidence of anaemia among infants.

- If you are feeding your baby an infant formula that is not fortified with iron, he will require an iron supplement by the fourth month. You may, at this point, give your baby an iron-fortified formula or an iron supplement in the form of ferrous sulfate.
- If your baby is fed an evaporated whole cow's milk formula, he will require an iron supplement by the third month, in the form of ferrous sulfate.

The chart below shows *total* daily amounts (not supplements) recommended for infants in Canada.

Table 7
Iron: Daily Recommended Amounts for Infants in Canada

0.3 mg	0 to 4 months
7 mg	5 to 11 months
6 mg	12 to 24 months

Iron Supplement Available

- Fer-In-Sol (ferrous sulfate), in drop form
(See the chart, Baby Supplements, on page 114.)

Possible Side Effects
The additional iron found in iron-fortified infant formulas or in ferrous sulfate drops very seldom causes adverse reactions but can sometimes lead to cramps, constipation, and gas. The only noticeable difference caused by iron supplements is the colour of the stools, which become dark brownish, greenish, or black.

If your baby does have an annoying gastrointestinal reaction when you introduce the iron-fortified formula, alternate between the iron-fortified and the non-fortified formula until the symptoms slowly disappear.

Once Your Baby Is Eating Solids
When your baby is eating enough iron-rich foods, her need for an iron supplement will slowly decrease. If, for example, she eats at least 90 millilitres (or 6 tablespoons) of iron-fortified infant cereals each day, she will receive a fair amount of iron.

A study has also shown that meat intake can improve iron status in late infancy because the iron it contains is easily absorbed by the body. A 27-gram serving per day (less than one ounce) can make a difference.

No specific research has been done on the impact of other foods rich in iron such as tofu and cooked legumes, but these foods can enhance the iron content of the baby's diet.

Vitamin B_{12}

Scientific journals have reported on a few tragic cases of B vitamin deficiencies that have caused babies to suffer major neurological problems before the age of 12 months. These babies were breastfed by strict vegetarian or vegan mothers. These lactating mothers had not eaten any food of animal origin (no meat, egg, milk, cheese, fish) during pregnancy or lactation. Nor had they taken adequate vitamin supplements during that time. Their breast milk became deficient in vitamin B_{12} and could no longer support the infant's normal growth and brain development.

Vitamin B_{12} is found in foods of animal origin such as dairy products, meat, fish, poultry, and eggs, and especially liver. In adults who become strict vegetarians after having eaten a mixed diet for many years, a vitamin B_{12} deficiency takes years to develop. This is because body stores can last up to eight years. But infants born to vegans can develop a deficiency in their first year of life because they had no stores at birth.

Vitamin B_{12} is involved in the growth and division of cells. It works along with folic acid, another B vitamin, to produce red

blood cells. A deficiency leads to a progressive degeneration of
nerve fibres and causes a variety of neurological symptoms. In
infants, it can be fatal.

Lacto-ovo or lactovegetarian mothers do not need to worry because milk products and eggs provide ample amounts of vitamin B_{12}.

Soon after Birth

If you are a strict vegetarian and have not taken any vitamin B_{12} supplement during your pregnancy, give your baby a supplement beginning in the second week of life — the equivalent of 0.3 micrograms per day.

The chart below shows *total* daily amounts (not supplements) recommended for infants in Canada.

Table 8

Vitamin B_{12}: Daily Recommended Amounts for Infants in Canada

0.3 mcg	0 to 4 months
0.4 mcg	5 to 11 months
0.5 mcg	12 to 24 months

Vitamin B_{12} Supplements Available

(See the chart, Toddlers' Supplements, on page 115.)

- nuborn (nu-life), a multivitamin in liquid form
- Floradix Kindervital, a multivitamin in liquid form

Fluoride

Fluoride given in appropriate quantities can decrease the incidence of dental caries (tooth decay) by up to 50 percent. It acts before eruption of the teeth through the gums by improving the quality of the enamel. After eruption, it limits degradation of the enamel.

Breast milk has a very low fluoride content even if you take a supplement and even if you drink fluoridated water. Infant formulas are now prepared with defluoridated water, so their fluoride content is less than three parts per million.

The Latest Recommendation . . .
An increase in the availability of fluoride in toothpaste, mouthwashes, and food and drinks made with fluoridated water has led the Canadian Paediatric Society and the Canadian Dental Association to modify their recommendations. These associations no longer recommend fluoride supplements at birth and have decreased the recommended doses during the first six years of life.

– No supplement is recommended during the first six months.
– 0.25 mg per day is recommended from 6 to 24 months, if your water supply is not fluoridated.

Fluoride Supplement Available
• Karidium (2 drops provides the equivalent of 0.25 mg of fluoride)

Other Ways of Preventing Tooth Decay
There are other ways of preventing tooth decay during the first two years of life:

– Never let your baby fall asleep with a bottle of milk or juice in his mouth. This causes the teeth to be bathed in beverages containing sugar. Even lactose in milk can trigger the multiplication of dental bacteria and lead to tooth decay.
– After 12 months, establish a ritual around toothbrushing, at bedtime.
– Avoid giving your baby sticky, sweet foods, especially between meals.

Different Milks, Different Supplements

Breast milk is the most beneficial milk for your newborn, but it may require some supplementation in certain instances.

- A vitamin D supplement of 10 mcg (400 IU) is needed by the beginning of the second week of life if your baby has darker skin, has limited exposure to sunlight, is born between the end of August and the end of March, or if you are a strict vegetarian.
- 0.3 mcg of vitamin B_{12} per day is needed by the beginning of the second week of life if you are a strict vegetarian.
- A maximum dose of 15 mg of iron per day is needed by the beginning of the third month if your baby is premature and/or had a low birth weight.

Iron-fortified infant formulas, milk- or soy-based, provide all the vitamins and minerals your baby needs. There is no need for a supplement.

Regular infant formula, milk- or soy-based, provides all the vitamins and minerals needed until your baby is four months old. An iron supplement or iron-fortified formula is then recommended.

Evaporated milk formula is deficient in iron. An iron supplement in the form of ferrous sulfate drops is needed when your baby reaches three months.

Once Your Baby Is Eating Solid Foods

During the first 12 months of life, breast milk (or any other type of milk) remains the most important source of nutrients, even when solid foods are part of the daily menu.

Once your baby begins eating iron-fortified cereal, meat, or legumes, his intake of iron will slowly increase. His intake of fruit and vegetables will supply other vitamins and minerals. If he has a good appetite and eats a variety of healthy foods on a daily basis, there is no need for supplements at this time.

After 12 months, your baby's appetite will slowly decrease because his growth rate is decreasing. So his intake of fruit, vegetables, and meat can really shrink. He can even go on "hunger strikes." If the strikes become repetitious, a multivitamin for toddlers can become useful. The liquid form is easier to give and to absorb.

Liquid Supplements Available for Toddlers: A selection

• Multivitamins with iron and extra vitamin C
• Floradix Kindervital
• nuborn liquid
(See the chart, Toddlers' Supplements, on page 115.)

Beware of Toxic Doses

Excessive supplementation can happen in early years. Young children taking megadoses (large doses) of vitamins are at risk of developing toxic reactions. Many vitamins and minerals taken in large quantities can cause harm.

Although 10 micrograms (400 IU) of *vitamin D* is recommended to prevent rickets, excessive doses of vitamin D (levels of 35 micrograms (1,400 IU)) may actually retard growth.

Vitamin A in the form of retinol can cause serious problems such as confusion, leg pains, vomiting, and dehydration when taken in doses from 10,000 to 40,000 micrograms (50,000 to 200,000 IU) per day, compared with the recommended dose of 400 micrograms (2,000 IU).

Beta-carotene, which is the vitamin A precursor (the nutrient that produces vitamin A), is much less toxic but can make the skin of some babies turn slightly orange. The symptom is harmless and gradually disappears once the consumption of carrots or other vegetables rich in beta-carotene is decreased.

Iron taken in excess can cause toxic disorders in the liver. Iron supplements are the second source of drug poisoning among toddlers in the United States.

Fluoride taken in excess can cause irreversible tooth mottling (white spots on the teeth). Before you give a fluoride supplement to your baby, make sure your local water does not already contain fluoride, naturally or artificially.

A supplement is essential
when it fills a nutritional gap.

	D-Vi-Sol[1] or D-Ovit[2]	Tri-Vi-Sol[1] or Triovit[2]	Fer-In-Sol[1]	Tender Age Liquid[3]	Tender Age ADC[3]
	1 mL	1 mL	1 mL	0.6 mL	0.6 mL
Vitamin A		1,500 IU		1,500 IU	1,500 IU
Beta-carotene					
Vitamin D	400 IU	400 IU		400 IU	400 IU
Vitamin C		30 mg		30 mg	30 mg
Vitamin B$_1$				0.5 mg	
Vitamin B$_2$				0.6 mg	
Vitamin B$_3$				4 mg	
Iron			15 mg		

Table 9
Baby Supplements

Manufacturers:
1. Mead Johnson Nutritionals
2. Euro-Pharm International Canada Inc. These products are distributed only in Quebec.
3. Jamieson

Table 10
Toddlers' Supplements

	Multivitamins[1] (with iron and extra C)	Floradix Kindervital[2]	nuborn liquid[3]
	1 tablet	5 mL	1 mL
Vitamin A	5,000 IU	1,250 IU	
Beta-carotene			1,000 IU
Vitamin D	400 IU	100 IU	
Vitamin D_3			50 IU
Vitamin E		6.25 IU	4 IU
Vitamin C	100 mg	25 mg	35 mg
Vitamin B_1	1.5 mg	0.375 mg	0.3 mg
Vitamin B_2	1.2 mg	0.375 mg	0.4 mg
Vitamin B_3	10 mg	2.5 mg	6 mg
Vitamin B_6	1 mg	0.375 mg	0.4 mg
Vitamin B_{12}	6 mcg	1.5 mcg	0.5 mcg
Iron	5 mg		
Folic acid		0.025 mg	0.2 mg
Pantothenic acid	10 mg		2 mg
Calcium		50.1 mg	
Choline			4.5 mg
Inositol			5 mg
Magnesium		7.25 mg	
PABA			1 mg

Manufacturers:
1. Jamieson
2. Status Hans
3. nu-life

TWELVE

How to Wean Your Baby

*W*eaning is an important period in your life and your baby's life. It's a very natural process that occurs sooner or later, but it is not always an easy step. It often coincides with your return to work and goes much beyond the passage from breast to bottle or cup. It implies a transition that can affect you emotionally and disturb your baby's comfortable routine.

When you wean, you more or less detach yourself from your baby, but at the same time, you allow your baby to discover a whole new world of food experiences.

Your baby will live through other food changes during her first year of life. Each of these changes can be compared to a weaning or a passage from one type of food to another, toward new foods, new textures, new discoveries.

Possible Weaning Scenarios

These scenarios can vary according to your circumstances or your personal plan.

- You may have to leave for an unexpected trip or you may suddenly become ill and be forced to end your breastfeeding rapidly. It is possible to wean this way, but it is more difficult emotionally and physically than if you spread out the weaning period over several weeks.
- You have probably developed a rough idea since your baby's birth of when you want to stop breastfeeding. If you can plan in this way, you are in a good position to stretch the weaning period and ease into the transition period.
- You may be enjoying your breastfeeding experience and may feel guilty about breaking up this unique rapport with your baby. You are postponing the weaning week after week and cannot find the strength to go through with it.

Whatever your starting point may be, the weaning process will eventually take place without harming your baby's health or nutritional status. The best scenario is the most convenient one for you, considering the circumstances.

The Perfect Timing . . .

There is no unique rule, no perfect timing for all babies, but there is a certain logic that can help you decide the right moment for you and your baby to pass on to another eating experience.

Nutritionally speaking, in the case of a normal-weight, term jbaby, breast milk supplies all the necessary nutrients for the first six months. After that age, breast milk no longer provides enough iron, and at about 12 months, it no longer meets the infant's protein needs. The contribution of other foods, therefore, becomes a must in the second half of the first year.

From a maternal perspective, weaning is an answer when you are completely exhausted, when your baby hurts you by biting your breasts, when your breasts have become too heavy, when your baby's appetite is too great, or when you have to return to work. All these reasons can help you make the decision and initiate the process.

In other cases, the baby can become gradually disinterested in the breast and find the bottle easier to handle.

The decision can be yours or your baby's — or it may be influenced by circumstances. Prepare yourself mentally and plan a smooth transition.

Introducing a Bottle

If you have chosen to breastfeed but plan an eventual return to work, or if you would simply like to enjoy a longer break between feedings once in a while, introduce an occasional bottle quite early on, to allow your baby to become acquainted with it. Plan the "bottle exposure" after your milk supply is well established but before the baby reaches three months. If you wait three or four months before introducing a bottle, your baby may go on a "bottle strike" and make the transition quite painful.

Express your milk manually or with a pump, and offer it in a bottle. This helps maintain good milk production and allows your baby to feel at home with the taste of your milk. Choose a bottle nipple that closely resembles the natural nipple and breast during feeding.

Ask the father, the babysitter, or another person to offer the bottle. To make things easier, leave the room during the feeding. Remember, in your arms or close to your odour, your baby will not expect a bottle and might initially refuse it.

Nicole, 35, had a four-month-old baby and had major surgery scheduled in approximately two months. To wean her baby smoothly, she decided to gradually introduce a bottle during the fourth month. Her baby refused the bottle for a couple of weeks but finally accepted it. Nicole had no choice; she had to proceed. Before long, everything settled down, for both mother and child.

Supplementing Breast Milk

If you would like to supplement breast milk with an infant formula, make sure your milk production is already well established. Never forget that your supply responds to the baby's demand, and the more often you feed him, the more milk you produce. If you eliminate a feeding too soon, you will worsen the potential problem of inadequate breast milk supply instead of helping it.

Here are a few general guidelines:

– If your baby is not gaining enough weight, begin by nursing him more often for two or three days before adding any supplementary feeding.
– If more frequent feedings do not work, offer the formula immediately after your baby has sucked from both breasts.

Weaning Smoothly

If you are planning to alternate breast milk with infant formula before six months, always breastfeed in the morning and at the night feeding. Offer a bottle at the other feedings.

Gradually replace one feeding at a time with a formula feeding. After your baby has adjusted to this first substitution, replace a second feeding, thus slowly decreasing the lactation process.

The slower you do it the better, for you as well as for the baby.

Even with the best of intentions, weaning is not always as smooth as you would like.

Mary, 36, had a nine-month-old baby who had travelled with her in many countries and had grown accustomed to sleeping close to her. The baby had become a night owl and was taking 75 percent of her daily breast milk ration during the night. The baby's daily nutritional content was not threatened, but Mary's energy level was.

After a few weeks of trial and error, Mary finally accepted that she would have to listen to her baby cry at night, for a few nights. She developed new rituals and taught her baby to fall asleep on her own. The process was long, but in the end, both were better off.

A Premature or Abrupt Weaning

If you need to stop breastfeeding suddenly, the lactation process continues for more than a month, and your body will require time to adjust. Pumping your milk can help relieve some of the pain while still maintaining the milk supply. To decrease total milk production, it is better to space out milk expression sessions. At the beginning, you may experience considerable discomfort, including "milk fever," with chills and malaise. This is not a type of flu but a natural reaction from your system, which can last three to four days. You may feel depressed for both physiological and emotional reasons. But remember that premature or unexpected weaning is not a failure; it is an accident.

Who Decides?

Who initiates the weaning process and when? In most cases, you will do so — for all kinds of reasons. This is natural and acceptable.

Health professionals around the world encourage mothers to breast-feed for at least six months, but no one has set an upper limit. You are the best person to decide. You may wish to breastfeed for three months. If so, congratulate yourself for this achievement. You may prolong the experience to up to 12 months or beyond. The choice is yours. Every day of breastfeeding is worth it.

Some babies initiate the weaning process, showing less and less interest in the breast. This can happen during the first year, at about 4 to 5 months, 7 months, or 9 to 12 months. By responding to your baby's message, you can plan a gradual and easy weaning.

Other babies suddenly refuse to nurse for various reasons: when your first period occurs, when you've eaten foods that flavour the milk with an unpleasant taste, when you've changed your body odour with a new soap or a new perfume, when you are very tense, or when the baby is teething. There are remedies for such things, and you can counteract the "strike" by improving all aspects of the feeding strategy. But do not insist. If the baby's message persists, slowly introduce infant formula.

Introducing a Cup

A cup can be introduced quite easily. Some babies go from breast to cup at about seven to eight months without any problem. Once the baby has started solid foods, slowly introduce a cup with a special spout. After the noon meal or in the afternoon, offer milk in this cup. Babies enjoy the sound of their teeth on the rim of the cup, and they will swallow more and more liquid as days go by.

A Bottle Is Not a Lifelong Friend!

The American Academy of Pediatrics encourages parents to start weaning their baby from the bottle at about 9 months and to complete the process soon after 12 months.

The prolonged use of the bottle well into the second or third year of life is not a sound practice. When babies fall asleep with a bottle of milk or juice in their mouth, it can even give rise to dental caries in a pattern called baby bottle tooth decay. Sometimes this is so extensive that the extraction of teeth is required in toddlers as young as 18 months.

The Introduction of Solids and Texture

The introduction of solid foods is a very important issue that will be discussed in the next chapter. It can be done easily, without interrupting the breastfeeding routine. But beware! Do not prolong the puree period beyond the eighth or ninth month. If you do, your baby may become lazy and refuse new textures altogether. You may have heard of toddlers who eat baby food and nothing else. You can avoid such a problem by introducing textured solid foods gradually at an early stage.

Consider the weaning process as a transition
and try to live through this period as smoothly as possible.

THIRTEEN

Solid Foods: Slowly but Surely

*Y*ou may be eager to introduce solid foods into your baby's menu, but you need to know why, when, what, how, and how much. Your baby is always hungry and is not yet sleeping through the night. Your neighbour offered her baby solids at two months and noticed a difference.

Early in this century, babies waited for solid foods until they were 12 months old. They were exclusively milk-fed and were often anaemic.

In the fifties, research teams started adding strained meat to infant formulas by age six weeks in order to prevent iron deficiency.

Who is right?

After so many trials and errors, experts in the field have come to the general conclusion that babies fed breast milk or iron-fortified formulas *do not need any solid food before the age of four months.*

Some can even wait until six months without any risk. In the document *Nutrition for Healthy Term Infants* (1998), the Canadian Paediatric Society, Dietitians of Canada, and Health Canada have concluded that *"Infants between 4 and 6 months of age are physiologically and developmentally ready for new foods, textures and modes of feedings."*

If you are uncertain about the best timing, please do not rush the introduction of solid foods before understanding their role in your baby's diet.

Why?

Solid Foods Cannot Replace Milk

Solids are not introduced into the baby's diet to replace milk but to complement it when milk alone can no longer provide all the essential nutrients. If solids are introduced too early, the baby's milk intake drops, and the total nutritional content of his diet is not improved. Studies have compared the nutritional value of infant diets consisting of only milk with diets composed of milk and solids. The milk-and-solids diet did not provide additional nutritional value because the baby ate some solids and drank less milk. For the same amount of calories, solids provide fewer essential nutrients than milk.

Stephen had been breastfed for seven weeks. He seemed to be hungry all the time. The family doctor had recommended the addition of cereal at three weeks of age, weaning from breast milk and the introduction of a formula at eight weeks, and supplements of sugared water in bottles between feedings, to prevent him from getting too much milk. At ten weeks, the infant was famished, cried part of the night, had cramps, and needed to take laxatives to relieve a constipation problem.

Following my advice, the mother abandoned the sugared-water

*supplements and the cereal. She fed her baby an infant formula
on demand. His daily intake increased rapidly, from 700 mL to a
litre (24 to 34 fl. oz.) per day. The baby's sleeping pattern gradually improved, and the constipation decreased. This is just an
example of one misuse of solid foods and its impact on the baby's
overall health and behaviour.*

The Maximum Amount of Milk You Can Give

To satisfy a hungrier baby before the age of four months, it is wiser
to increase the number of milk feedings per day than to introduce
solids. The total volume of milk per day is not an issue at that age.
Up to the age of five months or more, a baby needs at least four milk
feedings a day. She can take 1.2 litres (40 fl. oz.) of milk per day and
develop normally without solids.

In other words, it is impossible to give too much milk before the
baby is four months old, whether it be breast milk or infant formula.

Solid Foods Do Not Affect Infant Growth

One study tried to determine whether the early introduction of solid
foods had an impact on growth or body composition during the first
year. For a full year, 165 infants were observed. The researchers compared babies who started solids at three months with babies who
started at six months. They found that there was no difference in
growth or body composition at twelve months. Early introduction of
solids did not lead to more rapid growth.

Solid Foods Do Not Affect the Baby's Sleep

Many parents think that cereals given at bedtime promote a full
night's sleep, but this solution is a dream, not a reality! Recent
research carried out in the Cleveland area showed that babies given
cereals at five weeks did not sleep any longer than babies who were
fed milk exclusively until the age of four months. They observed
that most babies slept six consecutive hours at around 12 weeks and

slept eight consecutive hours at around 20 weeks, notwithstanding their food intake.

A British study came to a similar conclusion, reporting that 70 percent of infants sleep from midnight to 6 a.m. by three months of age, while 13 percent sleep through at about six months, and yet another 10 percent never sleep through, regardless of solid-food intake. Prolonged sleep reflects the baby's total neurological development and has very little to do with the food she eats — colic being one exception.

Solid Foods Need to Be Swallowed

Before the age of three to four months, a baby does not have a lot of saliva, and her tongue cannot push solid food toward the back of her mouth. She can suck very well, but the extrusion reflex inhibits normal swallowing when she is trying to chew. Feeding her solids at that stage is in fact forcefeeding. By 16 to 18 weeks, the extrusion reflex gradually disappears, and the baby has acquired neuromuscular coordination, which enables her to swallow solid foods.

Solid Foods Need to Be Digested and Assimilated

At birth, the baby is able to digest breast milk or anything similar. She does not yet possess the complete array of digestive substances. She has only a fraction of the digestive enzymes needed to cope with a normal variety of foods. Before three months, she cannot properly digest cereals or other starches. Before six months, she cannot assimilate different fats. A baby who eats solids too early has great difficulty coping with certain substances and cannot totally assimilate them. A lot of undigested foods are found in her stools.

Solid Foods Impose an Extra Burden on the Renal System

A newborn baby has immature kidneys that react very poorly to protein excesses. Foods such as undiluted whole cow's milk, meat, or egg yolk may cause serious problems in fragile babies if they are given too early.

Solid Foods Increase the Risk of Allergies

The baby's immune system is still quite vulnerable during the very early months. Normal production of antibodies gradually increases during the first year, peaking at about seven months of age. Once the baby has a larger army of antibodies at his disposal, once the mucosal barrier has matured, the risks of developing allergic reactions to food are diminished. A slow introduction of solids at the age of about six months is, therefore, especially beneficial for a baby whose family has a history of food allergies.

A Slow Introduction Respects Your Baby's Needs

Before the age of four to six months, breast milk or infant formula provides all the nutrients a full-term baby needs. After that age, iron needs are not fully met. Protein, zinc, and energy needs also increase. Solid foods now begin to play a true nutritional role in the baby's diet.

When to Begin?

After Four Months, When Your Baby Is Ready

The best time to start solid foods for your second baby may not be the same as with your first child. Although many agree on an ideal time for the introduction of solid foods, there is no standard timing for all babies. Each baby has its own calendar of growth and needs. Your baby's growth and general behaviour are your best indicators. Signs such as the following can lead you to the final decision:

- A breastfed baby requires more than 8 to 10 feedings per 24 hours, empties both breasts at each feeding, and always seems hungry.

- A formula-fed baby drinks at least 1.2 litres (40 fl. oz.) per day, empties all bottles, and still seems hungry.
- Your baby has doubled his birth weight and is always hungry.

Just make sure your baby is crying for food and not for attention. Use solid foods as a last response to a cry after eliminating other causes of discomfort such as dirty diapers, uncomfortable position, need for light, need for water, or need for affection.

After Four Months, Your Baby Can Tell You "I've Had Enough"

At five or six months, a baby also has better control of her head and neck. She can express needs and wants, show hunger by moving the head forward, indicate how full she is by moving her head backward. These movements send distinct messages and allow you to respond to your baby's appetite. The harmony between your baby's need for solids and your feeding response can be met more easily by a slow introduction of solids at five or six months. This harmony fosters the development of good eating habits for a lifetime.

Do Not Wait Longer Than Seven Months

At six months, a baby is ready and able to chew solid foods, even though she has no teeth. If the introduction of solid foods is delayed until nine or ten months, the baby may resist and refuse foods having consistency and texture for years. For the same reason, introduction of textured foods is also a need at about six to seven months. Pureed foods should not be served forever!

What to Serve?

The First Solid Food Should Be Rich in Iron

When your baby is five or six months old, he will be able to digest and assimilate a variety of foods — much more easily than when he was two or three months old.

The first solid food to offer could be either meat, tofu, or infant cereal — because of their richness in iron and protein.

My advice is to follow the traditional sequence of introduction, and to begin with iron-fortified cereal (see the next chapter (Chapter 14, Infant Cereals) for all the details). Then introduce vegetables, fruit, and finally protein-rich foods such as meat and its alternatives.

The first feeding schedule might look like this:

Table 11	
Feeding Schedule between Four and Five Months	
(If Your Baby Needs Solid Foods)	
at dawn	breast milk or iron-fortified formula
breakfast	breast milk or iron-fortified formula
	infant single-grain cereal
lunch	breast milk or iron-fortified formula
supper	breast milk or iron-fortified formula
	infant single grain cereal
evening	breast milk or iron-fortified formula
night-time	breast milk or iron-fortified formula

How and How Much?

Adopt the Following Feeding Ritual

– Always offer solid food *after* the milk feeding until the age of nine months. In this way, you will not reduce the intake of breast milk or infant formula.
– Always offer solid food with a spoon, not in a bottle, to give your baby chewing exercise.
– Begin with 5 mL (1 tsp.) of solid food the first day and gradually increase the quantity.
– Introduce one new food at a time and avoid mixed foods at the beginning.

- Repeat the same new food three, five, or even seven days in a row, before introducing another food, to allow sufficient time to identify a food allergy, if applicable.
- Never force your baby to finish, even if this means throwing out some food after the meal.
- Never let your baby eat alone.
- Feed your baby in a reclining seat so that he can hold his head up straight.
- Avoid feeding your baby in the car to reduce risks of choking.

The Second Solid Food: Vegetables

Two or three weeks after the cereals have been introduced, add pureed vegetables to the menu. Babies enjoy their flavour, especially if vegetables are tasted before the sweet flavour of fruits. Vegetables bring vitamins, minerals, and fibre with very few calories. They also bring colour to the plate. Try these easy techniques:

- Introduce one vegetable at a time. Wait three, five, or even seven days before offering a new vegetable.
- Start with yellow vegetables like squash and carrots. Follow these up with greens like zucchini, asparagus, and green peas. Save broccoli and cauliflower for the end because they can give your baby gas.
- Offer beets, turnip, and spinach after nine months, because of their nitrate content.
- Offer plain vegetables before mixed vegetables.
- Always serve cooked vegetables at this stage: homemade purees or commercial baby food.
- Always feed your baby with a small spoon, rather than a bottle, so that he learns to chew.
- Serve vegetables at noon, after breast milk or formula feeding, until nine months. In this way, you won't reduce your baby's milk intake.

- Do not add any salt, sugar, or fat.
- Heat a small amount in a glass container in a double boiler or in the microwave. Always stir and test the temperature with the tip of your tongue to make sure the food is not too hot.
- Discard any leftover food from the baby's dish.
- Start with 5 mL (1 tsp.) the first day. Gradually increase up to 150 mL (10 tbsp.) by the end of the first year. This is not a maximum amount but represents the average daily intake.
- If your baby refuses to eat a new vegetable but is still hungry, do not insist but serve another vegetable that he has already tried and enjoyed.

The day my daughter introduced asparagus into Emilie's menu, the baby's reaction was so negative that my daughter did not know what to do to compensate. I recommended offering green peas, which Emilie had already enjoyed and to give asparagus another try in a few days.

The Third Solid Food: Fruit

Two or three weeks after vegetables have been introduced is a good time to introduce fruit. Fruits add sweetness to the menu, as well as vitamins, minerals, and fibre. Here's how to proceed:

- Offer one fruit at a time before offering mixed fruit.
- Never add sugar, and wait until later to introduce spices.
- Always spoonfeed.
- Serve homemade purees or commercial baby food.
- Offer the fruit cooked, rather than raw — except for bananas, papayas, and mangoes, which can be fork-mashed or blended without cooking.
- Avoid small fruit with seeds, such as strawberries, raspberries, and grapes, until the child is well over two years of age. Strained or pureed strawberries or raspberries can be given with other

fruit or yogourt at the end of the first year.
- If there is a family history of allergies, avoid citrus fruit juices (lemon, orange, or grapefruit) or citric acid before 12 months.
- Avoid commercial fruit desserts filled with sugar.

Fruit Juice in a Cup

Babies love fruit juice and can easily drink too much of it. This ruins their appetite and can cause problems (see Chapter 17, Frequent Problems — and Solutions, page 190).

- Introduce fruit juice once your baby can drink from a cup or a glass.
- Do not offer juice in a bottle. You don't want your baby to play with it and keep small quantities of juice in his mouth, which can trigger dental caries even if your baby has no teeth.
- Dilute juice with an equal amount of safe tap or well water or bottled spring water.
- Serve fruit juice cold but not chilled.
- Limit your baby's daily intake to 125 mL (4 fl. oz.) knowing that 60 mL (2 fl. oz.) supplies enough vitamin C to meet daily requirements until the age of three.
- Start with apple juice or grape juice to reduce any risk of allergies. Then offer orange or grapefruit juice — freshly squeezed or frozen and reconstituted and strained.
- Avoid flavoured fruit crystals, fruit drinks, or punches that contain very little fruit (and sometimes none!) and too much sugar, food colouring, and other additives.

Table 12

Feeding Schedule between Five and Six Months

(or beginning one month after the

first solid food has been introduced)

at dawn	breast milk or formula
breakfast	breast milk or formula
	infant cereal
lunch	breast milk or formula
	vegetable puree
supper	breast milk or formula
	infant cereal
	fruit puree
evening	breast milk or formula

The Fourth Solid Food: Something Rich in Protein

Meat, poultry, fish, or substitutes such as tofu or pureed beans can be introduced gradually, two to three weeks after the addition of fruit, once the baby is at least six months old. This food group provides high-quality protein, iron, zinc, more or less fat depending on the food, and calories. One serving a day is sufficient. Follow this pattern:

– Start with white meat such as chicken, turkey, or fish.
– Continue with beef, veal, liver, or lamb.
– Introduce mashed tofu — the silken type.
– Avoid processed meats such as ham and bacon because of their high sodium and nitrite content.
– Choose fish that have fewer PCB residues, such as small, farmed fish or ocean fish: sole, flounder, grouper, haddock, halibut, monkfish, salmon, or tuna.
– Introduce one new meat every three to four days.

- Offer homemade or commercial baby food.
- At first, serve only 5 mL (1 tsp.) alone, not mixed with vegetables.
- Offer this food group at the noon meal.
- Never add salt or seasonings.
- Gradually increase to a maximum of 90 mL (6 tbsp.) daily by the end of the first year.

Sébastien was initiated to silken tofu as his first protein-rich food, and he loved it. He ate tofu for several months alone at the beginning. Then he ate it mixed with cooked vegetables. Tofu is the easiest food to serve, requires no cooking, is easily mashed with a fork and has a delicate flavour that suits babies. It's a bargain and babies have no negative opinion about it yet!

- Avoid seafood such as shrimp, lobster, clams, mussels, and scallops before the age of 12 months (because of the baby's vulnerability to allergies).
- If there is a family history of food allergies, delay the introduction of fish and seafood altogether until 12 months — or even 2 to 3 years.
- Never force your baby to eat!

Table 13

Feeding Schedule between Six and Nine Months

at dawn	breast milk or formula
breakfast	infant cereal
	fruit puree
	breast milk or formula
lunch	pureed meat
	pureed vegetables

Table 13 (cont'd)

Feeding Schedule between Six and Nine Months

lunch (cont'd)	fork-mashed fruit
	breast milk or formula
snack	teething foods (see pages 137–38)
	water
supper	infant cereal
	vegetables or fruit
	cottage cheese or yogourt
	breast milk or formula
bedtime	breast milk or formula

Egg Yolk and Whole Egg

Once your baby is eating infant cereal, vegetables, fruit, and protein-rich foods on a regular basis, you can introduce another food, such as *egg yolk*. Egg yolk supplies protein, vitamins, and minerals but is no longer considered a good source of iron. It is not an essential food in the baby's diet but can be mixed into the noon meal a few times a week. Serve it as follows:

– Hard boil and sift a small quantity into a vegetable or meat dish.
– Start with 5 mL (1 tsp.) a day, and gradually increase to a maximum of two egg yolks per week.
– Keep leftover yolk in the refrigerator for up to three days. Use any leftovers in salads and sandwiches for the rest of the family.
– *Never* offer *raw* egg yolk or *raw* egg. If you do, you risk giving your baby *salmonella poisoning*.

Delay the introduction of whole eggs until your baby is 11 months old, to avoid any risk of allergy as a result of the egg whites. Once your baby's immune system is better developed, you can offer her a poached or hard-boiled egg three to four times a week. Eggs are easy to digest and can be served easily at supper with colourful vegetables. Once the whole egg is introduced into the menu, there is no need to continue serving the egg yolk.

Yogourt and Fresh Cheese

Yogourt supplies calcium, vitamins, protein, and lactic cultures in a very smooth-tasting package. It can be added to the menu once the baby is eating cereal, vegetables, fruit, and foods from the protein group.

– Start with plain yogourt made with whole milk.
– Try homemade yogourt for a milder taste.
– Avoid fruit-flavoured yogourts and frozen yogourts loaded with sugar and very little fruit.
– Once the baby is accustomed to plain yogourt, add fruit purees or mashed bananas for extra flavour.
– 125 mL (4 fl. oz.) of yogourt can replace 125 mL (4 fl. oz.) of whole cow's milk.
– Fresh cheese prepared with whole milk, such as cottage or ricotta cheese, provides good-quality protein and can be introduced into the baby's menu at the same time as yogourt. When mixed with pureed vegetables or fruit, it becomes a protein-rich food that can be offered as a main dish.
– Sweetened fresh cheeses such as Minigo and Petit Danone do not contain the lactic bacteria found in real yogourt, but they do supply more sugar. They can be offered as desserts once in a while.

Foods to Avoid

Foods to avoid during the first year or so are foods that contain questionable ingredients — such as large amounts of bad fat, sodium, sugar, or food colouring or other additives:

- Processed meats such as bacon, smoked sausages, commercial pâtés, smoked or cured meats, and canned luncheon meats.
- Puddings, cakes, sweet cookies, candies, chocolate, and packaged gelatine desserts.
- Fried foods and french fries.
- Soft drinks — because of their high sugar content.
- Diet foods, including diet drinks sweetened with sugar substitutes — babies *need* the calories!
- Foods prepared with fat substitutes — babies need the essential fatty acids to develop normally.
- Foods associated with risk of choking, such as raw fruit and vegetables (until the end of the first year); seeded fruit, such as berries and grapes, and dry cereal (until well over one year); popcorn, nuts, seeds, chips, and small candies (until three or four years of age).
- Honey and corn syrup, to avoid any risk of botulism (before 12 months of age).

Foods That May Cause Choking
Some foods that are very nutritious can at the same time expose your baby or your toddler to choking because of their shape or texture. You must avoid them unless you take careful precautions.

- Unpeeled raw fruit. Peel and cut into small pieces.
- Raw vegetables. Peel and cook a few minutes to soften.
- Seedless grapes. Cut each grape in half or into three pieces, lengthwise.
- Nuts and seeds. Grind them and add them to yogourt or applesauce, if desired.
- Smoked sausages, hot dogs, and tofu dogs. Not recommended, but if you *do* serve them, cut in half lengthwise and then into small pieces.

– *Avoid* popcorn and small candies. Do not even allow your baby near them.

Teething Foods

Your baby will always welcome teething foods. He needs to chew between meals during the prolonged teething period, from 4 to 24 months. Using the safe and sound teething foods, proceed as follows:

– Offer a piece of Melba toast, dry whole-wheat toast cut in strips, or a bread crust.
– Prepare small popsicles with water for a very soothing effect.
– Offer a dentally approved teething ring. This can do a great job.
– Avoid raw carrots and celery sticks, to prevent choking during the first year. However, you can offer slightly cooked carrots and celery. Make sure the pieces have been cooked for 2 to 3 minutes.
– *Avoid* teething biscuits. They contain sugar and are therefore not recommended.

*The introduction of solid foods is an exciting period.
It allows your baby to discover a whole range of
new flavours and textures.*

FOURTEEN

Infant Cereals

⟨ornament⟩

Infant cereals can be quite important in your baby's diet because most of them provide a good dose of iron at a critical time. They are often introduced as the *first* solid food and remain essential all through the first 24 months of life. Some have been fortified with iron and are adapted to the infant's nutritional needs; others are not.

To help you choose the right cereal at the right time, this chapter presents the whole assortment and provides guidelines on the best choices to make before and after 12 months of age. New infant cereals appear on the market on a regular basis. The ones described here were available as of September 1999.

Cereals Available for Babies under 12 Months

Pre-cooked, Iron-fortified Cereal

- brown rice cereal (Earth's Best)
- refined rice, oatmeal, or barley, with or without fruit (Heinz, Pablum)
- multigrain cereal (whole oat, brown rice, and millet) (Earth's Best)
- refined mixed cereal (Heinz, Pablum)
- refined mixed cereal with soy (Infantsoy by Heinz)

Infant cereals in this category are adjusted to the baby's nutritional needs. Some have been on the market for many years. To prepare them, you must add milk or formula.

A few of these cereals are made from whole grains such as brown rice, but most are made with refined grain such as white rice or refined oatmeal. Some are composed of a single grain such as rice or barley. Others contain two or more grains and are called mixed or multigrains. Many varieties include fruit and flavourings. All these grains have been pre-cooked to gelatinize the starches and facilitate the baby's digestion. All are fortified with iron, B vitamins, calcium, and phosphorus. (See feeding ritual on page 144.)

You will notice by reading the labels that some of the Heinz cereals (barley, rice, rice with apple, rice with bananas and vanilla, rice with pear and orange) still contain, as of September 1999, vegetable oil shortening. This hydrogenated oil is not recommended for anyone, and especially not for infants.

Pre-cooked, iron-fortified cereal supplies between 8 and 14 mg of iron per 100 mL (6 1/2 tbsp.) depending on the brand.

Pre-mixed Cereal with Iron-fortified Infant Formula

- one-grain cereal (rice, barley, oatmeal), with or without fruit (Milupa, Nestlé)
- multigrain cereal mixed with fruit (Milupa, Nestlé)

Infant cereals in this category are refined, pre-cooked, and pre-mixed, with a small amount of iron-fortified infant formula. They contain less iron than the first category but are easier to prepare. You just need to add a certain amount of water instead of milk or formula.

There is no whole-grain product in this category but no hydrogenated oil is present either.

Pre-mixed cereal with iron-fortified infant formula supplies approximately 4 mg of iron per 100 mL (6 1/2 tbsp.).

Whole-grain Cereal without Added Iron

- brown rice cereal (Healthy Times)
- mixed grains with fruit and wheat germ (Familia)
- oatmeal with banana puree and apple juice (Healthy Times)

Infant cereals in this category are composed of either single, mixed-sprouted, or crushed grains, blended with other ingredients. They are usually available in natural food stores.

There is no oil or other fat present in this type of cereal.

The Healthy Times–type cereal supplies approximately 0.25 mg of iron in 100 mL (6 1/2 tbsp.).

Cereal Cookies

Some of these cookies have been on the market for years; others have just arrived.

The *Farley-type cookie* is made with enriched white flour, sugar, palm oil, vitamins, and in the case of banana cookies, banana powder. It is fortified with iron, calcium, and B vitamins. One cookie supplies 2.7 milligrams of iron.

The *Healthy Times–type cookie* is made with three organic flours (whole wheat, oatmeal, and soy), molasses containing no sulphur as preservative, milk powder, and natural flavours. The iron content is not indicated on the label.

The Right Cereal before 12 Months

The right cereal at the right time depends on your infant's nutritional needs and the type of milk he drinks. Cereal is usually introduced when your baby reaches between four and six months (when he usually needs extra iron). The objective is to provide him with at least 7 milligrams of iron per day.

1. *If you plan to continue to breastfeed your baby beyond four months,* breast milk is still excellent but it does not supply enough iron. To compensate and fulfill your baby's needs, go for an iron-fortified cereal.

   – Begin with a single-grain cereal that is iron fortified. The brown rice cereal (Earth's Best) would be my first choice: It has six times more fibre than regular rice cereal, and it contains more magnesium, more vitamin B$_6$, and no vegetable oil shortening. Any other single-grain cereal fortified with iron or mixed with iron-fortified formula would also be suitable.
   – Once your baby has tasted the three basic single grains (oats, rice, and barley), introduce the mixed or multigrain cereals fortified with iron.
   – Choose plain cereals without added fruit because of their higher protein content and their lower risk of bringing on

food allergies. Once you have introduced fruit, add fruit or fruit puree to the infant cereal, to provide more vitamins and fibre than those present in the pre-mixed cereal and fruit.

- If you prefer a whole-grain cereal that is not fortified with iron, give your baby a daily iron supplement that supplies approximately 7 mg of iron. (Fer-In-Sol drops provide 7.5 mg of iron in a 0.5-mL drop.)
- If your baby was born prematurely and had a low birth weight, consider giving an iron supplement until he eats at least 100 mL (6 1/2 tbsp.) of iron-fortified cereal per day.
- If you have a family history of gluten intolerance, serve rice cereal until 12 months (whole or refined) because it is the only gluten-free cereal.
- Do not offer cereal cookies as a substitute for infant cereals. You may introduce these cookies as snacks later on in the first year of life when your baby is hungry. The ones made of mixed whole-grain flours can contribute to the baby's healthy diet by increasing fibre and mineral intake.

2. *If your baby is fed an iron-fortified formula* (see Chapter 10, Other Milks — Before and after Six Months, pages 87–89) *or a transition formula* (see Chapter 10, pages 96–97), he is getting enough iron to satisfy his daily needs.

- Choose any category of single-grain infant cereal, with or without formula, fortified or not fortified with iron.
- Once your baby has tasted the three basic single grains (rice, oats, barley), introduce mixed grains.
- Do not count on mixed grains with fruit to supply any significant amount of vitamins or fibre. Once you have introduced fruit into your baby's diet, add fruit to infant cereal for extra taste and for extra vitamin and fibre intake.

3. *If your baby is fed whole cow's milk, whole goat's milk, an evap-orated milk formula, or a formula that is not iron fortified,* follow the guidelines given for the breastfed baby (under no. 1, above).

Feeding Ritual for Babies under 12 Months
– Begin with a single-grain cereal such as rice because it offers lit-tle risk of allergies.
– Mix 5 mL (1 tsp.) of infant dry cereal with breast milk or for-mula until it has the consistency of a thick soup.
– Serve with a small spoon after you have breastfed your baby or given her the formula. This strategy helps maintain an adequate milk intake and offers cereal as a plus.
– Begin by serving the cereal at the morning meal after the milk feeding. After a few days, offer the same cereal at suppertime.
– Always spoonfeed rather than bottle-feed, to provide chewing exercise and to prevent choking.
– After four or five consecutive days with the same cereal, intro-duce another single-grain cereal such as barley or oatmeal. If there is a family history of allergies, introduce wheat only after 12 months.
– Never add sugar.
– Once the single-grain cereals have been offered, introduce mixed grains.
– Gradually increase the amount to a maximum of 200 mL (3/4 cup) of dry cereal per day by the end of the first year.

Cereals Available for Babies over 12 Months

Other Cereal
There is quite an assortment of breakfast cereals for babies and for adults. Some are ready to eat, some require cooking and are served hot. Some you grind and serve raw or cooked. Among them, some respect the young child's nutritional needs; others do not.

Cereal for Toddlers 12 Months and Over
This relatively new product line for one-year-olds and older is available everywhere.
– *Nutrios* (Heinz). This is a dry cereal made of oat and corn flour with a touch of refined sugar (3 g per 100 g). It is fortified with calcium, B vitamins, and iron.
– *Fruit Crisps* (Heinz). This dry cereal is made of rolled oats, cornmeal, and rice flour, mixed with skim milk powder, a small amount of dried fruit (apple powder or dried blueberries or raspberries), and natural flavouring. It is heavily sweetened (13 to 15 g of sugar per 100 g) and fortified with calcium, B vitamins, and iron.

Nutrios supply 6 mg of iron per 30 g (250 mL).
Fruit Crisps supply 6 mg of iron per 28 g (45 mL).

Regular Ready-to-Eat Cereal
A vast number of ready-to-eat cereals are on the market. For instance, basic oatmeal cereal (e.g., Cheerios), corn cereal (e.g., Corn Flakes), and rice cereal (e.g., Rice Krispies) are refined, sweetened, and fortified with a certain amount of iron and B vitamins. Others are made of wheat with added bran (e.g., Bran Flakes) and added iron, while still others are made of whole wheat (e.g., Shredded Wheat); they are whole grain but are not fortified with iron. Read the labels to check their complete contents.

Table 14		
Corn Flakes, Rice Krispies	100 mL (6 1/2 tbsp.)	1.3 to 2 mg of iron
Bran Flakes, Raisin Bran	100 mL (6 1/2 tbsp.)	2.7 mg of iron
Shredded Wheat	100 mL (6 1/2 tbsp.)	0.8 mg of iron
Grape Nuts	100 mL (6 1/2 tbsp.)	6.4 mg of iron
Grape Nut Flakes	100 mL (6 1/2 tbsp.)	1.8 mg of iron

Cooked Cereal

Among the most common cooked cereals, cream of wheat is refined and highly fortified with iron, while oatmeal and cream of brown rice are whole grains not fortified with iron. Read labels to check their complete contents.

Before serving, always test the temperature by putting a drop of food on the tip of your tongue or on your wrist.

Table 15		
iron-fortified cream of wheat	100 mL (6 1/2 tbsp.)	7 mg of iron
cream of brown rice	100 mL (6 1/2 tbsp.)	3 mg of iron
oatmeal	100 mL (6 1/2 tbsp.)	1.8 mg of iron

Freshly Ground Whole Grains

You can grind whole grains such as millet, quinoa, or amaranth in a coffee grinder and obtain a whole-grain flour. This type of flour can be cooked 5 to 10 minutes in a small amount of water and contribute a fair level of iron.

Table 16		
freshly ground quinoa	100 mL (6 1/2 tbsp.)	5.4 mg of iron
freshly ground millet	100 mL (6 1/2 tbsp.)	7.9 mg of iron
freshly ground amaranth	100 mL (6 1/2 tbsp.)	6.4 mg of iron

The Right Cereal after 12 Months

Once your baby has reached 12 months, you can either breastfeed or give him whole cow's milk or whole goat's milk, but never forget the importance of iron in his daily diet. The recommended amount is 6 milligrams of iron per day.

Your baby may be eating some iron-rich foods on a regular basis — such as meat, legumes, tofu, or green vegetables — but he may be eating these foods in large quantities only rarely. He can easily develop an iron deficiency — as do many other young children before the age of two. That is why he can still benefit from a daily intake of iron-fortified cereals until 24 months.

- Camouflage the pre-cooked, iron-fortified infant cereal or the freshly ground whole grains in muffins or pancakes.
- Substitute cookies with a toddler-type cereal that has little sugar, for snacks and desserts.
- Avoid overly sweetened cereals, which will only trigger your child's desire for sweets.
- For a hearty winter breakfast, mix pre-cooked, iron-fortified cereal with regular oatmeal before adding the water and cooking. Add raisins or pureed prunes for extra flavour and iron.

Do not underestimate the importance of cereal in your baby's menu.

FIFTEEN

Commercial Baby Food

*Y*ou may be wondering whether baby food sold in little jars can be useful in your baby's diet. The question is not always easy to answer.

Commercial baby food has been on the market since the thirties. Their composition has changed over the years to comply with research in nutrition and with consumers' reactions, so the products available today are quite different from those sold years ago. Among the most notable changes are the following:

– Small metal can containers were replaced with glass containers in the early 1960s, to decrease the lead content.
– MSG (monosodium glutamate), a flavour enhancer, was removed in 1969.
– Added salt was removed in 1977.
– Added sugar was reduced in the late seventies.

- Nitrite-cured meats (ham, bacon) were replaced by nitrite-free cured meats in the seventies. Pureed meats are heat-processed at a high temperature for a sufficient time to kill any trace of botulism-causing bacteria.
- Hydrogenated vegetable oils have recently been replaced with sunflower, palm, soy, or canola oil in most products.

Preservatives and artificial colouring and flavouring are not currently used. For all of these reasons, commercial baby foods are safer today than they were 20 years ago.

Since the departure of Gerber, H.J. Heinz Company of Canada Ltd. commands over 90 percent of Canada's baby food market. It offers a complete line of products that includes all the food categories, partly because it owns Pablum cereals, Farley's biscuits, and Earth's Best products. However, a survey I undertook recently provides evidence that within each category, there is a limited choice of products, with variable nutritional value.

I have been checking the content of commercial baby foods for the past 25 years and was one of the first in Canada to criticize the sugar and salt content in these foods, back in the seventies. I have witnessed many changes over the years, some good, some not so good. I have surprises every time I check. If you find a new and interesting baby food, please let me know.

Vegetables in Little Jars

Beginner* vegetable purees contain a single vegetable, and water. The variety is limited to carrots, squash, green beans, wax beans, peas, and sweet potatoes (Heinz). Other available vegetable purees

---

* "Beginner" is a type of baby food (for young babies), not a brand name. The other two types, used as babies get older, are "Strained" and "Junior."

are prepared with organic vegetables but the variety is even more limited (Earth's Best).

Strained vegetable purees consist of the same variety of vegetables, with added potatoes, celery, and rice (Heinz). This actually dilutes the vitamin content of the vegetable. Recently, in some strained vegetable purees, modified starches have been replaced by split green or yellow peas. Nonetheless, these purees provide less vitamin C and less thiamine, riboflavin, and niacin — the B vitamins — than the Beginner vegetable purees or the homemade purees.

A recent analysis done by the Center for Science in the Public Interest in Washington has shown that Heinz Company of Canada's Beginner vegetables have an average of 20 percent less vegetable and more added water than the same Heinz product sold in the United States.

The strained vegetable purees are perhaps time and energy savers, but they cannot compete with the nutritional value and taste of homemade purees, fresh or frozen. They have been heat-treated more extensively and seldom supply a lot of vitamin C because they are rarely prepared with vitamin C–rich vegetables like broccoli, cauliflower, or snow peas.

After six months, your baby can enjoy fresh vegetables cooked at the last minute, fork-mashed, and unsalted. This provides more nutrition than manufactured vegetable purees.

Your wisest choice: If you need to rely on these commercial purees, choose Beginner vegetable purees that contain a single vegetable and water, and nothing else. You will need this type of puree only for a few weeks — until your baby can handle more texture.

Each company (Heinz, Earth's Best) offers six varieties of vegetable puree with water, and nothing else.

From Fruit Purees to Fancy Desserts

The range of Beginner fruit purees, strained fruits, and strained desserts for babies is absolutely incredible.

Surprisingly enough, water is often the first ingredient in strained desserts, and the list of thickeners (such as modified cornstarch, modified tapioca, rice flour, or wheat flour) is usually quite long. These thickeners are not harmful on their own, but in a fruit salad or a pear dessert, although they improve the texture, they dilute the vitamin content.

In the past, some fruit purees were sweetened, and this was not clearly identified on the label. But the good news is that now you can identify the fruit purees with a light blue label and the sweetened desserts with a darker blue label.

Beginner fruit purees, for very young infants, contain only one fruit and sometimes water (Heinz, Earth's Best).

Strained fruits contain water and at least two different fruits, concentrated fruit juice, and fruit paste (Heinz).

Mixed organic fruit purees contain two fruits and water (Earth's Best).

A study on baby food carried out by Stallone and Jacobson and published a few years ago by the Center for Science in the Public Interest has found that many popular fruit desserts were prepared with thickening agents and half the amount of fruit contained in the Beginner fruit puree. When they compared a fresh apricot with a commercial apricot dessert containing tapioca, they noted that the commercial apricot dessert for babies supplied four times less potassium and half the amount of beta-carotene found in a fresh apricot.

A *second category of strained fruits* is made with organic fruit, water, and fruit paste (Earth's Best). These purees contain less fruit than the fruit purees mentioned above.

Strained desserts are rich in calories but poor in vitamin content. Water is often the first ingredient in a long list of ingredients. The dark blue label on strained desserts can help you differentiate them from the non-sweetened, strained fruits, which have a light blue label.

Sébastian, seven and a half months, refused to eat commercial banana baby food but really enjoyed fresh, ripe, mashed banana. The citric acid and concentrated lemon juice present in the commercial food may explain his reaction.

Strained yogourts are yogourts with a lactic culture that has been inactivated through heat treatment. This means that these yogourts have no impact on intestinal flora — unlike regular yogourts. (Active bacteria in the lactic cultures found in regular yogourts can help maintain healthy intestinal flora.) Strained yogourts also contain sugar and cornstarch. When compared with the same amount of regular yogourt mixed with 60 millilitres (4 tablespoons) of mashed banana, the commercial baby food banana yogourt supplies half the amount of protein, six times less fat, three times less vitamin A and riboflavin, five times less potassium, and two and a half times less calcium.

Your wisest choice: Beginner fruit purees are your best choice (Heinz, Earth's Best) when you introduce fruit into your baby's diet — even if these baby foods contain less fruit and more water than the U.S. version of the same product.

After six months, your baby will be better off with fresh fruit — lightly poached if needed but unsweetened. If you want to increase the vitamin C content, add fortified apple juice to the mixture.

Strained fruits and strained desserts (sweetened) can be occasional treats, but they do not offer any significant nutritional benefit.

In the case of yogourt, the commercial baby food type offers your baby no advantage. Besides, it does not have the real taste of plain yogourt made with whole milk. By eating real yogourt, your baby obtains the benefits of the active lactic culture, less sugar, and better nutritional value.

Strained Juices and Drinks

Strained juices are one of the latest additions to the family of baby foods. They are prepared with water and concentrated juice and are fortified with 40 milligrams of vitamin C per 100 millilitres.

- Ten different kinds of juices and drinks are available from Heinz. Among them, seven contain concentrated apple juice.
- Heinz's apple–sweet potato mix is an interesting exception because it contains a significant amount of beta-carotene (1,540 IU per 100 g).
- These juices and drinks cost at least three times more than a regular, adult-type juice, made from a concentrate.
- A reconstituted frozen orange juice or a freshly squeezed orange, strained if desired, supplies 50 to 65 mg of vitamin C in 125 mL (4 fl. oz.) — and at a lower cost!

Beware: Fruit juices, even if unsweetened, are a much sweeter beverage than infant formula or whole milk. They rapidly become a favourite food and can limit the intake of milk. It is always a good idea to serve juice diluted with an equal amount of water, to reduce the sugar content and limit overconsumption.

From Strained Meats to Vegetable Combinations

There is a wide variety of products in this category.

Strained meats are meats for young infants (about six to eight months) such as beef, veal, chicken, lamb, and turkey. They are mixed with other ingredients — in one case, broth, lemon juice, and beef fat (Heinz). Strained liver puree is no longer on the market. The protein content of these purees is high, and the product is sometimes easier to swallow than homemade pureed meats.

Meat dinners have a short list of ingredients, including water, meat, carrots, and green or yellow split peas as a thickener, with rice and potatoes. The protein content is half the amount found in commercial, strained meats, and the carbohydrate content is higher.

Strained vegetables and meat combinations have a long list of ingredients, including water, vegetables, potatoes, lentils, meat, pasta or rice, and seasonings — but no salt. The presence of carrots in every combination explains the interesting beta-carotene content in these purees. Apart from that, these combinations provide four times less protein, three times fewer calories, and half the amount of iron supplied by commercial, strained meats. They cannot replace a meat meal.

Your wisest choice: Choose strained meats to introduce your baby to this group of food. Once your baby has tried all five available, mix these purees with your own pureed vegetables or with Beginner vegetables to increase the vitamin content.

Toddler Meat and Vegetable Combinations

Toddlers 12 months old or more have a wide variety of meals from which to choose, including beef stroganoff, chicken cacciatore, and country casserole with chicken. Most of these dishes contain a fair amount of carbohydrates, including rice, modified cornstarch, and pasta, and they are seasoned with salt. The protein content is low, and so is the iron content — two important nutrients that are usually found in meat dishes. These meals can surely save time, but an 18-month toddler can easily eat and enjoy other simple homemade combinations — and will gain more protein and iron from them (see Chapter 20, Transition Menus and Recipes for Nine Months and Beyond).

Vegetarian Meals

To respond to more and more parents who have opted for a vegetarian diet, and to offer variety to babies who do not need two meat meals a day, vegetarian meals can play a role in the baby's diet after nine months, once all food groups have been introduced.

Vegetarian meals for babies are available (Earth's Best) and often contain pasta, cheese, vegetables, and canola oil. Some have lentils or chickpeas and brown rice.

Some *vegetable and cheese combinations* (Heinz) can also constitute a meatless meal, if desired.

Your wisest choice: Consult the list of ingredients and choose the meal with the healthiest ingredients. However, a nine-month-old can fare as well with fork-mashed silken tofu and mashed cooked vegetables.

Nutritional Value, Taste, and Cost

Commercial baby foods can be a great help when there is no time to cook. Beginner purees of vegetables, fruit, and strained meats designed for the very young can introduce your baby to different solid foods for a few weeks and provide important nutrients.

But if you are not careful in choosing the right commercial baby foods, you may buy one with a protein, mineral, and vitamin content that is significantly lower. In fact, commercial baby foods cannot really compete with the nutritional value of homemade purees that are prepared with top-quality ingredients.

A study was done with 165 infants, comparing those who were fed homemade foods with those who were fed commercial foods during the first 12 months of their lives. The results showed that babies fed commercial baby food had a lower caloric intake, with less protein and less fat. This difference had no effect on growth or body composition. However, experts in Canada do not recommend a low-fat diet in early infancy.

Try both homemade and commercial baby food, and see for yourself. The commercial products are not as tasty.

Commercial baby food costs about twice as much as homemade purees, and commercial organic baby food is even more expensive. When fresh fruit and vegetables (regular or organic) are in season, you can really save many dollars by making your own purees.

> ***Commercial baby food has improved,***
> ***but cannot really compete with homemade purees***
> ***— in taste or in nutritional value.***

SIXTEEN

Homemade Baby Food

*I*f you want to feed your baby the healthiest, freshest foods possible, without any added sugar, tapioca, or thickener, make your own purees! Prepared with the freshest ingredients available, they will always taste better and provide more nutrients than commercial baby foods.

As far as preparation is concerned, you have more than one option. Choose the one that suits your work schedule best. You can use the blender-freezer method, stocking purees to avoid last-minute preparation. You can cook and puree for the day. Or you might want to prepare small amounts of food at the last minute, for extra flavour. With all three options, follow the guidelines concerning choice of ingredients and preparation.

You also have the option of alternating homemade and commercial baby food once in a while. But if you are planning to make your own purees at least part of the time, start your baby off with the homemade ones, so he or she will first become accustomed to the taste of real food. Then introduce your child to commercial baby foods.

The Benefits of Homemade Baby Food

With homemade purees, you increase the nutritional value of your baby's menu and control the quality. You expose your baby to a wide range of foods still not found in commercial products for babies.

For instance, in the vegetable group, you don't have to limit yourself to carrots, peas, sweet potatoes, squash, or green beans — the only vegetables in Beginner vegetable purees. Try zucchini, asparagus — even lettuce! You can use broccoli and cauliflower, which are so rich in vitamin C, calcium, and folic acid. You even have the possibility of making your purees with organic vegetables if you wish to reduce pesticide residues to a minimum.

Fruit purees can be prepared in no time. Some, like apples and pears, need cooking, but others, like fresh pineapple, melon, papaya, and mango, can be pureed uncooked. Bananas and avocados can simply be mashed with a fork.

> When Sophie was approximately six months old, she had already tried commercial green beans and green peas. She was then offered homemade fresh asparagus puree. She reacted very negatively and made a big mess. To calm things down, she was offered a well-liked vegetable for a couple of days and then was offered homemade broccoli puree. Her reaction was very good. She now alternates between homemade and commercial food without any problem.
>
> Do not give up after one refusal, but try introducing your own purees before offering commercial baby foods.

Chicken purees are relatively simple to make, with boneless, skinless breast of chicken, grain fed if desired. Liver puree, which is no longer available commercially, provides lots and lots of iron and is easy to prepare. Fish purees are the easiest to make — with fresh fish fillets. They are rich in protein and supply precious omega 3 fatty acids.

Homemade purees taste better than the commercial variety. Cooking time is limited, and the flavours available depend on what's in season. Babies initiated to these purees love them; babies that have been used to the blander taste of commercial baby foods can temporarily react. Later on, babies accustomed to homemade foods make an easier transition to regular family foods.

From the tender green of asparagus and zucchini to the deep orange of carrots and papaya, homemade purees are attractive, not only for your baby's eyes but also for your own.

The texture of homemade purees can vary, depending on your baby's development. And no thickening agent needs to be added — a net advantage.

Homemade Purees Save You Money

Preparing your own purees saves you money, since the commercial products cost approximately twice as much as those you can make — all groups of foods included. Your savings will be even greater during the summer months, when fresh vegetables and fruits are in season, even if you use organic vegetables and fruits.

You Control the Quality

Make sure your baby food is safe and nutritious. If you follow the guidelines outlined below, your homemade purees will surpass commercial baby foods in every way. Choose top-quality foods, since the final product depends on the quality of the basic ingredients. This rule applies to all recipes, but is even more important when it comes to baby foods.

The following method has been used by thousands of parents and has produced good results.

Choose Top-Quality Ingredients

Firm but ripe fresh fruit and fresh vegetables, in season, are your best choices. When fresh fruit and vegetables do not look good, are not available, or are too expensive, suitable alternatives include unsweetened frozen fruit and unsalted frozen vegetables, with no sauce or other flavourings.

To reduce pesticide residues in your baby's menu, buy *certified organic fruit and vegetables.* Babies are more sensitive to environmental contaminants and pesticides than adults because of their small body size. They take in more food per kilogram of body weight than adults and more contaminants per kilogram as well. If organic products are not available or too expensive, wash fruits and vegetables thoroughly and peel before cooking.

Canned fruit and vegetables are not appropriate. Even if some canned fruit and vegetables are available without added salt or sugar, they have been heat-treated and have lost some vitamin and mineral value. The whole idea of making your own baby food is to obtain a more nutritional product, not the opposite!

Fresh or frozen meats (lean parts in particular) and fresh or frozen poultry (organic or regular) are all suitable choices. Processed meats of all kinds are not acceptable.

Fresh or frozen fish is a valid choice. For fewer PCBs and other residues, choose farmed or ocean fish, the smaller the better. Canned fish contains too much sodium and is not recommended before 12 months.

Follow a Few Rules of Hygiene

To eliminate the possibility of food contamination and protect your baby from unnecessary infections, follow these simple guidelines:

- Wash your hands before handling any food that will be used in the baby food.
- Use impeccably clean utensils, containers, and cookware.
- Once the food is cooked and blended, cover and refrigerate it immediately. Never let cooked food sit at room temperature.
- When you prepare small quantities of food to be eaten immediately, do not keep the food more than three days in the refrigerator.
- Do not refreeze a thawed puree.

Assemble All Utensils You Need

Since homemade purees are introduced between the ages of four and six months, very smooth purees without lumps are required for only a few months at the most. By the time your baby has reached seven to eight months, she can chew more easily and can eat food mashed with a fork.

A blender or a food processor makes your job much easier, but you can manage with an inexpensive manual food mill to prepare smaller quantities. You also need: pots and pans, measuring cups and measuring spoons, individual ice-cube containers, freezer bags with ties — 500-millilitres (1-pint) and 1-litre (1-quart) sizes — labels, and small aluminum plates.

Cook Rapidly

Well-cooked foods are easier to digest, but overcooked foods lose many vitamins and minerals.

Vegetables can be steamed or cooked in the microwave. Both methods use very little water and require very short cooking times, and have been shown to minimize nutrient losses. Frozen vegetables should not be thawed before cooking and should be cooked rapidly.

Meat, fish, and poultry are cooked in small amounts of liquid.

Fruit is peeled and poached a few minutes in a small amount of water or fruit juice. This can be done on top of the stove or in the microwave. Ripe bananas, papayas, and mangoes can simply be mashed with a fork or pureed in the blender and served without any cooking.

Process no more than 375 to 500 millilitres (1 1/2 to 2 cups) of food at one time. Reduce this quantity to 250 millilitres (1 cup) in the case of poultry or meat. Large quantities of food hamper the blender's operational capacity and affect the quality of the final product.

Do Not Add Any Salt or Sugar

Babies do not need any seasonings during the first year of life. They enjoy the real flavour of vegetables without added salt and will never refuse apples, pears, bananas, or other fruit *au naturel.*

The addition of salt during these early months may overload the baby's renal system (kidneys) while the addition of sugar cultivates the need for sweets. Even honey is not recommended before 12 months because it can cause botulism (serious food poisoning).

To avoid such additions, never add salt to the cooking water and never season the foods before reducing them to a puree. If you want to serve some of the same foods to the rest of the family, add salt or seasonings once you have set aside the food for the baby.

Pour into Ice-Cube Trays

Once the puree is completed, pour it into ice-cube containers. Each cube used for the following recipes contains 60 millilitres (2 oz.) of food. Cool the puree in the refrigerator before freezing. If you prepare only a small quantity of food, you can store the puree in a covered container in the refrigerator for two or three days.

One mother decided to fill each cube only half full while introducing a new food, to minimize losses. This is a great idea.

Cover the ice-cube containers with a sheet of waxed paper and place them in the coldest part of the freezer, far from the door. Allow 8 to 12 hours for complete freezing to take place.

Place Frozen Purees in Plastic Bags

Once the purees are frozen, remove the ice-cube trays from the freezer and empty the cubes into small freezer bags, one type of food per bag. Seal the bag by withdrawing the air with a straw. Label each bag with the type of food and the date. Quickly return the bags to the freezer.

Purees can be kept this way in the freezer for varying lengths of time depending on the ingredients:

Table 17

Storage Time for Frozen Purees*

vegetables	6 to 8 months
fruits	6 to 8 months
cooked meat and poultry	1 to 2 months
cooked fish	1 to 2 months
meat and vegetable dinners	1 to 2 months
purees containing milk	4 to 6 weeks
cooked legumes and tofu	2 to 3 months

*   The first figure refers to the maximum storage time in the freezer compartment of the refrigerator, and the second figure refers to storage time in a deep freezer.

Reheat at the Last Minute

You can reheat the purees in a double boiler or in the microwave. At mealtime, remove the number of cubes needed from the freezer bags and put them in a glass container or a glass bowl. Warm up the cubes for a few minutes in a double boiler or for 30 seconds in the microwave. Avoid overheating. Always stir the food with a spoon to distribute the heat evenly.

Before serving, always test the temperature by putting a drop of food on the tip of your tongue or on your wrist.

There are exceptions to the rule . . .

Emily, seven months, enjoys fruit purees and can swallow up to three cubes at one meal. When she first tried mango puree that had been frozen, she did not like it when served lukewarm. The next day, it was served half thawed; it had a sherbet-like consistency and she loved it.

Even if tofu is ready to eat and does not require any cooking, pureed tofu was more easily accepted by Jonathan when it was only slightly reheated: 10 to 15 seconds in the microwave for 60 mL (1/4 cup).

You Don't Need Purees for More Than Four to Six Weeks

You don't need to fill up your freezer with carrot or apple puree! When you add vegetables and fruits to your baby's menu, he will be between five and six months old, and he will need food of a very smooth consistency. But this is not necessary for more than four to six weeks. When your baby reaches the age of about seven or eight months and has tasted a good variety of vegetables and fruits, he will be capable of chewing and will want thicker purees, even though he has no teeth.

However, if you feed your baby purees for a longer period, you can easily bypass this intermediate stage. At about nine months of age, he will be ready to eat mixed foods and fork-mashed foods.

You will enjoy making your own purees and,
at the same time, you'll expose your baby
to a wider range of healthy food.

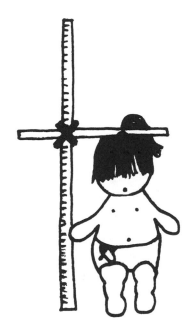

Asparagus Puree

A spring delicacy.

Ingredients

- 1/2 kg (1 lb.) tender, young asparagus, in season
- water

Preparation

Snap off tough ends and discard. Wash tips and tender stalks. Cut into 5-cm (2-in.) pieces.

Steam asparagus over boiling water approximately 10–15 minutes or until tender.

Or, in the microwave, place asparagus pieces in a covered glass dish with 60 mL (1/4 cup) of water. Cook at high power 6–9 minutes. Stir with a fork after half the cooking time.

Remove from heat and cool slightly.

Put half the asparagus into the blender with a small amount of water. Puree. Repeat with the remaining asparagus.

Pour puree into ice-cube trays and freeze.

Yield: 1 ice-cube tray full

Storage life: 6 months

Beet Puree

Serve with one bib on you and another on the baby! Do not serve until your baby is nine months old, because of high nitrate content. The same restriction applies to spinach and turnip.

Ingredients

- 1/2 kg (1 lb.) young beets
- water

Preparation

Scrub beets. Cut off all but 5 cm (2 in.) of the tops. Do not peel. Leave whole.

Steam 30–40 minutes in pressure cooker. Or microwave beets in covered glass dish with 30 mL (2 tbsp.) of water at high power for 12 minutes or until tender.

Cool slightly. Peel and slice cooked beets. Put into the blender with 60–80 mL (1/4–1/3 cup) of fresh water. Puree.

Pour into ice-cube trays and freeze.

Yield: 1 ice-cube tray full

Storage life: 6 months

Broccoli Puree

Bright green broccoli has a sweet, pleasant flavour. It is rich in vitamins C and A, iron, calcium, and folic acid.

Ingredients

— 1 bunch fresh broccoli (approx. 750 g (1 1/2 lb.))
— water

Preparation

Cut off and discard the stalks. Keep only the flower part for the puree. (Use the stalks for soups or stir-fries for the rest of the family.)

Steam broccoli over boiling water 10–15 minutes until it is tender but still very green.

Or, in the microwave, place broccoli in a covered glass dish with 30 mL (2 tbsp.) of water. Cook at high power 7–10 minutes. Stir with fork halfway through cooking time.

Remove from heat and cool slightly.

Place half the broccoli with 60 mL (1/4 cup) of water into the blender. Puree. Repeat with the remaining broccoli.

Pour into ice-cube trays and freeze.

Yield: 1 ice-cube tray full

Storage life: 6 months

Carrot Puree

Babies love the colour and flavour of carrots. Choose organic carrots when possible, to reduce nitrate content.

Ingredients

- 1 kg (2 lb.) fresh carrots
- water

Preparation

Remove tops. Wash. Scrape, peel, and scrub well with a stiff brush. Cut into 2.5-cm (1-in.) pieces.

Steam carrots over boiling water 15–20 minutes or until tender.

Or, in the microwave, place prepared carrots in covered glass dish with 15–30 mL (1–2 tbsp.) of water. Cook at high power 15–18 minutes. Stir with fork after half the cooking time.

Allow to stand 3 minutes before pouring into the blender.

Place 375 mL (1 1/2 cups) of cooked carrots and 80 mL (1/3 cup) of fresh water into the blender. Puree. Repeat with the remaining carrots.

Pour into ice-cube trays and freeze.

Yield: 2 ice-cube trays full

Storage life: 6 months

Cauliflower Puree

Cauliflower, a member of the cabbage family, is very rich in vitamin C.

Ingredients

- 1 small head of cauliflower
- water
- 125 mL (1/2 cup) whole milk or soy milk

Preparation

Separate into small florets. Remove any green stalks. Wash well.

Steam over boiling water 15–20 minutes or until tender.

Or, in the microwave, cook florets in a covered glass dish at high power 9–11 minutes. Stir with a fork after half the cooking time.

Allow to stand 3 minutes before putting into blender.

Place into blender 375 mL (1 1/2 cups) of florets with 250 mL (1 cup) of water and 60 mL (1/4 cup) of whole or soy milk. Puree. Repeat with the remaining ingredients.

Pour into ice-cube trays and freeze.

Yield: 2 ice-cube trays full or less, depending on the size of the cauliflower

Storage life: 4 to 6 weeks

Green Bean Puree

The younger the green beans, the better the puree. Frozen green beans can also be used.

Ingredients

- 750 g (1 1/2 lb.) tender, fresh green beans
- water

Preparation

Wash and snap off ends. Cut beans into thirds.

Steam over boiling water approximately 10–15 minutes or until tender.

In the microwave, put beans into a covered glass dish with 60 mL (1/4 cup) of water. Cook at high power 8–10 minutes. Stir with a fork after half the cooking time.

Allow to stand 3 minutes before putting into the blender.

Place half the cooked beans and 80 mL (1/3 cup) of water into the blender. Puree. Repeat with the remaining beans.

Pour into ice-cube trays and freeze.

Yield: 2 ice-cube trays full

Storage life: 6 months

Green Pea Puree

Very green, very rich in iron, and quite sweet!

Ingredients

- 1 kg (2 lb.) fresh green peas, unshelled or 500mL (2 cups) shelled
- water

Preparation

Shell and wash just before cooking.

Steam peas over boiling water 12–15 minutes or until tender.

Or, in the microwave, put peas into a covered glass dish with 60 mL (1/4 cup) of water. Cook at high power 8–11 minutes. Stir with fork after half the cooking time.

Allow to stand 3 minutes.

Pour into the blender with 60 mL (1/4 cup) of water. Puree.

Pour into ice-cube trays and freeze.

Yield: 1 ice-cube tray full

Storage life: 6 months

Winter Squash Puree

Winter squash and pumpkin are filled with beta-carotene.

Ingredients

- 1 large winter squash (acorn, butternut)
- water

Preparation

Wash the outside of the squash.

Bake whole in a 180° C (350°F) oven for about 1 1/2 hours.

Or, for the microwave, cut squash in half and remove seeds. Place cut side down in a shallow glass dish. Cover. Cook at high power 12–16 minutes or until tender.

Let stand 3 minutes.

Put the flesh into the blender with 60 mL (1/4 cup) of water. Puree.

Pour into ice-cube trays and freeze.

Yield: 1 ice-cube tray full or more, depending on the size of the squash

Storage life: 6 months

Zucchini Puree

Zucchini has a sweet and soft flavour. The puree is a pretty spring green. Babies enjoy!

Ingredients

- 750 g (1 1/2 lb.) zucchinis
  (7 to 8 small ones)
- water

Preparation

Wash, scrub lightly, but do not peel. Remove stem and blossom ends. Cut into 1.25-cm (1/2-in.) slices.

Steam zucchini 10–12 minutes or until tender.

Or, in the microwave, place zucchini into a covered glass dish. Cook at high power 11–13 minutes. Rotate dish after half the cooking time.

Allow to stand 3 minutes.

Put half the cooked zucchini into the blender without adding any water. Puree. Repeat with the remaining zucchini.

Pour into ice-cube trays and freeze.

Yield: 2 ice-cube trays full

Storage life: 6 months

Legume Puree

Legumes are easy to digest but may cause gases. Start by giving your baby small amounts before serving legume puree as a meal.

Ingredients

— 250 mL (1 cup) lentils or peas
or
250 mL (1 cup) red kidney beans or
white beans, pre-soaked in water

Preparation

In a saucepan, cover legumes with water and cook for about an hour. When legumes are tender and can be mashed easily with a fork, remove saucepan from heat. Let legumes cool, then drain.

Place half the legumes in the blender with 500 mL (2 cups) of fresh water. Puree until smooth. Repeat with the remaining legumes and water.

Pour into ice-cube trays and freeze.

Yield: 500 to 750 mL (2 to 3 cups)

Storage life: 2 to 3 months

Tofu Puree

Tofu puree is simple to make. It does not need any preparation or cooking. With its mild flavour and smooth texture, your baby will love this easy-to-swallow puree. Once you have introduced your child to most solid foods, you can also serve pureed vegetables or fruits stirred into the tofu.

Ingredients

— 30 to 60 g (1 to 2 oz.) soft tofu (silken type)

Preparation

Mash tofu on a plate with a fork and serve.

Yield: 1 serving

Storage life: Tofu can be stored in water, in refrigerator, for 7 to 10 days.

Applesauce

Organic apples are a wise choice if you cook the apples with the skin. Cooking time varies according to type of apples used. Ripe McIntosh apples in season produce a soft pink and sweet puree. Once your baby is 12 months or older, modify this classic recipe by adding cinnamon for extra taste.

Ingredients

— 8 to 10 apples and water

Preparation

Scrub and wash the apples well. Do not peel unless your blender is not powerful enough to pulverize all the peel. Remove cores, cut into quarters, and slice.

Place apples in a saucepan with 125 mL (1/2 cup) of water. Bring to a boil, reduce heat, and simmer for about 20 minutes or until tender.

Or, in the microwave, put apples into a covered glass dish with 125 mL (1/2 cup) of water. Cook at high power for 12–15 minutes or until tender.

Allow to stand 5 minutes to cool.

Place 500 mL (2 cups) of cooked apples into the blender and puree until the peel has completely disappeared. If the blender is not powerful enough to pulverize all the peel, pass the puree through a sieve or peel the apples before cooking. Repeat the same operation with the remaining apples.

Yield: 2 ice-cube trays full

Storage life: 6 months

Pear Puree

~

Different pears provide different flavours. You may wish to prepare half the recipe with Bosc or French pears and the other half with red Anjou pears. When your baby has been introduced to all fruit, cook the pears in apple juice or make a pear-and-apple puree by using both fruits in the same puree. This can be fork-mashed later on.

Ingredients

— 9 to 11 fresh, medium pears
— water

Preparation

Peel pears, quarter, and core.

Put into a saucepan with 125 mL (1/2 cup) of water. Simmer for 20–30 minutes or until pears are tender.

Or, in the microwave, put pears into a covered glass dish with 125 mL (1/2 cup) of water. Cook at medium power 10–15 minutes.

Allow to stand at least 5 minutes before pouring into the blender.

Put half the cooked pears into the blender with 30 mL (2 tbsp.) of the cooking water. Puree. Repeat with the remaining pears.

Pour into ice-cube trays and freeze.

Yield: 2 ice-cube trays full

Storage life: 6 months

Apricot Puree

Apricots are a good source of beta-carotene, but they are in season for only a short time. If you are lucky, you will be able to offer this special puree to your baby.

Ingredients

- 1 L (4 cups) fresh, ripe apricots
- water

Preparation

Wash very well. Do not peel. Pit and slice the apricots.

Place fruit into a saucepan, bring to a boil, reduce heat, and simmer for about 15 minutes, until apricots are tender.

Or in the microwave, put fruit into covered glass dish with 125 mL (1/2 cup) of water. Cook at medium power for 8 minutes or until the fruit is tender.

Allow to stand 5 minutes.

Place half the cooked apricots into the blender with 60 mL (1/4 cup) of cooking water. Puree. Repeat with the remaining apricots.

Pour into ice-cube trays and freeze.

Yield: 2 ice-cube trays full

Storage life: 6 months

Peach Puree

Fresh peaches are a seasonal luxury. Nectarines are easier to find and may serve as a replacement when peaches are out of season. Simply fork-mash when your baby is more than eight months old.

Ingredients

- 1 L (4 cups) fresh peaches, pitted, and sliced
- water

Preparation

Put peaches and water into a saucepan. Bring to a boil, reduce heat, and simmer gently for about 15–20 minutes or until peaches are tender.

Or, in the microwave, put peaches into a covered glass dish with 125 mL (1/2 cup) of water. Cook at medium power for 7–8 minutes or until tender.

Allow to stand 5 minutes before processing in the blender.

Put 500 mL (2 cups) of cooked peaches into the blender with 15 mL (1 tbsp.) of cooking water. Puree. Repeat with the remaining peaches.

Pour into ice-cube trays and freeze.

Yield: 2 ice-cube trays full

Storage life: 6 months

Prune Puree

Prunes are quite sweet, rich in iron, and rich in fibre. A sure favourite! Once the baby has been introduced to all fruit, mix an equal share of this puree with applesauce for a different treat.

Ingredients

- 375 mL (1 1/2 cups) pitted prunes
- 500 mL (2 cups) hot water
- 250 mL (1 cup) cold water

Preparation

Soak prunes in hot water for 5–15 minutes. Drain.

Put the prunes and cold water into a saucepan. Bring to a boil. Reduce heat and simmer for about 20 minutes.

Remove from heat and cool slightly.

Put half the prunes into the blender with 80 mL (1/3 cup) of cooking liquid. Puree. Repeat with remaining fruit.

Pour into ice-cube trays and freeze.

Yield: 1 ice-cube tray full

Storage life: 6 months

Beef Puree

The same directions can be used to prepare a puree of veal.

Ingredients

- 1/2 kg (1 lb.) lean, tender beef, cut into 2.5-cm (1-in.) cubes
- 1 stalk of celery, chopped
- 3 carrots, peeled and cut into pieces
- 2 medium potatoes, peeled and quartered
- 15 mL (1 tbsp.) minced onion

Preparation

Place beef and 550 mL (2 1/4 cups) of water into a saucepan. Simmer for about 45 minutes. Add celery, carrots, and potatoes. Cook another 35 minutes or until tender.

Remove from heat and cool slightly.

Separate the beef from the vegetables. Place 200 mL (3/4 cup) of cooked meat into the blender with 80 mL (1/3 cup) of cooking water. Puree until nice and smooth. Repeat with remaining beef.

Pour into ice-cube trays and freeze.

Yield: 10–12 cubes

Storage life: 10–12 weeks

Tip: Puree the cooked, discarded vegetables with extra broth and serve as a garden soup to the rest of the family.

Chicken Puree

Use turkey breast for variety and economy, depen
the market specials. Organic chicken is also a recomm
product.

Ingredients

- 2 boneless, skinless chicken breasts
- water or unsalted vegetable broth

Preparation

Place the chicken breasts into a steamer. Steam over boiling water 15 minutes or until the chicken flesh is cooked.

Remove and cut the chicken into big pieces.

Place 125 mL (1/2 cup) of chicken meat with 80 mL (1/3 cup) of broth or water into the blender. Puree until nice and smooth. Repeat with remaining chicken.

Pour into ice-cube trays and freeze.

Yield: 1 ice-cube tray full

Storage life: 10–12 weeks

Chicken Liver Puree

Liver is a very rich source of iron, and chicken livers have a softer texture and flavour than others.

Ingredients

- 5 to 6 chicken livers (from grain-fed chickens)
- homemade chicken broth, unsalted
  or vegetable broth

Preparation

Cut livers in half and remove the white membrane. Place into a saucepan with 250 mL (1 cup) of broth. Simmer gently for 10 minutes or until livers are a gray-brown inside. Remove from heat and cook slightly.

Put a few chicken livers into the blender with a small amount of cooking liquid. Puree until smooth. Repeat with remaining liver.

Pour into ice-cube trays and freeze.

Yield: 6 cubes

Storage life: 10–12 weeks

Fish Puree

Babies enjoy the taste and texture of fish. Mothers enjoy the short preparation involved! Fish is an excellent source of protein and of omega 3 fatty acids.

Ingredients

- 250 g (1/2 lb.) fish fillets (ocean or farmed fish: sole, salmon, flounder, grouper, haddock, halibut, monkfish)
- 125 mL (1/2 cup) whole milk
  (Do not use 2% or skim milk until the baby is 1 year old.)

Preparation

Pour 60 mL (1/4 cup) of milk into a pan and gently heat. Add the fish fillets. Cover and poach over low heat 5–10 minutes or until the fish flakes easily with a fork. Remove from heat and cool slightly.

Place half the cooked fish and cooking milk into the blender. Blend until smooth. Add more milk if needed. Repeat with the remaining fish.

Pour into ice-cube trays and freeze.

Yield: 8 cubes

Storage life: 4–6 weeks

Tip: Once your baby has been introduced to all basic foods, add 30 mL (2 tbsp.) of minced onion during poaching for extra flavour.

SEVENTEEN

Frequent Problems — and Solutions

Questions relating to feeding are quite frequent during the early months after birth. Concerns about eating behaviour become stronger after your baby reaches six months. Parents also want to be sure that their child will not suffer from obesity or bad cholesterol later in life. This chapter deals with these issues and provides answers that will help you manage such challenges better.

Your Baby Is Spitting Up

Spitting up, or regurgitation, is a fairly common problem during the first months of life. It is quite different from vomiting and can be described as spitting up small amounts of food that then dribble from the mouth during and after a meal. This is caused by the immaturity of the digestive tract and should not be interpreted as an allergic reaction. It does not affect your baby's growth or her appetite and slowly disappears by the third month of life.

You can nevertheless minimize the problem by trying the following strategies:

- Lay your baby on his stomach after each feeding instead of putting him in an infant seat. The use of infant reclining seats, also called Chalasia chairs, has been shown to cause such problems.
- Avoid overfeeding your baby by responding to the cues she gives to show that she is full.
- Make sure your baby is never left alone to feed from a propped bottle.
- Avoid playing with or exciting your baby just after a feeding.
- Make sure your baby burps at least once during a feeding.

Your Baby Is Vomiting

Vomiting is another problem altogether. It is a forceful expulsion of large quantities of food or milk, during or after a meal. It is usually associated with fever or a gastrointestinal infection and requires medical attention.

When your baby vomits, you must rehydrate him rapidly. Give him liquid on a regular basis — the equivalent of 125 millilitres (4 fl. oz.) every hour, 15 millilitres (1 tablespoon) every five minutes or even 5 millilitres (1 teaspoon) at a time, if your baby is under six months.

The best liquid to give him will be one that imitates the composition of body fluids. Commercial preparations sold in drugstores — such as Pedialyte or Gastrolyte — fit this criterion. If you cannot obtain this type of preparation or if your baby refuses it, prepare your own home mix with unsweetened orange juice, water, and a bit of salt. Follow the exact proportions given in the following recipe.

The Rehydration Drink

600 mL (20 fl. oz.) bottled spring water or tap water*
360 mL (12 fl. oz.) orange juice prepared as usual
2 mL (1/2 tsp.) salt

Mix well and keep in refrigerator.
Take out of the refrigerator a few minutes before giving it to the baby.

* Boil it at least 2 minutes if your baby is under four months.

Do not let your baby become dehydrated before consulting your doctor or a health unit. If your baby vomits over and over again, if his urine is smelly, and/or if he is very tired, go to emergency immediately.

Your Baby Has Colic

Colic is a manifestation of acute pain that usually begins during the third or fourth week of life and gradually disappears by the fourth month. It occurs as often in breastfed infants as among formula-fed babies.

If your baby has colic, she will cry, even scream, for hours, usually in late afternoon or early evening. Her abdomen will be hard and distended and she will find no comfort, even in your arms. There are many possible causes of infantile colic: under- or overfeeding, poor burping technique, food intolerance, air swallowing, or a greater need for affection.

If you are breastfeeding:

– Do not hesitate to feed your baby on demand to satisfy your
baby's frequent needs for food, but make sure you empty the

first breast before offering the second. Short feedings on each breast provide too much lactose and not enough milk fat, which in turn causes hunger, colic, and crying.

- Check your feeding position and make sure your baby is not swallowing too much air.
- Try eliminating all milk products from your diet for five to ten days (see the end of Chapter 7, Improving Your Menu for Better Breastfeeding, page 64, for a balanced menu without milk products).

If you see some results but your baby still goes through painful sessions, try eliminating other proteins, such as beef or chicken or soy. Plan your menus around protein-rich foods that you did not eat frequently during your pregnancy. See how it works. If you see no results after five to ten days of elimination, resume your usual diet and look for another solution (such as using medication prescribed by your doctor).

If you are formula feeding:

- Try a protein-hydrolysate-based formula (see Chapter 10, Other Milk — Before and after Six Months, page 91), for a few weeks. If the problem is relieved, continue on with this formula until the fourth month.
- Massage your baby's abdomen and take her in your arms more often.

Never forget that colic is a temporary problem. If it lasts beyond four months, it may require special medical investigation.

Your Baby Has Diarrhea

It is important to know the difference between a mild diarrhea and a gastroenteritis or a flu. This section deals with mild diarrhea.

Before 12 months. A breastfed baby can have eight to ten stools per day and never have diarrhea. After a few months, stools become less frequent but remain soft and yellowish until solid foods are introduced.

A formula-fed baby can have loose stools following the introduction of a new food. The problem is minor and does not require any intervention.

If the soft stools persist, your baby may have an intolerance to milk protein or to lactose. Try a soy-based formula. If there is a family history of food allergies, try a therapeutic formula (see Chapter 10, Other Milk — Before and after Six Months, pages 91–92).

After 12 months. Your baby may have chronic mild diarrhea if he drinks too much fruit juice — apple juice in particular. The problem is quite easy to solve. Just cut down the intake of juice to a minimum — that is, to approximately 125 millilitres (4 fl. oz.) per day. Dilute the juice with an equal amount of water and gradually increase his milk intake.

Your Baby Has Gastroenteritis

Gastroenteritis is a severe diarrhea that can happen anytime and is rarely caused by food. It is a viral infection. It manifests itself through liquid stools and is often accompanied by vomiting and fever. It is considered a serious health problem and requires immediate action to prevent the dehydration that causes 500 deaths and 200,000 hospitalizations per year among young children in the United States, according to the Center for Disease Control and Prevention.

To adequately rehydrate your baby, constantly give him a rehydration drink that contains the right proportion of water, sodium, and sugar. Use your own home mix or commercial preparations such as Pedialyte or Gastrolyte, sold in drugstores (See "Rehydration Drink" recipe on page 188).

- Give him approximately 125 mL (1/2 cup) per hour, in a bottle or on a spoon. If your baby vomits, give him 5 mL (1 tsp.) every 5 to 10 minutes until the vomiting has stopped.
- A baby less than 12 months of age can require 1 L (4 cups) of drink per day.
- Avoid fruit juices, sodas, or carbonated drinks because they do not contain the right proportion of water, sodium, and sugar. They can actually worsen the situation and delay recovery.
- Consult your doctor or your health unit.
- Continue to breastfeed or formula-feed your baby as often as possible.
- If your baby is already eating solid foods, continue to feed him. Infant cereal, bananas, meat, and tofu are easy to digest.

Even if the stools remain quite watery, this strategy will prevent weight loss, shorten the period of diarrhea, and help your baby recuperate more rapidly.

To prevent contamination, wash your hands with soap and warm water after every diaper change and before meal preparation.

Your Baby Is Constipated

Breastfed babies have soft stools and are rarely constipated. Formula-fed babies have firmer stools.

Constipation can happen the day after you introduce the first solid food or when you introduce the formula, or cow's milk. It manifests itself through infrequent, drier, and firmer stools. In some cases, the elimination becomes so painful that babies retain their stools to avoid the pain.

Constipation is a frequent problem among infants and children. In a U.S. study (Issenman et al.), 16 percent of parents of 22-month-olds reported that their child had a constipation problem.

Stephanie was breastfed five months before having any solid food. She used to eliminate five to six stools per day. After two days of infant cereal, she stopped eliminating and did not have any stool for the next six days. At seven months, she has now adapted to solid foods and eliminates every day or second day, but she still reacts after a new solid is introduced.

Before Six Months

- In the rare case of a constipated, breastfed baby, increase feedings to increase the amount of fluid.
- In other cases, alternate iron-fortified formula with a non-fortified formula, to allow the baby to adapt.
- Increase the amount of fluid in your baby's diet by offering cooled boiled water — approximately 15 mL (1 tbsp.) between each feeding.
- After 3 months, give your baby diluted prune juice, 15 mL (1 tbsp.) of juice with 15 mL (1 tbsp.) of water, once or twice a day.
- If the problem persists, have your baby examined by your doctor, to eliminate the possibility of an anal fissure.

Between 6 and 12 Months

- Increase the intake of bottled or safe tap or well water, between meals.
- Serve a whole-grain infant cereal instead of a refined cereal (see Chapter 14, Infant Cereals).
- Replace the milk-based formula with a soy-based formula (see Chapter 10, Other Milks — Before and after Six Months, pages 89–90). If you do not notice any change after two weeks, try other measures.
- Offer your baby pureed prunes alone or with other fruits.

- If the preceding suggestions produce no results, mix 5 to 15 mL (1 to 3 tsp.) of natural bran with the infant cereal in the morning and at night. This small amount of bran cannot significantly reduce caloric intake or mineral absorption.
- In lieu of natural wheat bran, add 5 mL (1 tsp.) cold pressed flaxseed oil to the cereal.

Constipated babies who do not respond to increased fluid intake, increased dietary fibre, or other natural laxatives such as prune juice and flaxseed oil may be intolerant of cow's milk protein. An interesting study published in The New England Journal of Medicine *suggests that possibility.*

The researchers studied 65 young children (11 to 72 months of age) with constipation problems and compared the effect of cow's milk and soy milk. They saw that soy milk given for 2 weeks helped 44 of these children solve their constipation problem.

After 12 Months

- Offer raw, grated vegetables on a daily basis, and pieces of raw fruit.
- Offer water between meals.
- Serve whole-grain cereal products, rich in dietary fibre, such as brown rice, whole-wheat bread, and whole-wheat pasta, instead of white rice, white bread, and white pasta.
- Limit the daily intake of cow's milk to 1 L (32 fl. oz.) per day.
- For two weeks, replace cow's milk with a soy-based formula or a soy drink fortified with calcium and vitamin D (e.g., So Good, So Nice). If you notice an improvement, continue with the soy formula.
- Add 15 to 30 mL (1 to 2 tbsp.) of natural wheat bran to the cereal or in yogourt. This small amount cannot affect caloric intake or mineral absorption.

– Add 5 mL (1 tsp.) cold pressed flaxseed oil to the cereal or even add 5 mL (1 tsp.) of ground flaxseeds.

When your baby has a tendency to be constipated, he will require a regular routine to function properly. Allow sufficient time for toilet training after your child has reached 18 months. This will favour normal elimination.

Your Baby Refuses to Eat

Never force your baby to eat — never! This advice is valid for all ages and in all circumstances.

Babies are hungry some days and less hungry on other days. Appetite normally slows down when growth slows down at the end of the first year, and hunger strikes can happen any day at that time.

Your response can enhance the development of a happy eating relationship or do the opposite. A relaxed attitude is your surest strategy from the time of birth on, but it is also the most difficult one to manage.

To reduce your anxiety, always offer the most nutritious foods, but allow your child to determine the quantity. Remember the Clara Davis study that showed that top-quality, unprocessed foods always work in favour of your child's growth and development (see beginning of Chapter 1). Maintaining a positive interaction with your child even if she refuses some foods is your surest route to a healthy feeding relationship.

During the second year of life, when your baby's appetite drops normally, you may want to do these things:

– Offer very small helpings of individual foods.
– Remove uneaten foods without any nasty remarks.
– Offer water instead of milk or juice between meals, to build up your baby's appetite for mealtime.

– Accept day-to-day changes in eating behaviour and appetite.

What foods are most often refused? Your baby may have been happy with all your food purees during the first 12 months, swallowing the whole range of vegetables with great appetite. Then, suddenly, she began to show signs of food refusal. Don't worry, your baby is normal!

Vegetables are the food most frequently refused by babies and children in our society. Cooked vegetables are much less popular than raw ones. Partially cooked carrot sticks with a yogourt dip can win many children over.

Red meat refusal comes second and can last for many months while your baby continues to resist new textures. Chicken, tofu, and filleted fish are much easier to chew and swallow.

The list of refusals only increases as parental pressure becomes greater. But once that pressure comes off, things can take a turn for the better. My own experience with my first daughter is worth a dozen reports from the experts. I got into serious negotiation with my very sensitive little girl over every mouthful of vegetables from the time she began walking until the day I gave up insisting — four or five years later! From that moment on, she started to taste and enjoy vegetables, and still does.

Your Family Has Food Allergies

This is an area of great concern and growing scientific evidence. Research done in the last 20 years allows us to understand the issue better, but a lot of answers are yet to come. We do know that:

– Babies are much more vulnerable to adverse food reactions during the first few years of life, but skin tests do not help identify the offending foods in this age group.

- 58 percent of babies born into families where both parents have a history of allergies risk developing reactions to food.
- 29 percent of babies born into families where only one parent has allergies risk developing reactions, while only 12 percent of babies born into families with no history of allergies risk these reactions.
- Most food reactions occur during the first 12 months.
- Most eliminated foods can be reintroduced by the third year without any risk.
- Symptoms associated with adverse food reactions include diarrhea, vomiting, colic, skin rashes, eczema, and chronic nasal congestion — but such symptoms are not always caused by offending foods.
- Most allergens are found in protein-rich foods such as milk, eggs, and peanuts. These three foods, as well as soy, nuts, and wheat, are responsible for about 95 percent of food allergies in infants.
- It is rare for an infant to have allergies to more than two or three foods.
- Allergies to peanuts, other nuts, wheat, fish, and seafood are the most severe and tend to be lifelong.

The good news is that it seems possible to prevent adverse reactions in the early months and to delay eventual allergic reactions. The following proposed strategy is especially recommended for infants born into families with a history of food allergies.

Before 12 Months

- Breastfeed for at least six months or give hypoallergenic formula (with a casein or whey hydrolysate) for at least six months (see Chapter 10, Other Milks — Before and after Six Months, pages 91–92).

A five-year follow-up study has shown that infants with a family history of allergies can be fed in a way that reduces the incidence of food allergies. High-risk babies, whose mothers had chosen not to breastfeed, were put on a partial whey hydrolysate (Good Start) for six months and compared with high-risk infants who were either breastfed or fed a regular milk- or soy-based formula. The occurrence of eczema and asthma was the lowest in the breastfed and whey hydrolysate groups.

- If symptoms occur, eliminate other potentially offensive foods from your menu — such as beef, fish, soy, or peanut butter — but continue breastfeeding as long as you can.
- Delay introduction of all solid foods until six months.

When Introducing Solids

- Introduce one new food every seven days instead of following the regular calendar.
- Among infant cereals, leave out wheat cereal until after 12 months.
- Avoid mixing foods together before each food component has been introduced separately.
- Leave out egg and orange juice until 12 months.
- Leave out all fish and peanut butter until at least 12 months.
- Delay introduction of whole cow's milk until after 12 months, offering breast milk or a protein-hydrolysate-based formula until that age.

After 12 Months

- Continue a slow introduction of new foods.
- If a reaction occurs, eliminate the suspected food for one to two weeks, and see whether the symptoms disappear.
- Reintroduce the eliminated food in a small quantity and observe the reaction. If the symptoms reappear, leave out the offending food for another two or three months, but reintroduce it after

that period. In the majority of cases, there is no need to eliminate any food for a lifetime.

A Low-Fat Diet Is Not Helpful for Infants and Toddlers

Low fat intake is not suitable for an infant or a young child; it can even work against the baby's growth and development. Today's recommendation for healthy adults is to lower the total fat intake to 30 percent of total calories. Some programs for cardiac patients, such as Dr. Dean Ornish's program for reversing heart disease, suggest an even more drastic drop, to 10 percent of total calories. These programs are suitable for vulnerable adults but present risks for growing children.

Dr. Dean Ornish from Sausalito, California, became a worldwide hero when his research showed that it was possible to reverse heart disease with diet, exercise, and meditation. He followed very closely a small number of high-risk heart patients, who could no longer have their arteries unblocked with surgery. His prescription was a very low-fat diet, regular exercise, and meditation sessions.

Evaluation was done through angiograms of the blocked arteries (inside photos of the artery) before and after the treatment. After 12 months, Dr. Ornish saw that the intervention had significantly decreased the arterial blockage. This was the first research to show such results.

Such a low-fat diet can be valuable for high-risk patients but is not meant for the general population — and especially not for infants and toddlers.

Breast milk, which is considered the perfect food for infants for at least the first six months of life, stores 40 to 50 percent of its calories in the form of fat and 150 milligrams of cholesterol per litre.

Dietary fat present in breast milk and other foods such as vegetable oils provide essential fatty acids that are critical ingredients for brain development. At birth, the infant's brain weighs about half a kilogram (1 lb.) but reaches 1.35 kilograms (3 lb.) by age three. Essential fatty acids are one of the most important brain materials acquired during that period.

Cholesterol is also an essential ingredient for nerve and nervous system membrane development in the early years.

For these reasons, the Canadian Paediatric Society's Committee on Nutrition does not recommend a low-fat diet during childhood. It recommends breast milk for at least six months and whole cow's milk after nine months once the baby is eating 180 millilitres (12 tablespoons) of solid foods per day. The use of skim or partially skimmed milk is strongly discouraged before 24 months of age. After 24 months, skim milk can be tolerated if there is need for it because of a serious weight or genetic problem.

In all other cases, proper growth and development are to be achieved through a wholesome menu, not a low-fat diet.

Your Child Is Chubby

Childhood obesity is a growing problem in North America, but weight gain during the first year of life is not a predictor of future obesity. At the end of the first year, a baby will normally have tripled his or her birth weight and often has a double chin. But most chubby babies return to a normal weight by school age and never become obese.

Excessive weight gain does become a problem around the age of four or five, and studies show that a child who is obese before school age is quite likely to develop long-term obesity. The family context has a lot to do with such a situation. Heavy parents tend to have obese children more often than lean parents. Genetics and eating habits are both implicated.

A widespread myth is that obese children always eat more than others. Research has shown, however, that susceptible babies become overweight while eating no more calories than normal-weight babies.

Another myth is that breastfeeding and the slow introduction of solid foods prevent long-term obesity. While no one can deny the overall benefits provided by these two excellent feeding practices, no study has ever shown such a long-term result.

The last myth is that dieting can solve the problem! But weight-reduction diets don't work even during childhood. Worse, diet restrictions in early childhood can lead to nutritional deficiencies, lowered body temperature, reduced capacity to fight infections, and reduced capacity to be physically active. Such complications are unacceptable and avoidable.

If you are overweight and your two-year-old has a tendency to gain more weight than is desirable for normal growth, please don't put your child on a diet! The best long-term feeding strategy is to respond very early to your baby's cues by never forcing him to finish a bottle or a plate and by helping him never to overeat. Five minutes of storytelling can very easily replace two chocolate-chip cookies.

If your child is a big eater, slowly increase the fibre content of the menu to provide her with more satisfaction and fewer calories in the long run. Work on a family approach to physical activity to increase everybody's regular energy expenditures. Limit television viewing and walk the dog instead.

Build a family menu around winning foods, and systematically avoid foods that are loaded with added sugar, fat, or salt. If everyone else eats the same healthful meals, it will become much easier for your child to limit heavy snacks and desserts.

If your child has always had a normal weight and suddenly gains more than 7 kilograms (15 lb.) in a preschool year, take time to figure out how that has happened. Sudden weight changes often hide emotional discomfort. By tackling the real cause instead of counting calories, your child will learn to avoid misusing food on a long-term basis.

A few years ago, a young girl and her mother visited me at my nutrition clinic. They were consulting me about a weight problem. Barbara was nine years old and had gained 20 lb. in 12 months. After carefully reviewing the little girl's food intake, I tried to find out what had changed in her life during that period. The family had moved from one side of the city to the other and Barbara had changed schools and had had to give up her violin lessons. This little girl loved playing violin three to four times a week but could no longer do that, since the distances did not allow for it anymore. She missed this and watched more television instead. This meant she also exercised less.

My advice to the mother was to improve Barbara's menu but also to find another musical activity for her daughter. This little musician needed to express her talent; that was a must!

**When there is a problem,
there is always a solution.**

EIGHTEEN

Flowers Talk about Nutrition

~

To help you remember some of the best sources of all the nutrients discussed throughout this book, this chapter leads you through a special garden! Each flower presents a different nutrient, a vitamin, or a mineral. The centre of the flower describes the role of each nutrient, the petals indicate major food sources, and the leaves translate the child's daily nutritional needs into servings of food.

In these pages, you will find energy-producing nutrients such as proteins, carbohydrates, and fats; the fat-soluble vitamins A, D, and E; and the water-soluble vitamins, including the B-complex vitamins thiamine, riboflavin, niacin, vitamin B_6, folic acid, vitamin B_{12}, and vitamin C.

You will discover good sources of dietary fibre, as well as the key minerals, including iron, calcium, magnesium, and zinc. If your child's menu contains enough of the first three minerals (calcium, iron, and magnesium), the overall quality of his or her menu is guaranteed.

Not all vitamins and minerals are presented, but I have chosen the most important ones as they relate to your baby's growth and development.

As you will notice, winning foods appear on many flowers and provide more nutrients in every mouthful. Winning foods not only provide long-term health. They are also fun to cook and fun to eat!

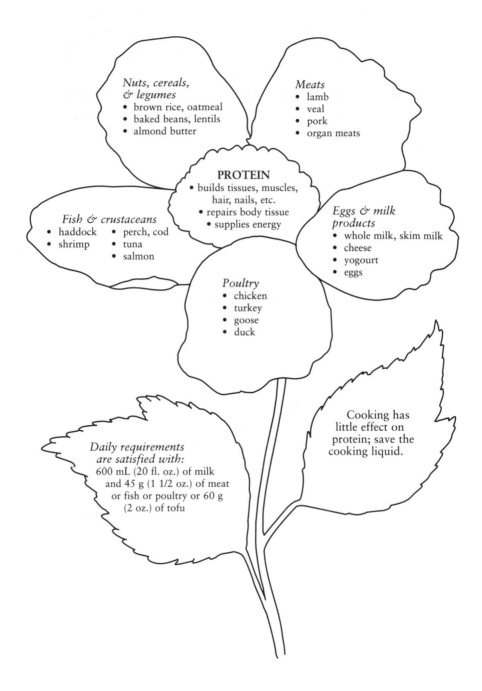

Nuts, cereals,
& legumes
- brown rice, oatmeal
- baked beans, lentils
- almond butter

Meats
- lamb
- veal
- pork
- organ meats

PROTEIN
- builds tissues, muscles,
  hair, nails, etc.
- repairs body tissue
- supplies energy

Fish & crustaceans
- haddock
- shrimp
- perch, cod
- tuna
- salmon

Eggs & milk
products
- whole milk, skim milk
- cheese
- yogourt
- eggs

Poultry
- chicken
- turkey
- goose
- duck

Daily requirements
are satisfied with:
600 mL (20 fl. oz.) of milk
and 45 g (1 1/2 oz.) of meat
or fish or poultry or 60 g
(2 oz.) of tofu

Cooking has
little effect on
protein; save the
cooking liquid.

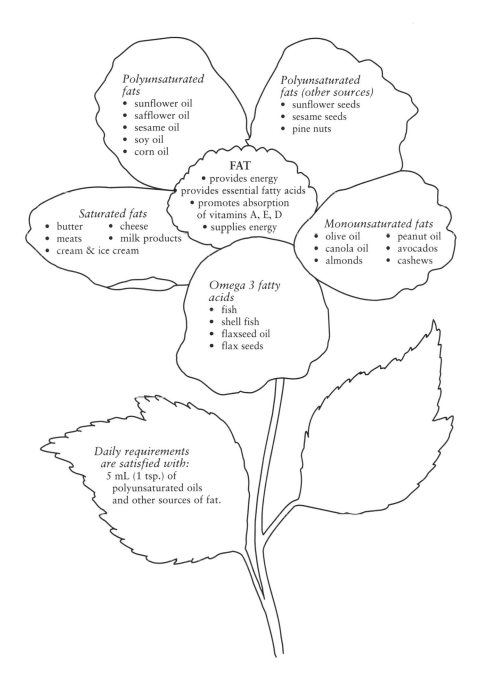

Polyunsaturated
fats
• sunflower oil
• safflower oil
• sesame oil
• soy oil
• corn oil

Polyunsaturated
fats (other sources)
• sunflower seeds
• sesame seeds
• pine nuts

FAT
• provides energy
provides essential fatty acids
• promotes absorption
of vitamins A, E, D
• supplies energy

Saturated fats
• butter   • cheese
• meats   • milk products
• cream & ice cream

Monounsaturated fats
• olive oil   • peanut oil
• canola oil   • avocados
• almonds   • cashews

Omega 3 fatty
acids
• fish
• shell fish
• flaxseed oil
• flax seeds

Daily requirements
are satisfied with:
5 mL (1 tsp.) of
    polyunsaturated oils
    and other sources of fat.

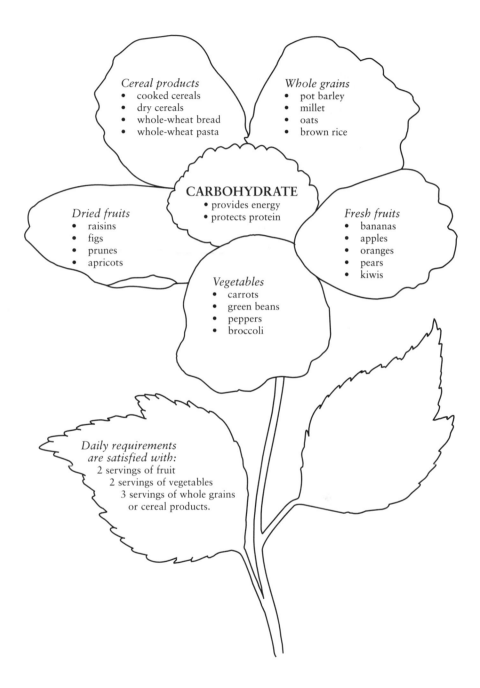

Cereal products
- cooked cereals
- dry cereals
- whole-wheat bread
- whole-wheat pasta

Whole grains
- pot barley
- millet
- oats
- brown rice

CARBOHYDRATE
- provides energy
- protects protein

Dried fruits
- raisins
- figs
- prunes
- apricots

Fresh fruits
- bananas
- apples
- oranges
- pears
- kiwis

Vegetables
- carrots
- green beans
- peppers
- broccoli

*Daily requirements
are satisfied with:*
2 servings of fruit
2 servings of vegetables
3 servings of whole grains
or cereal products.

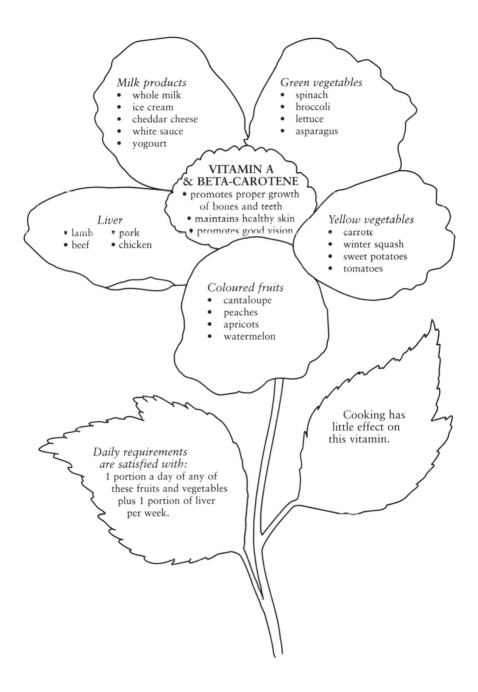

Milk products
- whole milk
- ice cream
- cheddar cheese
- white sauce
- yogourt

Green vegetables
- spinach
- broccoli
- lettuce
- asparagus

VITAMIN A & BETA-CAROTENE
- promotes proper growth of bones and teeth
- maintains healthy skin
- promotes good vision

Liver
- lamb
- beef
- pork
- chicken

Yellow vegetables
- carrots
- winter squash
- sweet potatoes
- tomatoes

Coloured fruits
- cantaloupe
- peaches
- apricots
- watermelon

Daily requirements are satisfied with:
1 portion a day of any of these fruits and vegetables plus 1 portion of liver per week.

Cooking has little effect on this vitamin.

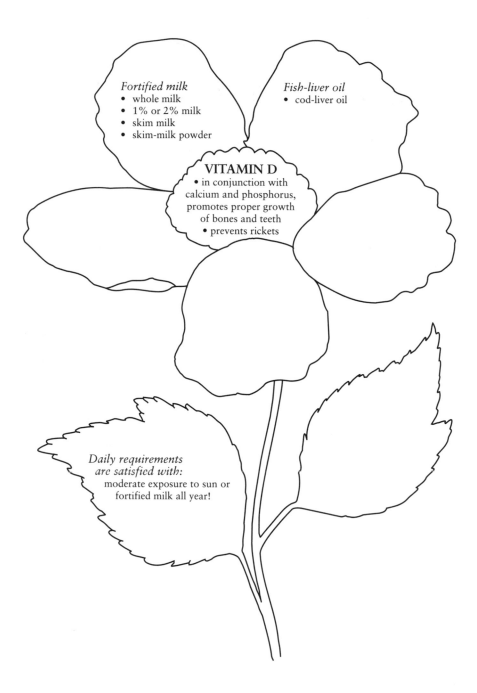

Fortified milk
- whole milk
- 1% or 2% milk
- skim milk
- skim-milk powder

Fish-liver oil
- cod-liver oil

VITAMIN D
- in conjunction with calcium and phosphorus, promotes proper growth of bones and teeth
- prevents rickets

Daily requirements are satisfied with: moderate exposure to sun or fortified milk all year!

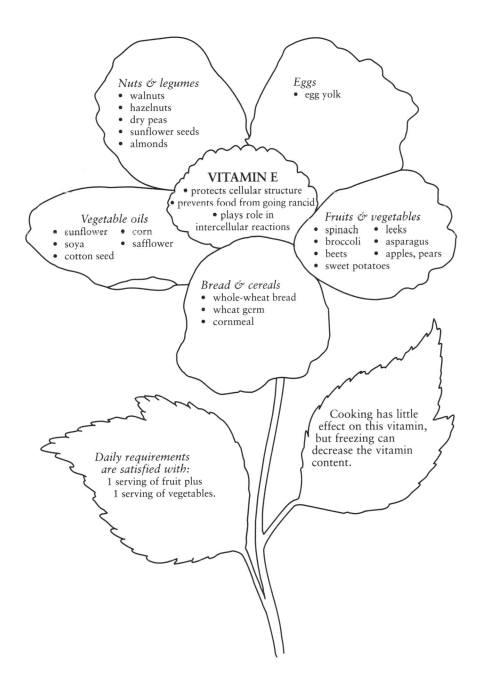

Nuts & legumes
- walnuts
- hazelnuts
- dry peas
- sunflower seeds
- almonds

Eggs
- egg yolk

VITAMIN E
- protects cellular structure
- prevents food from going rancid
- plays role in intercellular reactions

Vegetable oils
- sunflower   • corn
- soya   • safflower
- cotton seed

Fruits & vegetables
- spinach   • leeks
- broccoli   • asparagus
- beets   • apples, pears
- sweet potatoes

Bread & cereals
- whole-wheat bread
- wheat germ
- cornmeal

Daily requirements are satisfied with:
1 serving of fruit plus
1 serving of vegetables.

Cooking has little effect on this vitamin, but freezing can decrease the vitamin content.

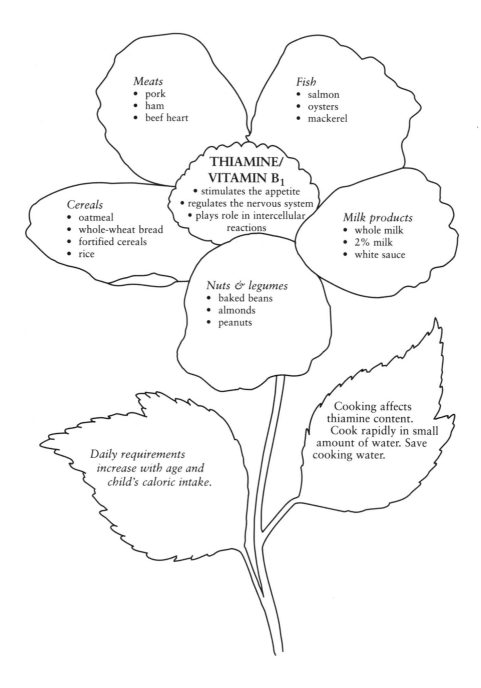

Meats
- pork
- ham
- beef heart

Fish
- salmon
- oysters
- mackerel

THIAMINE/ VITAMIN B$_1$
- stimulates the appetite
- regulates the nervous system
- plays role in intercellular reactions

Cereals
- oatmeal
- whole-wheat bread
- fortified cereals
- rice

Milk products
- whole milk
- 2% milk
- white sauce

Nuts & legumes
- baked beans
- almonds
- peanuts

Daily requirements increase with age and child's caloric intake.

Cooking affects thiamine content. Cook rapidly in small amount of water. Save cooking water.

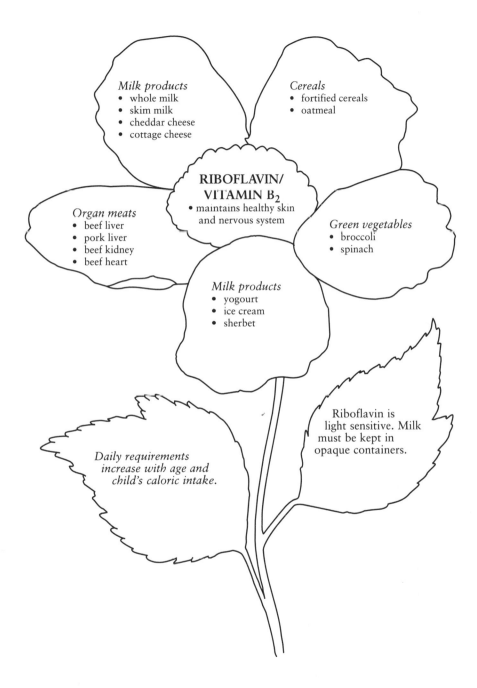

Milk products
- whole milk
- skim milk
- cheddar cheese
- cottage cheese

Cereals
- fortified cereals
- oatmeal

RIBOFLAVIN/ VITAMIN B$_2$
- maintains healthy skin and nervous system

Organ meats
- beef liver
- pork liver
- beef kidney
- beef heart

Green vegetables
- broccoli
- spinach

Milk products
- yogourt
- ice cream
- sherbet

Daily requirements increase with age and child's caloric intake.

Riboflavin is light sensitive. Milk must be kept in opaque containers.

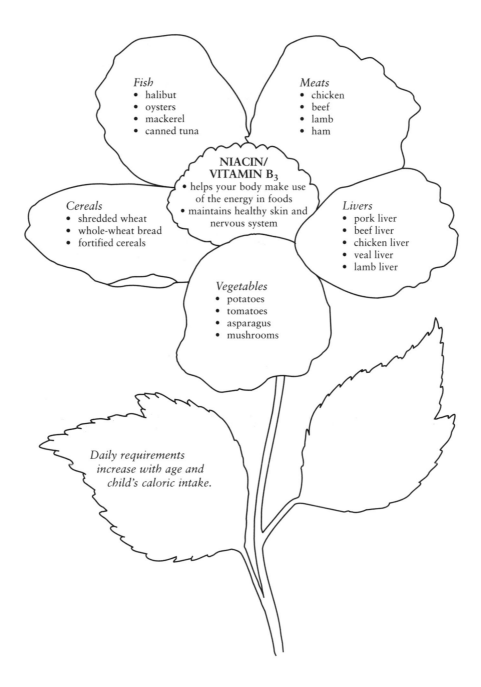

Fish
- halibut
- oysters
- mackerel
- canned tuna

Meats
- chicken
- beef
- lamb
- ham

**NIACIN/
VITAMIN B$_3$**
- helps your body make use
  of the energy in foods
- maintains healthy skin and
  nervous system

Cereals
- shredded wheat
- whole-wheat bread
- fortified cereals

Livers
- pork liver
- beef liver
- chicken liver
- veal liver
- lamb liver

Vegetables
- potatoes
- tomatoes
- asparagus
- mushrooms

*Daily requirements
increase with age and
child's caloric intake.*

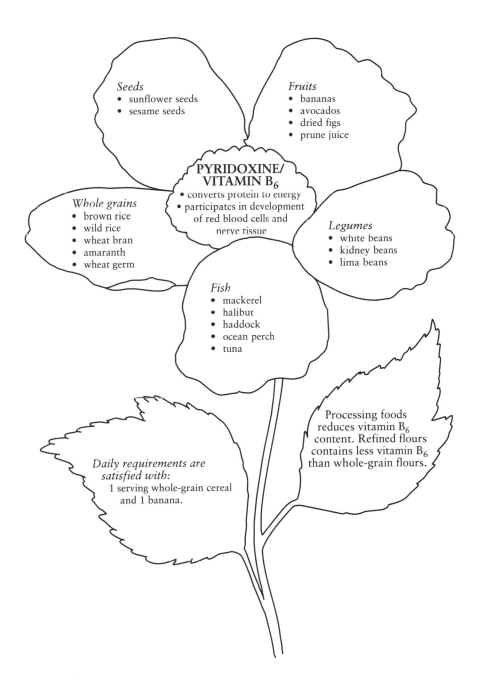

Seeds
- sunflower seeds
- sesame seeds

Fruits
- bananas
- avocados
- dried figs
- prune juice

PYRIDOXINE/ VITAMIN B_6
- converts protein to energy
- participates in development of red blood cells and nerve tissue

Whole grains
- brown rice
- wild rice
- wheat bran
- amaranth
- wheat germ

Legumes
- white beans
- kidney beans
- lima beans

Fish
- mackerel
- halibut
- haddock
- ocean perch
- tuna

Daily requirements are satisfied with:
1 serving whole-grain cereal and 1 banana.

Processing foods reduces vitamin B_6 content. Refined flours contains less vitamin B_6 than whole-grain flours.

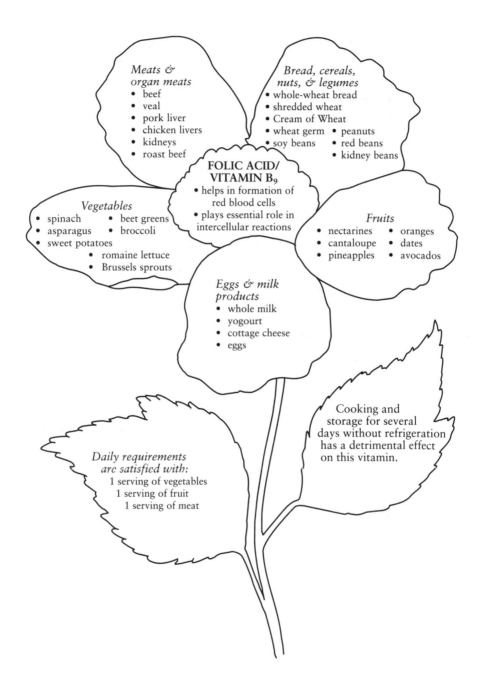

Meats &
organ meats
- beef
- veal
- pork liver
- chicken livers
- kidneys
- roast beef

Bread, cereals,
nuts, & legumes
- whole-wheat bread
- shredded wheat
- Cream of Wheat
- wheat germ   • peanuts
- soy beans   • red beans
                • kidney beans

FOLIC ACID/
VITAMIN B_9
- helps in formation of
  red blood cells
- plays essential role in
  intercellular reactions

Vegetables
- spinach   • beet greens
- asparagus   • broccoli
- sweet potatoes
                • romaine lettuce
                • Brussels sprouts

Fruits
- nectarines   • oranges
- cantaloupe   • dates
- pineapples   • avocados

Eggs & milk
products
- whole milk
- yogourt
- cottage cheese
- eggs

Daily requirements
are satisfied with:
1 serving of vegetables
1 serving of fruit
1 serving of meat

Cooking and
storage for several
days without refrigeration
has a detrimental effect
on this vitamin.

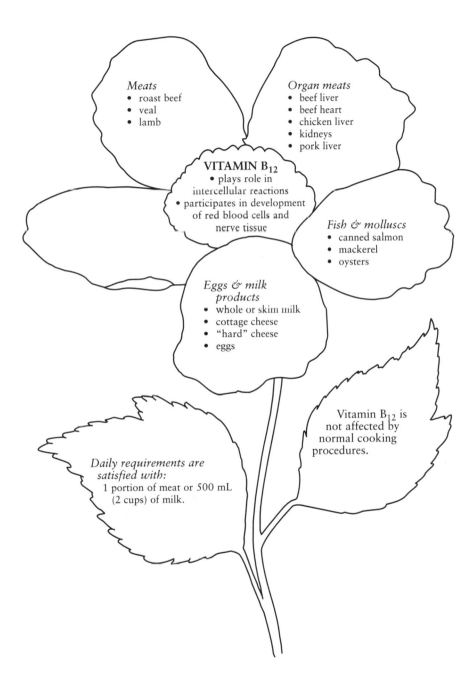

Meats
- roast beef
- veal
- lamb

Organ meats
- beef liver
- beef heart
- chicken liver
- kidneys
- pork liver

VITAMIN B$_{12}$
- plays role in intercellular reactions
- participates in development of red blood cells and nerve tissue

Fish & molluscs
- canned salmon
- mackerel
- oysters

Eggs & milk products
- whole or skim milk
- cottage cheese
- "hard" cheese
- eggs

Vitamin B$_{12}$ is not affected by normal cooking procedures.

Daily requirements are satisfied with:
1 portion of meat or 500 mL (2 cups) of milk.

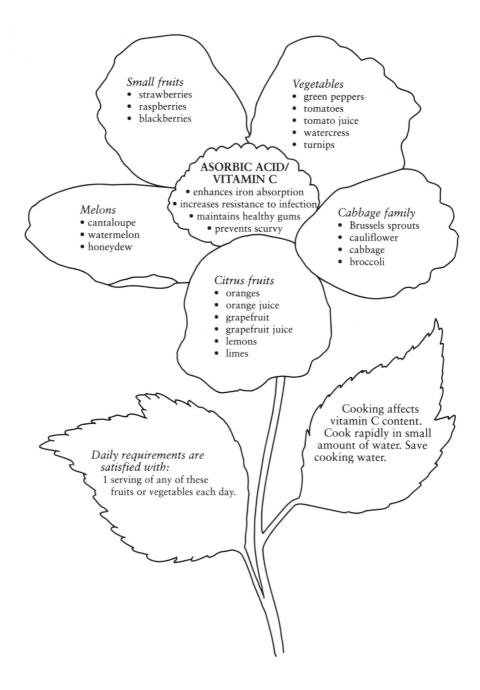

Small fruits
- strawberries
- raspberries
- blackberries

Vegetables
- green peppers
- tomatoes
- tomato juice
- watercress
- turnips

ASORBIC ACID/ VITAMIN C
- enhances iron absorption
- increases resistance to infection
- maintains healthy gums
- prevents scurvy

Melons
- cantaloupe
- watermelon
- honeydew

Cabbage family
- Brussels sprouts
- cauliflower
- cabbage
- broccoli

Citrus fruits
- oranges
- orange juice
- grapefruit
- grapefruit juice
- lemons
- limes

Daily requirements are satisfied with:
1 serving of any of these fruits or vegetables each day.

Cooking affects vitamin C content. Cook rapidly in small amount of water. Save cooking water.

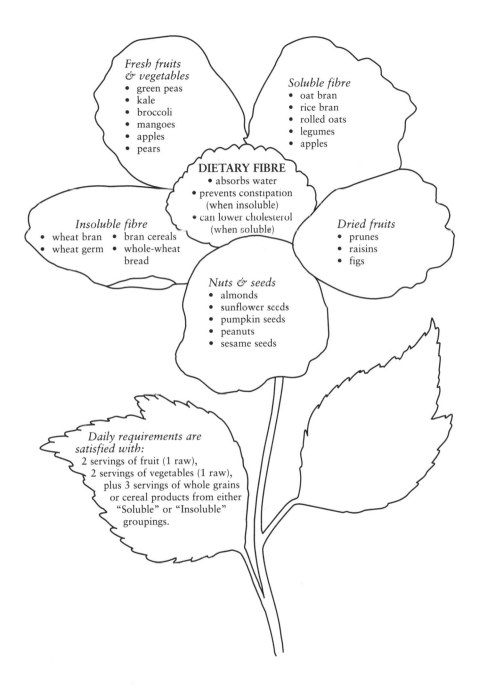

Fresh fruits & vegetables
- green peas
- kale
- broccoli
- mangoes
- apples
- pears

Soluble fibre
- oat bran
- rice bran
- rolled oats
- legumes
- apples

DIETARY FIBRE
- absorbs water
- prevents constipation (when insoluble)
- can lower cholesterol (when soluble)

Insoluble fibre
- wheat bran
- wheat germ
- bran cereals
- whole-wheat bread

Dried fruits
- prunes
- raisins
- figs

Nuts & seeds
- almonds
- sunflower seeds
- pumpkin seeds
- peanuts
- sesame seeds

Daily requirements are satisfied with:
2 servings of fruit (1 raw), 2 servings of vegetables (1 raw), plus 3 servings of whole grains or cereal products from either "Soluble" or "Insoluble" groupings.

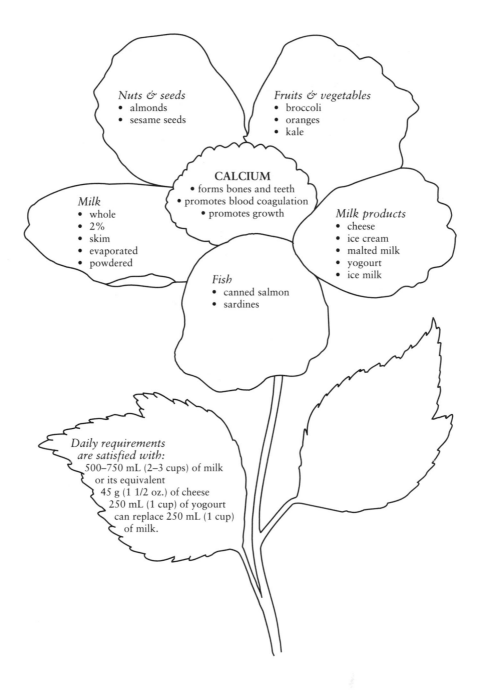

Nuts & seeds
- almonds
- sesame seeds

Fruits & vegetables
- broccoli
- oranges
- kale

CALCIUM
- forms bones and teeth
- promotes blood coagulation
- promotes growth

Milk
- whole
- 2%
- skim
- evaporated
- powdered

Milk products
- cheese
- ice cream
- malted milk
- yogourt
- ice milk

Fish
- canned salmon
- sardines

Daily requirements
are satisfied with:
  500–750 mL (2–3 cups) of milk
  or its equivalent
  45 g (1 1/2 oz.) of cheese
  250 mL (1 cup) of yogourt
  can replace 250 mL (1 cup)
  of milk.

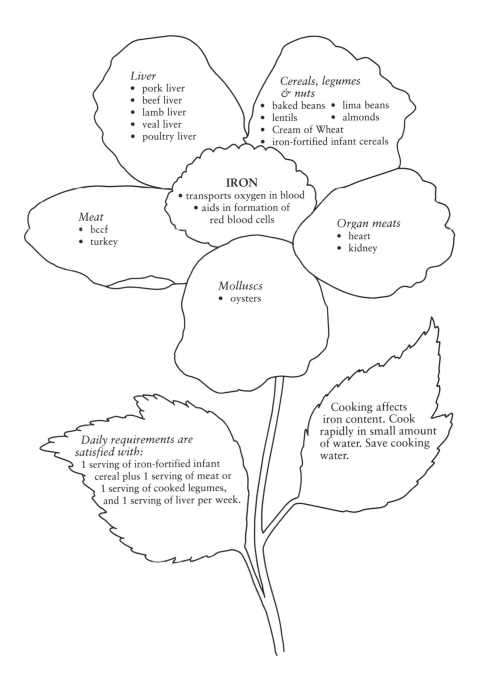

Liver
- pork liver
- beef liver
- lamb liver
- veal liver
- poultry liver

Cereals, legumes
& nuts
- baked beans
- lentils
- Cream of Wheat
- iron-fortified infant cereals
- lima beans
- almonds

IRON
- transports oxygen in blood
- aids in formation of red blood cells

Meat
- beef
- turkey

Organ meats
- heart
- kidney

Molluscs
- oysters

Daily requirements are satisfied with:
1 serving of iron-fortified infant cereal plus 1 serving of meat or 1 serving of cooked legumes, and 1 serving of liver per week.

Cooking affects iron content. Cook rapidly in small amount of water. Save cooking water.

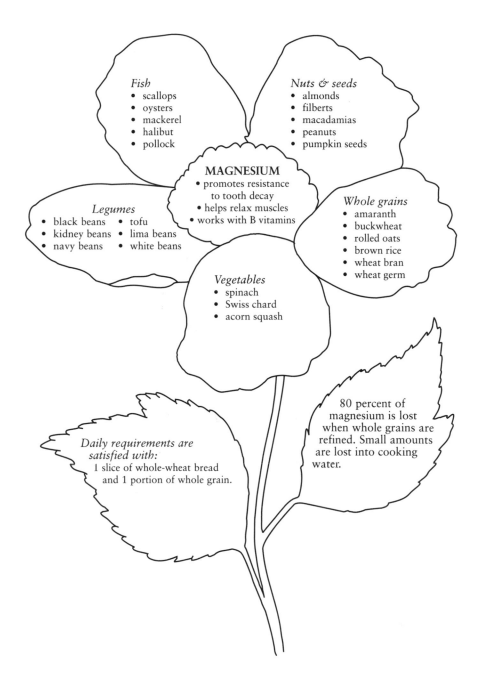

Fish
- scallops
- oysters
- mackerel
- halibut
- pollock

Nuts & seeds
- almonds
- filberts
- macadamias
- peanuts
- pumpkin seeds

MAGNESIUM
- promotes resistance to tooth decay
- helps relax muscles
- works with B vitamins

Legumes
- black beans
- kidney beans
- navy beans
- tofu
- lima beans
- white beans

Whole grains
- amaranth
- buckwheat
- rolled oats
- brown rice
- wheat bran
- wheat germ

Vegetables
- spinach
- Swiss chard
- acorn squash

Daily requirements are satisfied with:
1 slice of whole-wheat bread and 1 portion of whole grain.

80 percent of magnesium is lost when whole grains are refined. Small amounts are lost into cooking water.

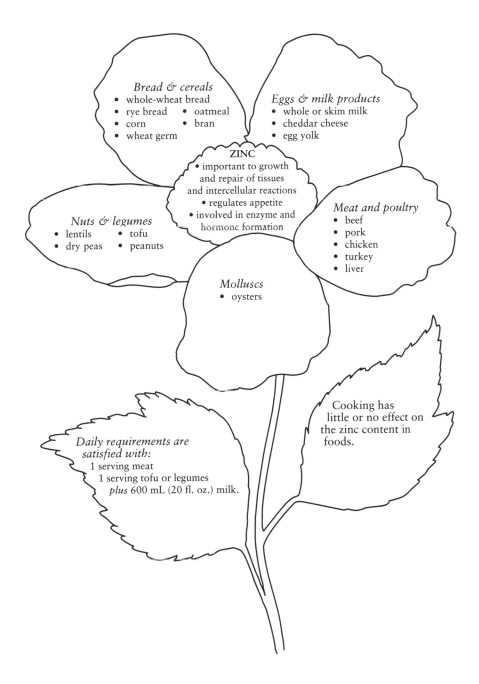

Bread & cereals
- whole-wheat bread
- rye bread
- oatmeal
- corn
- bran
- wheat germ

Eggs & milk products
- whole or skim milk
- cheddar cheese
- egg yolk

ZINC
- important to growth and repair of tissues and intercellular reactions
- regulates appetite
- involved in enzyme and hormone formation

Nuts & legumes
- lentils
- tofu
- dry peas
- peanuts

Meat and poultry
- beef
- pork
- chicken
- turkey
- liver

Molluscs
- oysters

Daily requirements are satisfied with:
1 serving meat
1 serving tofu or legumes
plus 600 mL (20 fl. oz.) milk.

Cooking has little or no effect on the zinc content in foods.

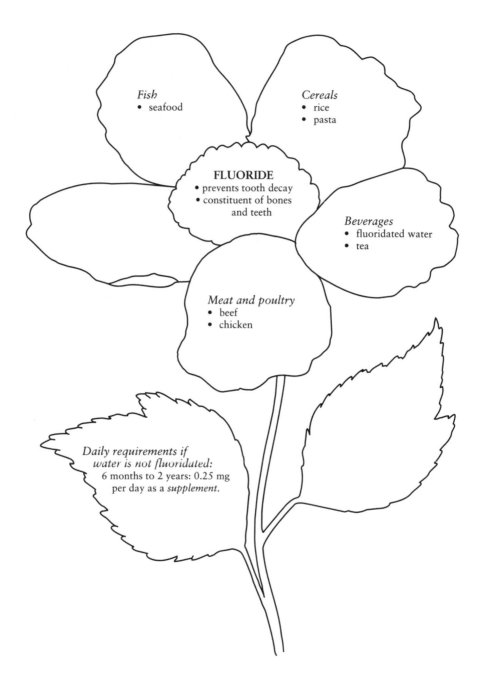

Fish
• seafood

Cereals
• rice
• pasta

FLUORIDE
• prevents tooth decay
• constituent of bones
and teeth

Beverages
• fluoridated water
• tea

Meat and poultry
• beef
• chicken

Daily requirements if
water is not fluoridated:
6 months to 2 years: 0.25 mg
per day as a *supplement.*

NINETEEN

The Feeding Challenge after Nine Months

Feeding a 10- or 15-month-old baby is quite a different challenge from feeding a hungry newborn. New foods and textures are introduced, but at the same time, new eating behaviours are taking shape.

Your baby's appetite is slowly becoming unpredictable, and mealtime is more tense. You are losing some control over the feeding situation. Your child is gaining power!

Your child now likes playing with his food instead of eating it. At 11 months, he has more fun picking up food with his thumb and finger than putting it in his mouth. He can afford to drop food on the floor because he is not as hungry as a few months ago. He expects you to understand the situation and not argue over spoonfuls of food. Your acceptance of his new eating behaviour is critical. It can ease a lot of tension and make mealtimes more positive for years to come. Your non-acceptance can ruin your child's relationship to food.

The reality is that a child who eats too little attracts five times as much attention as the one who eats too much. When you think of the growing incidence of obesity during childhood, the reverse should be the case.

An alarming fact is that many parents start misusing food during the preschool years. Food becomes the vehicle for reward or punishment or a means of bargaining:

– Vegetables become the passport to dessert.
– Sweets become the supreme reward.
– An empty plate wins favours, while leftovers are seldom accepted.

A child also learns to use food to his advantage, swallowing extra mouthfuls to please, not to respond to hunger. A child is encouraged to overeat, while he should be learning to respect his appetite.

Your child's growth rate is slowing down, and his appetite follows.

Growth Spurts

A child grows in spurts after the first 12 months, and these growth fluctuations affect her whole eating behaviour. During the first year of life, your baby gains approximately 25 centimetres (10 inches) and triples her birth weight. That is a once-in-a-lifetime accomplishment.

A baby born at 3.5 kilograms (7.5 lb.) easily weighs 10.5 kilograms (23 lb.) at one year and normally weighs 20 kilograms (45 lb.) at six. This corresponds to a normal growth curve. After 12 months, your child continues to grow but at a much slower pace. Her yearly growth reaches approximately 7.5 to 10 centimetres (3 to 4 inches) and about 2 to 2.5 kilograms (4.5 to 5.5 lb.) until she reaches school age, compared to 25 centimetres (10 inches) and 7.5 kilograms (16.5 lb.) during the first year of life.

This slower growth rate explains the great drop in appetite, but it is hard to accept. Your seven-month-old baby who was always ready to swallow food has now developed into what you consider a "fussy eater." What makes things more difficult is that you can never predict a sudden decrease in appetite or understand the sudden disinterest in food of a 15- or 20-month-old child. That is part of the feeding challenge after nine months.

The only good news is that the younger your child is, the more willing he or she is to try new foods. A study shows that three out of four babies between the ages of 12 and 24 months will try new foods while only one in ten toddlers will do the same between the ages of two and four. This interesting fact allows you to introduce small quantities of a wide variety of foods during the transition period between baby food and table food.

Mealtime Atmosphere

It can make a difference: a calm and relaxed environment helps your child eat well, while a noisy background, including a blaring television or radio, turns off your child's need for food. A child's attention cannot be split the same way as an adult's. Forgetting to eat is common among young children, especially when lively conversations or harsh noises fill the air.

A regular mealtime schedule promotes better eating. If a meal is served too late, a tired 18-month-old will not eat a bite. Three meals a day are a minimum. Snacks are acceptable as long as they do not replace meals.

Physical comfort at mealtime is also an important appetite enhancer! Make sure your child has:

– a high chair with foot support,
– a table suited to his needs,
– small utensils,
– a good bib,

- a small but wide and unbreakable cup or glass (always half full),
- a bowl or a convex plate, rather than a flat plate, and
- a colourful placemat or tablecloth.

Motor and Social Development

As months go by, your child's manual abilities and social development evolve.

From 6 to 12 months:

- The child learns to use his hands.
- He shows interest in texture.
- He discovers the world with his nose and hands.

At around 15 months:

- He can grasp a spoon and place it on the plate but cannot really fill it up properly.
- Once the spoon is close to his mouth, he often holds it upside down.
- The child often drops his spoon and cup.
- His appetite is decreasing.
- Everything but food goes into his mouth.

At 18 months:

- The word "NO" is adopted for all purposes.
- The child drinks well from a cup.
- The child has some difficulty putting the cup down on the table.
- He can now turn the spoon in his mouth.
- Growth rate is slow.
- Appetite decreases considerably.

- The child loves rituals.
- He enjoys finding his placemat, his spoon, etc.
- He agrees to be fed when tired.

At 24 months:

- Your child can drink from a glass held in one hand.
- He can put a spoon in his mouth without turning it.
- The child has whims.
- He is happy with the same food day in and day out.
- He needs a more or less rigid schedule.
- Your child still enjoys rituals.

The feeding challenge after nine months requires much more work on your attitude than in the kitchen! Learning to respect your child's messages remains the key to your child's development as a happy and healthy eater.

*Your attitude can make a big difference
to your child's response to food.*

TWENTY

Transition Menus and Recipes for Nine Months and Beyond

The term "transition" includes the whole passage from semi-liquid purees to regular family meals. Some babies breeze through this period quite rapidly. Others are slower and less adventurous. The menus and recipes suggested in this chapter are adapted to the physiological and physical capacities of most children from the ages of 9 months to 15–18 months. They are easy to prepare but have some special features:

– The texture is more consistent than the first purees but still softer than regular foods.
– The flavours are still mild, but some seasonings (e.g., cinnamon, onions, and parsley) are added in moderate amounts. Salt is added to recipes in small quantities after 12 months.
– The variety of foods is much greater. Yogourt, cottage cheese,

firm cheese, cooked legumes, tofu, pastas, brown rice, some raw fruit, and vegetables are slowly incorporated into the menu.

Basic Foods and Portions

Vegetables are steamed over boiling water or cooked in the microwave with very little water. They are fork-mashed after cooking. Some, such as carrots and zucchini, can be grated and served raw.

Vegetables are never soaked in water before cooking, as soaking dissolves some of the minerals and vitamins. Cooking water can be kept to cook rice or pasta later.

Plan at least two servings of vegetables a day.

Meats are not easy to sell to babies. They need to be tender and juicy and easy to handle. Some meats are still blended until 12 months. Others are minced. After 12 months, meats should be finely cut up, depending on your baby's feeding skills. Fish needs to be poached, flaked, and easy to swallow.

Meat or fish loaves or croquettes are accepted nicely.

Plan one serving of meat per day.

Legumes (beans, lentils, chickpeas) are readily accepted at the end of the first year, when very well cooked. Blend at first, then fork-mash. Tofu can also be blended or gently mashed.

Plan one serving a day for a vegetarian baby. Tofu and legume dishes are good for all babies on a regular basis.

Fruits are popular. Serve as a single puree at first, then blend with other fruit: apple and pear, prunes and apple, pear and peach. Fruits may be lightly poached in fruit juice and fork-mashed, mixed with yogourt or blended with tofu, reduced in a puree, or used to fill up superb homemade jellied desserts. Gradually introduce raw fruits such as small pieces of cantaloupe, honeydew melon, watermelon, slices of kiwi, pear or peach, orange or clementine segments.

Always serve fruit without added sugar so your baby can develop the ability to appreciate the real flavour of fresh fruit.

Dilute fruit juice with an equal volume of water to avoid over-consumption of juice and deficient milk intake.

Plan two or more servings per day, including a vitamin C–rich fruit. (See Vitamin C flower, page 216.)

Whole grains such as brown rice, oatmeal, whole-wheat pasta, and whole-wheat bread provide minerals, protein, and a fair amount of fibre. Infant iron-fortified cereals made with whole grains remain the most nutritious choice in that category during the first 18 months.

Bread can be toasted or cut into strips or fingers. Whole-wheat pita can be served as an alternative. Homemade muffins can be offered. Brown rice and whole-wheat pastas make many happy meals.

Plan at least three servings per day, including a serving of infant iron-fortified cereals every day until 18 months.

Milk and milk products play a major role in your baby's menu. Once your baby is eating approximately 175 millilitres (3/4 cup) of solid foods per day, she can start drinking whole milk. Babies allergic to or intolerant of cow's milk can continue drinking a protein-hydrolysate formula or a soy-based formula (see Chapter 10, Other Milks — Before and after Six Months).

Partially skimmed, 1%, or skim milk are not recommended before the age of 24 months. After that age, you may serve 2% milk without any problem. Totally skimmed milk should be served after 24 months only when specific problems exist — such as a family history of severe cardiovascular disease or a genetically influenced weight problem.

Cottage cheese and yogourt should be incorporated into the diet after nine months, once the basic foods have been introduced.

Ice cream or ice milk remain treats to serve on special occasions only!

Chocolate milk is not a good substitute for whole milk. It contains more sugar and more calories.

Plan to serve 625 millilitres (2 1/2 cups) of milk per day, as a beverage in a cup, in soups, in cereal, or as a snack.

There is no place in your baby's diet for fried foods, processed meats, rich desserts, pastries, or sweets. Even if such foods are part of her environment, try avoiding them without creating taboos. Build a more favourable image around more wholesome foods.

Some foods are considered risky because they can cause choking:

- popcorn
- nuts and seeds
- chunks in peanut butter
- chewing gum
- hard candies
- raw carrot sticks
- hot dogs
- fruit with seeds, such as grapes

Other foods are good teething foods. They include

- Melba toast or dry bread crusts
- water popsicles

Some foods are easier to grasp and encourage your baby to self-feed. Such good finger foods include

- cooked vegetable pieces
- cooked pieces of poultry or meat
- cheese cubes
- bread crusts, dry toast
- pieces of poached fruit

All this discussion about adding new foods to your baby's diet improves the variety but does not necessarily increase your baby's appetite. Do not "push" food just because you are excited about a new menu addition. Take into account the nutritional needs of your baby, and do not fill the plate. Some babies ask for more food than others. Some need more. But if you never forcefeed your baby, you will teach him how to respond to his own limits.

Table 18
Suggested Portions for Babies up to 18 Months

Infant cereal:	up to 200 mL (3/4 cup) per day mixed with breast milk, formula, or whole milk
Fruit:	60 mL (1/4 cup) or 1/4 of a whole fresh fruit such as a pear or peach
Jellied fruit dessert:	60 mL (1/4 cup)
Fruit juice:	90 mL (3 fl. oz.) diluted with an equal amount of water
Vegetables:	30 mL (2 tbsp.) cooked or raw grated
Vegetable soup:	80 mL (1/3 cup)
Vegetables and meat dinners:	60 mL (1/4 cup)
Fish, meat, or poultry:	45 g (1 1/2 oz.)
Whole milk:	125 mL (1/2 cup)
Cottage cheese:	60 mL (1/4 cup)
Regular cheese:	15 g (1/2 oz.)
Yogourt:	80 mL (1/3 cup)
Whole-wheat bread:	1/2 slice
Brown rice:	60 mL (1/4 cup) cooked

Table 18 (cont'd)
Suggested Portions for Babies up to 18 Months

Whole-wheat pasta:	80 mL (1/3 cup) cooked
Legumes:	60 mL (1/4 cup) cooked
Firm tofu:	30 g (1 oz.)
Egg:	1 small

The following menus offer new foods and textures according to two balanced eating styles: one includes meat; the other takes a lacto-ovo vegetarian approach. Main dishes are composed of poultry, meat, legumes, tofu, cheese and pasta, fish, or eggs. The noon meal is the main meal; the night meal is slightly lighter. Whole-grain products are offered most often: brown rice, whole-wheat pastas, and whole-wheat bread. Your baby is apt to appreciate such flavours! Desserts consist mainly of fresh fruit or fruit purees.

Some foods listed in the menus are marked with an asterisk (*). This means a recipe has been included in the section following the menus. You can follow these recipes and also expand on them.

The freezer method is often suggested to make last-minute preparation easier, but you can always cook smaller quantities just before mealtime if you prefer. The goal is to serve a wide range of nutritious foods at an age when your baby is still willing to try!

The feeding schedule is a simple one. The baby is now ready for the family's timetable and can eat three meals a day plus one milk snack. The feeding capacity of your baby will slowly evolve. On certain days, he will want to feed himself; on other days, he will demand help! He is slowly learning to drink from a cup and can eat some foods with a spoon.

The world of real foods (table foods) will
slowly change your baby's eating routine.

A Seven-Day Menu
for the Transition Period

(from nine months on)

DAY 1

With Meat, Fish, or Poultry	*Lacto-ovo Vegetarian*

BREAKFAST

orange segments	orange segments
brown rice infant cereal with milk	brown rice infant cereal with milk
whole milk (in cup)	whole milk (in cup)

LUNCH

poached fresh fish (salmon)*	lentils, brown rice, and vegetables*
fork-mashed zucchini	
whole-wheat bread	whole-wheat bread
jellied fruit dessert (pear)*	jellied fruit dessert (pear)*
whole milk (in cup)	whole milk (in cup)

DINNER

creamed tofu & sesame butter*	creamed tofu & sesame butter*
whole-wheat pita bread	whole-wheat pita bread
banana milk*	banana milk*

SNACK

whole milk	whole milk

*Recipes available in this book. (See Index.)

DAY 2

With Meat, Fish, or Poultry   *Lacto-ovo Vegetarian*

BREAKFAST

apple juice (diluted with
  water)
barley infant cereal and
  milk with fresh banana
  and ground almonds
whole milk (in cup)

apple juice (diluted with
  water)
barley infant cereal and
  milk with fresh banana
  and ground almonds
whole milk (in cup)

LUNCH

chicken and brown rice
green beans in small
  pieces
slices of fresh kiwi
whole milk (in cup)

brown rice, vegetables,
  and cheese*
slices of fresh kiwi
whole milk (in cup)

DINNER

cream of vegetable soup
  (green peas)*
cornbread muffin
popsifruits*
whole milk (in cup)

cream of vegetable soup
  (green peas)*
cornbread muffin
popsifruits*
whole milk (in cup)

SNACK

whole milk

whole milk

*Recipes available in this book. (See Index.)

Transition Menus and Recipes for Nine Months and Beyond — 235

DAY 3

With Meat, Fish, or Poultry	Lacto-ovo Vegetarian

BREAKFAST

orange segments	orange segments
soy infant cereal with milk	soy infant cereal with milk
whole milk (in cup)	whole milk (in cup)

LUNCH

pureed pork and leek*	vegetables au gratin*
whole-wheat bread	whole-wheat bread
fruit kebabs*	fruit kebabs*
whole milk (in cup)	whole milk (in cup)

DINNER

scrambled tofu*	scrambled tofu*
asparagus in small pieces	asparagus in small pieces
1/2 slice whole-wheat bread	1/2 slice whole-wheat bread
jellied fruit dessert (strawberry)*	jellied fruit dessert (strawberry)*
whole milk (in cup)	whole milk (in cup)

SNACK

whole milk	whole milk

*Recipes available in this book. (See Index.)

DAY 4

With Meat, Fish, or Poultry   *Lacto-ovo Vegetarian*

BREAKFAST

apple juice (diluted with
   water)
oatmeal infant cereal
   with milk and ground
   sesame seeds
whole milk (in cup)

apple juice (diluted with
   water)
oatmeal infant cereal
   with milk and ground
   sesame seeds
whole milk (in cup)

LUNCH

mystery liver and beef
   loaf*
fork-mashed zucchini
whole-wheat bread
cantaloupe in small pieces
whole milk (in cup)

scrambled tofu*
fork-mashed zucchini
whole-wheat bread
cantaloupe in small pieces
whole milk (in cup)

DINNER

two-cheese macaroni
   with pieces of broccoli*
pureed apricots*
whole milk (in cup)

two-cheese macaroni
   with pieces of broccoli*
pureed apricots*
whole milk (in cup)

SNACK

whole milk   whole milk

*Recipes available in this book. (See Index.)

DAY 5

With Meat, Fish, or Poultry	Lacto-ovo Vegetarian

BREAKFAST

pieces of cantaloupe	pieces of cantaloupe
oatmeal infant cereal	oatmeal infant cereal
with milk	with milk
whole milk (in cup)	whole milk (in cup)

LUNCH

poached fresh fish (fillet of sole)*	pureed legumes with
fork-mashed carrots	vegetables*
whole-wheat bread	whole-wheat bread
1/4 ripe banana, mashed	1/4 ripe banana, mashed
whole milk (in cup)	whole milk (in cup)

DINNER

cottage cheese	cottage cheese
pureed prunes or	pureed prunes or
apples*	apples*
whole-wheat bread	whole-wheat bread
whole milk (in cup)	whole milk (in cup)

SNACK

whole milk	whole milk

*Recipes available in this book. (See Index.)

DAY 6

With Meat, Fish, or Poultry   *Lacto-ovo Vegetarian*

BREAKFAST

orange segments	orange segments
soy infant cereal with milk	soy infant cereal with milk
whole milk (in cup)	whole milk (in cup)

LUNCH

chicken, brown rice, and vegetables*	lentils, brown rice, and vegetables*
whole-wheat bread	whole-wheat bread
1/4 pear, mashed	1/4 pear, mashed
whole milk (in cup)	whole milk (in cup)

DINNER

whole-wheat pasta with fresh vegetable sauce and grated cheese	whole-wheat pasta with fresh vegetable sauce and grated cheese
1/2 ripe banana, mashed	1/2 ripe banana, mashed
whole milk (in cup)	whole milk (in cup)

SNACK

whole milk	whole milk

*Recipes available in this book. (See Index.)

DAY 7

With Meat, Fish, or Poultry	*Lacto-ovo Vegetarian*

BREAKFAST

orange juice (diluted with water)	orange juice (diluted with water)
barley infant cereal with milk	barley infant cereal with milk
whole milk (in cup)	whole milk (in cup)

LUNCH

beef, brown rice, and vegetables*	brown rice, vegetables, and cheese*
whole-wheat bread	whole-wheat bread
applesauce with cinnamon*	applesauce with cinnamon*
whole milk (in cup)	whole milk (in cup)

DINNER

finely grated carrot	finely grated carrot
soft-boiled egg	soft-boiled egg
whole-wheat bread sticks	whole-wheat bread sticks
1/4 peach cut into small pieces	1/4 peach cut into small pieces
whole milk (in cup)	whole milk (in cup)

SNACK

whole milk	whole milk

*Recipes available in this book. (See Index.)

Cream of Vegetable Soup

Prepare in minutes with the best vegetables on the market. Can be made with soy milk instead of whole milk. A nice way to sell invisible but good-tasting vegetables.

Ingredients

- 125 mL (1/2 cup) whole milk
- 60–125 mL (1/4–1/2 cup) raw or frozen vegetables: cauliflower, broccoli, flowers, asparagus, green peas, green string beans
- 1/2 slice whole-wheat bread
- 5 mL (1 tsp.) olive or sunflower oil

Preparation

Steam vegetables over boiling water or cook a few minutes in the microwave.

Put vegetables, cooking water, milk, bread, and oil into blender and blend for 30 seconds. Add more liquid as needed.

Reheat and serve. Freeze leftovers if desired.

Yield: 375 mL (1 1/2 cups), or 4 baby servings

Storage life: 3–4 days in refrigerator; 1 month in freezer

Chicken, Brown Rice, and Vegetables

Easy to prepare with boneless, skinless chicken breast. When your child is able to chew regular food, forget the blender and cut the chicken into little pieces.

Ingredients

- 1 boneless, skinless chicken breast
- 5 mL (1 tsp.) finely chopped parsley
- 750 mL (3 cups) water
- 30 mL (2 tbsp). minced onion
- 3 carrots, peeled and finely cut up
- 1 stalk celery, finely cut up
- 125 mL (1/2 cup) uncooked brown rice
- 250 mL (1 cup) green peas, fresh or frozen

Preparation

Put chicken breast, parsley, water, onion, carrots, and celery into large saucepan. Simmer 15 minutes.

Add brown rice. Simmer 20 minutes.

Add green peas and simmer another 20 minutes until all ingredients are tender and rice is done.

Remove from heat and cool a few minutes only.

Blend half the chicken with 125 mL (1/2 cup) of the cooking water. Empty the puree into a large bowl. Repeat with the rest of the chicken.

Drain and fork-mash rice and cooked vegetables. Mix well with the chicken puree.

Pour into glass or microwaveable containers in serving sizes of 60 mL (1/4 cup) each. Serve immediately or freeze.

Yield: about 750 mL (3 cups), or 12 baby servings of 60 mL (1/4 cup)

Storage life: 2–3 days in refrigerator; 10–12 weeks in the freezer

Beef, Brown Rice, and Vegetables

A dish that can be varied with different grains and different vegetables. It can also be made with minced turkey.

Ingredients

- 125 mL (1/2 cup) uncooked brown basmati* rice or millet
- 250 mL (1 cup) leftover vegetable cooking water and/or plain water
- 1/2 kg (1 lb.) lean minced beef
- 5 mL (1 tsp.) olive oil
- 375–500 mL (1 1/2–2 cups) water
- 200 mL (3/4 cup) each of fresh tomatoes (peeled and chopped) and finely chopped onions and green peppers
- 125 mL (1/2 cup) each: diced carrots, fresh or frozen green peas, and chopped zucchini — or any other seasonal vegetable mixture

Preparation

In a small saucepan, stir brown rice or millet into cooking water. Bring to a boil, then lower heat to simmer approximately 20 minutes.

After 20 minutes, in a medium saucepan, cook beef in olive oil for a few minutes. Add 375 to 500 mL (1 1/2 to 2 cups) of water, the selected vegetables, and the half-cooked brown rice or millet. Bring to a boil. Reduce the heat and simmer until vegetables are tender and rice is done.

* Fine-tasting and non-glutinous brown rice, found in health food stores.

Remove from heat and cool slightly.

Empty into small glass containers and freeze.

Yield: 750 mL (3 cups), or 12 baby servings before of 60 mL (1/4 cup)

Storage life: 2–3 days in refrigerator; 10–12 weeks in freezer

Reheat in the oven or the microwave. Stir the food once during reheating in the microwave. Also stir just before serving.

Pureed Pork and Leek

Any lean, cooked meat mixed with 250 mL (1 cup) of cooked vegetables can make a similar meal.

Ingredients

- 1 large leek
- 140–170 g (5–6 oz.) cooked roast pork, all fat removed
- 125 mL (1/2 cup) cooking liquid from the leek

Preparation

Wash and cut the leek, using the white part in this recipe. Save the green part for soups. Steam over boiling water 10–15 minutes or until tender.

Cut pork into small pieces. Put into blender with cooked leek and 125 mL (1/2 cup) of the cooking liquid. Blend until smooth.

Empty into small containers, 60 mL (1/4 cup) for 1 serving. Serve immediately or freeze.

Yield: 500 mL (2 cups), or 8 baby servings of 60 mL (1/4 cup)

Storage life: 2–3 days in the refrigerator; 10–12 weeks in the freezer

Mystery Liver and Beef Loaf

An excellent recipe to sell liver to your child and the rest of the family!

Ingredients

- 1/2 kg (1 lb.) chicken livers (from organic animal if possible; calf or lamb liver can also be used)
- 1 medium onion, quartered
- 160 mL (2/3 cup) uncooked regular oatmeal
- 250 mL (1 cup) tomato juice
- 625 g (1 1/4 lb.) lean minced beef
- 1 egg
- 2 mL (1/2 tsp.) salt (after baby is 12 months)

Preparation

Preheat over to 180°C (350°F).

Put cleaned, raw liver and onion into the blender. Blend to a smooth puree.

In a large bowl, soak oatmeal in tomato juice for about 10 minutes. Add liver puree, minced beef, and egg, and mix well.

Empty into a well-greased loaf pan.

Cook 60–75 minutes.

Let sit 5 minutes before slicing. Cut into small pieces for a baby during the transition period or into slices for an older child.

Yield: 16 baby servings; 8–10 toddler servings

Storage life: 2–3 days in refrigerator; 10–12 weeks in freezer

Poached Fresh Fish

Babies learn to enjoy the soft and real taste of fish with no batter, no frying fat. Choose fish with low PCB residues as mentioned in the list of ingredients.

Ingredients

- 60–125 mL (1/4–1/2 cup) whole milk
- 15–30 mL (1–2 tbsp.) finely chopped onion
- 225 g (8 oz.) fillets of fresh fish (choose small farmed fish or ocean fish such as sole, salmon, flounder, grouper, haddock, halibut, monkfish)

Preparation

Pour 60 mL (1/4 cup) milk into a skillet and gently heat. Add onion and simmer several minutes until soft.

Add fish fillets. Cover and cook over low heat 5–10 minutes or until fish is opaque and flaky.

Remove from heat and flake the fish with a fork, making sure all bones are removed.

Store in small containers to serve approximately 45 g (1 1/2 oz.) of fish per serving. Add a small amount of milk and onions. Cover and freeze or serve immediately.

Reheat in 200°C (400°F) oven for about 10 minutes or in the microwave for 1 minute at high. Stir once during reheating in the microwave and stir just before serving.

Yield: 5 baby servings of 45 g (1 1/2 oz.)

Storage life: 2–3 days in refrigerator; 4–6 weeks in freezer

Basic White Sauce
(medium thickness)

Can be prepared on the stove or in the microwave.

Ingredients

- 30 mL (2 tbsp.) oil
- 30 mL (2 tbsp.) whole-wheat, all-purpose flour
- 125 mL (1/2 cup) whole milk
- 125 mL (1/2 cup) chicken stock or leftover vegetable cooking liquid

Preparation

On the stove: In a saucepan, mix oil and flour, and heat for a few minutes. Gradually add milk and stock, stirring constantly until the sauce thickens. Cook 1 additional minute.

In the microwave: In a 1-L (4-cup) glass bowl, heat the oil on high for 30 seconds. Add flour and mix until smooth. Add milk and stock gradually, stirring constantly until smooth. Cook in microwave on high for 3–6 minutes or until sauce is thickened and smooth, stirring every 2 minutes.

Cool and use immediately or store in refrigerator or freezer.

Yield: 250 mL (1 cup)

Storage life: 3–4 days in refrigerator; 4 weeks in freezer

Brown Rice, Vegetables, and Cheese

Cheese can be replaced with tofu or mixed with it, half and half. Adjust seasonings with fresh herbs.

Ingredients

- 125 mL (1/2 cup) white sauce, medium thickness (No salt added to sauce before baby is 12 months.) (See recipe, p. 249)
- 125 mL (1/2 cup) cooked brown rice
- 125 mL (1/2 cup) fork-mashed vegetables (asparagus, zucchini, squash, carrots)
- 90 mL (6 tbsp.) grated, partially skimmed, mozzarella cheese

Preparation

Reheat white sauce in glass bowl in microwave or use a double boiler. Mix in all ingredients except cheese. Stir well.

Freeze in individual portions of 60 mL (1/4 cup) each or refrigerate to serve within a few days.

Reheat in a double boiler or in the microwave. Stir once during reheating in the microwave. Also stir just before serving, and add 5 mL (1 tsp.) of grated cheese to each portion.

Yield: 375 mL (1 1/2 cups), or 6–7 baby servings of 60 mL (1/4 cup)

Storage life: 2–3 days in refrigerator; 3–4 weeks in freezer

Scrambled Tofu

Looks like scrambled eggs and tastes even better!

Ingredients

- 115 g (4 oz.) firm tofu (silken type)
- 30 mL (2 tbsp.) minced onion
- 5 mL (1 tsp.) light tamari or soya sauce
- 1 mL (1/4 tsp.) turmeric (a spice that colours the mixture yellow when cooked)
- 10 mL (2 tsp.) oil

Preparation

In a bowl, mash tofu. Add next 3 ingredients and mix well.

Pour oil over skillet and heat on medium heat.

Add ingredients from bowl and cook 5 minutes or until warm throughout and coloured a light yellow. Serve immediately.

Yield: 2–3 baby servings

Storage life: 2–3 days in refrigerator

Pureed Legumes with Vegetables

A good vegetarian dish that introduces legumes into the child's menu. Use only half or third of recipe to begin with.

Ingredients

- 250 mL (1 cup) warm white sauce, medium thickness (See recipe, p. 249)
- 250 mL (1 cup) well-cooked legumes* pureed in a blender, food processor, or food mill
- 125 mL (1/2 cup) fork-mashed vegetables (carrots, zucchini, or asparagus)

Preparation

Reheat white sauce in large bowl in the microwave or use a double boiler. Add pureed legumes and vegetables. Mix well.

Divide into serving portions of 60 mL (1/4 cup). Pour into glass or microwaveable containers.

Store in freezer or refrigerator for a few days.

Reheat in double boiler or in microwave, a minute or so. Stir once during reheating in microwave. Also stir just before serving.

Yield: 625 mL (2 1/2 cups), or 10 baby servings of 60 mL (1/4 cup)

Storage life: 2–3 days in refrigerator; 4–6 weeks in freezer

* Canned, drained, and rinsed kidney beans, chickpeas, or dried peas can be used.

Lentils, Brown Rice, and Vegetables

Another nutritious vegetarian meal with lentils.

Ingredients

- 125 mL (1/2 cup) well-cooked brown or green lentils
- 60 mL (1/4 cup) cooked brown rice
- 125 mL (1/2 cup) white sauce, medium thickness (See recipe, p. 249)
- 60 mL (1/4 cup) cooked and finely cut vegetables: carrots, green beans

Preparation

Reheat white sauce in a large bowl in the microwave or use a double boiler.

Add cooked lentils, brown rice, and vegetables. Mix well.

Pour into small glass or microwaveable containers in serving portions of 60 mL (1/4 cup).

Serve immediately or freeze.

Yield: 375 mL (1 1/2 cups), or 6 baby servings of 60 mL (1/4 cup)

Storage life: 2–3 days in refrigerator; 3–4 weeks in freezer

Two-Cheese Macaroni

Babies love pastas, like the rest of the family!

Ingredients

- 500 mL (2 cups) cooked whole-wheat macaroni blended with 200 mL (3/4 cup) whole milk
- 2 eggs
- 250 mL (1 cup) whole milk
- 250 mL (1 cup) regular cottage cheese
- 60–90 mL (4–6 tbsp.) grated, partly skimmed mozzarella cheese
- 10 mL (2 tsp.) butter or olive oil
- 2 mL (1/2 tsp.) salt (after baby is 12 months)

Preparation

In blender, beat eggs; add milk, cottage cheese, grated cheese, and butter or oil. Blend well.

Pour mixture onto the cooked, blended macaroni. Mix well.

Place in small glass or microwaveable containers in 60 mL (1/4-cup) servings.

Reheat in the oven or in the microwave. If frozen, remove from freezer and cook in a 180°C (350°F) oven for about 40 minutes, or defrost and reheat in the microwave, stirring just before serving.

Yield: 750 mL (3 cups), or 12 baby servings of 60 mL (1/4 cup)

Storage life: 2–3 days in refrigerator; 4–6 weeks in freezer

Creamed Tofu and Sesame Butter

⸺

Delightfully smooth and tasty! Can be done with peanut butter as well.

Ingredients

- 115 g (4 oz.) firm tofu (silken type)
- 125 mL (1/2 cup) dark sesame butter*
- 10 mL (2 tsp.) honey

Preparation

Put tofu and sesame butter in blender or food processor. Blend until smooth. Add 5 mL (1 tsp.) honey and taste before adding more.

Serve as a spread with whole-wheat pita bread or as a dip with pieces of fresh fruit.

Yield: 250 mL (1 cup)

Serving size: 15–30 mL (1–2 tbsp.)

Storage life: 1 week in refrigerator

* *Dark sesame butter* is prepared with *whole* sesame seeds; *tahini* is prepared with *hulled* sesame seeds. The former contains much more calcium than the latter.

Vegetables au Gratin

Easy to prepare and to vary, according to the freshest vegetables on the market.

Ingredients

- 250 mL (1 cup) white sauce, medium thickness (See recipe, p. 249)
- 80 mL (1/3 cup) grated mozzarella cheese
- 250 mL (1 cup) cooked carrots, fork-mashed
- 250 mL (1 cup) cooked green vegetables, fork-mashed or pureed (broccoli, green peas, asparagus)

Preparation

Reheat white sauce in a large bowl in microwave or double boiler.

Add grated cheese and let it melt by stirring a few minutes. Add vegetables and mix well.

Serve immediately. Pour leftovers in small glass or microwaveable containers. Refrigerate or freeze.

Reheat a few minutes in double boiler or microwave. Stir just before serving.

Yield: 750 mL (3 cups), or 12 baby servings of 60 mL (1/4 cup)

Storage life: 2–3 days in refrigerator; 4–6 weeks in freezer

Jellied Fruit Dessert

Much more flavourful than commercial jellied desserts, filled with vitamin-rich fruit juice and purees. Try:

orange juice and banana puree

or white grape juice and pear puree

or apple juice and strained strawberry puree

Ingredients

- 60 mL (1/4 cup) cold water
- 1 package unflavoured gelatin (Knox type)
- 125 mL (1/2 cup) boiling water
- 250 mL (1 cup) fruit juice
- 250 mL (1 cup) fruit puree (fresh fruit pureed in blender with or without juice)

Preparation

Pour cold water into medium bowl. Sprinkle gelatin over water and allow to swell. Add boiling water and dissolve gelatin. Add fruit juice and fruit puree. Mix well.

If desired, pour into small, individual bowls.

Refrigerate a few hours, until gelatin is firm.

Yield: 675 mL (2 3/4 cups)

Baby serving: 30–45 mL (2–3 tbsp.)

Storage life: 2–3 days in refrigerator

Fruit Kebabs

Pretty to look at and easy to prepare. Vary the fruit: Use pitted prunes instead of peaches, pears instead of oranges, and enjoy! When your baby is older, add a third fruit such as banana or kiwi slices.

Warning: Make sure your baby does not handle the kebab stick or put it in his mouth.

Ingredients

- 1 fresh peach or nectarine, peeled and quartered
- 1 orange in segments

Preparation

Thread fruit onto 2 bamboo or wooden skewers, alternating between pieces of peach or nectarine and segments of oranges.

Keep in refrigerator until ready to serve.

Yield: 2 kebabs (one for you and one for baby)

Banana Milk

A dessert in a glass or cup.

Ingredients

- 1 small banana, cut into pieces
- 125 mL (1/2 cup) whole milk
- drop of vanilla

Preparation

Put banana and milk into blender and blend well. Add vanilla. Pour into cup or glass.

If not serving immediately, refrigerate and serve cold.

Yield: 250 mL (1 cup)

Popsifruits

Delicious sorbet-like homemade popsicles. Can be served in
a dish or as a popsicle. Try orange, grape, or apple juice. All flavours
are delightful.

Ingredients

- 500 mL (2 cups) plain yogourt
- 1 can, 178 mL (6 fl. oz.) of frozen, unsweetened
  fruit juice

Preparation

Into blender, pour yogourt and undiluted fruit juice. Blend until smooth.
Pour mixture into popsicle moulds or individual glass dishes. Freeze.

To serve, run popsifruit under very hot water to loosen it, or remove
bowl from freezer 15–30 minutes before serving so that popsifruit
acquires a good consistency.

Yield: 10 popsifruits

TWENTY-ONE

Learning to Love Good Foods

During the first few years of their lives, children spend a lot of time exploring their world. These years are filled with new sights, sounds, tastes, and smells.

A child discovers colours, textures, shapes, smells, and tastes. After the first few months, his eyes are attracted to the red toy rather than the little beige dog, to the orange carrot, rather than green beans. His fingers react to different textures and can differentiate between a plush doggy, a smooth ball, and a rag doll. His taste buds experience a whole range of new tastes, and even at this age, he makes his likes and dislikes known (mashed bananas may be eaten faster than pureed meats). His ears recognize the melody of the music box. He learns to sniff with his nose and enjoy pleasant smells.

Everything that is taken in and retained during the first years of life is accomplished through the baby's senses. The more opportunities a child has to see, touch, taste, smell, and hear, the more he gets to know the world around him and the better prepared he is to deal with it.

Senses must be exercised, just as muscles must be exercised. The child grows to love the things he knows: the pretty toy he looks at, the cat he strokes, the melon he tastes, the rose he smells, the song he hears!

Food is a part of the child's world. The more opportunities he has to learn about different foods, the greater the chances that he will like them.

Always keeping the objective of forming good eating habits in mind, this last chapter suggests activities, games, and experiences for the child that will enable him to discover and appreciate a wide variety of foods while having fun.

Let's Visit the Supermarket
(Two to Two-and-a-Half or Older)

It is a real pleasure for a child to go to the supermarket with her mother. She experiences the adventure of being wheeled around in a new place, and she discovers a whole new world of foods. This experience can be both pleasant for the mother and father and valuable for the child, even if it takes place only occasionally.

It is better to go shopping for food after your child has eaten. This protects you from listening to a lot of hunger cries. In the same vein, buying sweets or cookies to calm an overexcited child must not be done. If it's time for her snack, a child should be given an apple or a small package of raisins to nibble on.

During this visit, the child learns by watching her mother or father fill her shopping cart. In her mind, the food her parent buys is good food: good for the family and good for her! If all she sees is canned goods, frozen foods, and prepared dishes, she will not learn very much and will get a very poor idea of what a good diet is.

If, on the other hand, you buy basic foods (meat, fruit and vegetables, cereals, and milk products), and you explain why you are buying such-and-such a vegetable or cut of meat (to make a salad, to prepare some casserole), the child will feel that she is actively participating and will be very happy. Every now and then, the child should be allowed to make the choice between two kinds of cheeses, two vegetables, two fruits, or two fruit juices of equal nutritional value. If she has had a say in the actual choice of the food, she will be interested in getting to know it and will be less likely to refuse it when it appears on her plate.

Open-Air, or "Farmers'," Markets
(Suitable for Three-Year-Olds)

A family visit to this type of market at the height of the season is a treat that should be indulged. Between June and mid-October, it is possible to purchase fruits and vegetables in open-air markets. This is one activity a child should not miss.

He can savour the smell of fresh fruits and vegetables and will learn to recognize the characteristics of good vegetables and fruit: the whiteness of the cauliflower, the firmness of green peppers, the shiny skin of eggplants and zucchini, the deep colours of strawberries, and so on.

What a pleasure to taste the first carrots of the season!

There is no substitute for the smell of vegetables and fruits in season, and this is the perfect way to give your children a taste for them.

The Fish Market
(Suitable for Three-Year-Olds or Older)

The fish market presents nature's wonders to the curious and attentive child. No need to visit the ocean to see molluscs and crustaceans, mussels, clams, oysters, scallops, and snails. How surprising to see "green" lobsters swimming in saltwater tanks and yet find them "red" in the refrigerated display section. Or how about discovering frog's legs . . . or, better still, an octopus!

Fish is no exception to the rule. A child will like it if he has acquired a taste while very young and if his mother or father prepared it so that all of its flavour is retained. To double this pleasure, let the child choose her own favourite fish once in a while!

The Farm
(Suitable for Three-Year-Olds or Older)

To gather a still-warm freshly laid egg in the hen house, to see a cow being milked, to discover a pig's curly tail, to run in wheatfields, to go to a corn roast, to climb an apple tree and pick a ripe apple — these are but a few of the experiences that teach a child about the origins of his food. Many farms open their doors to families interested in sharing these experiences firsthand.

A Walk in the Country
(For Three-Year-Olds or Older)

With a pair of good, sharp eyes and a little luck, one can usually discover several edible plants growing wild during a simple walk in the country. Every month of the summer has something different to offer. In May you will find the young shoots of ferns known as "fiddleheads," a delicious and tender vegetable that is cooked in the same way as green string beans. Also in May, dandelion greens make an excellent salad and are rich in vitamin C. June brings wild strawberries and July, wild raspberries. In August tiny, delicious, flavourful blueberries are available. Autumn brings various nuts: walnuts and hazelnuts, for example, which are simply delicious.

A child soon learns to appreciate the flavour of these edible wild plants, which she has picked for herself in the countryside.

Warning: Do not pick any wild plant or mushroom that is unfamiliar to you. Some are poisonous.

Let's Plant Our Own Vegetables

All that is needed to grow one's own vegetables is earth, water, sunshine, and a lot of tender love and care. Even in the heart of the big city, a child can enjoy the fun of a vegetable garden.

Cherry Tomatoes
(For Three-Year-Olds or Older)

At the end of March, cherry tomato plants are available at garden stores. They can be planted in a pot 25 centimetres (10 inches) in diameter. The pot is then placed in a sunny window. The aspiring young gardener will be responsible for its care and watering — carefully and tactfully guided and supervised, of course. When the warm weather arrives, the pot should be put outdoors on a terrace or balcony in a sunny spot. The plants can then be trained to climb up a trellis or stake. If the young gardener has done her job well, she can proudly harvest and eat several miniature tomatoes.

Little Peas Grow into Big Peas
(For Three-Year-Olds or Older)

By sowing green peas, the child is able to observe every step in the development of a vegetable: seed, leaves, flowers, pods, and the green peas themselves. This experience is truly worthwhile!

Once spring arrives, a child can sow two or three pea seeds in a pot 25 centimetres (10 inches) in diameter, filled with planting soil. Place the pot near a sunny window and water regularly when the soil becomes dry.

In a few weeks, the child will notice seedlings and then some leaves. Place the pot in a warm, sunny corner of the garden or balcony, near a fence or trellis, since the pea plant is a climber. The child can then watch the successive stages of its growth — the flowers and then the pods. Tell him about the peas that will slowly form inside the pods.

Words can hardly express a child's happiness as he tastes the peas (raw or cooked) that he himself planted.

Let's Make Homemade Bread
(For Four-Year-Olds or Older)

What a thrill to discover in your own kitchen that yeast makes dough rise! And what a splendid smell hot bread has as it comes from the oven. What can be more delicious than devouring it warm!

A child who has walked in a wheatfield, watched the grain being ground, and helped to make the bread has had a unique and unforgettable experience!

Breadmaking is simple. However, four hours have to be set aside for the dough to rise and bake. Early morning or early afternoon is the ideal time to start the recipe that follows. The baking should coincide with mealtime, so tasting the bread will not spoil your child's appetite.

Nowadays, bread machines make things much easier but still show how flour is mixed with water, yeast, and some sugar can become a delicious bread.

Whole-Wheat Bread

Ingredients

- 60 mL (1/4 cup) honey
- 15 mL (1 tbsp.) butter
- 10 mL (2 tsp.) salt
- 250 mL (1 cup) boiling water
- 200 mL (3/4 cup) cold water
- 1 envelope of yeast, sprinkled over 60 mL (1/4 cup) lukewarm water
- 800–1000 g (5–6 cups) whole-wheat flour
- 75 mL (5 tbsp.) powdered skim milk
- vegetable oil

Preparation

(Mother or Father should carry out the first six steps.)

1. Measure honey, butter, and salt into a large bowl.
2. Pour in boiling water and mix well.
3. Add cold water and mix until preparation is lukewarm.
4. Add the soaked yeast and 750 g (3 cups) flour 250 g (1 cup) at a time. Mix until mixture is smooth.
5. Add powdered milk and beat for 2 minutes.
6. Add remaining flour and mix well.
7. Knead dough. Show the child how to do this, and let her try it for a few minutes.
8. When the dough has been well kneaded, brush a little vegetable oil over top of dough, cover with a damp cloth, and let dough rise until it has doubled in volume.
9. Once dough has doubled, show your child the change. Let her punch

the dough in the centre and watch it sink down.

10. Knead dough again with your child's help, and shape into 2 small loaves. Place in well-greased bread pans, cover, and let rise until double in volume. Alternatively: Divide dough into small pieces and let child "sculpt" her own little loaves. Cover with damp cloth and allow to rise until double in volume away from any draft. Explain to your child what yeast is and how it makes dough rise.

11. When dough has doubled in bulk, cook in a 180°C (350°F) oven until loaves are golden and crusty (45–60 minutes).

   Yield: 2 small loaves

Happy eating experiences and healthy foods
— a winning strategy!

Bibliography

ADA. Position of the American Dietetic Association. Nutrition Standards for Child Care Programs. *Journal of the American Dietetic Association* 94, no. 3 (1994): 323.

———. Position of the American Dietetic Association. Promotion of Breast Feeding. *Journal of the American Dietetic Association* 97 (1997): 662–66.

———. Position of the American Dietetic Association: Vegetarian Diets. *Journal of the American Dietetic Association* 93 (1993): 1317–19.

American Academy of Pediatrics. Committee on Drugs. The Transfer of Drugs and Other Chemicals into Human Milk. *Pediatrics* 93, no. 1 (1994): 137–50.

———. Committee on Environmental Health. PCBs in Breast Milk. *Pediatrics* 94, no. 1 (1994): 122–23.

———. Committee on Nutrition. On the Feeding of Supplemental Foods to Infants. *Pediatrics* 65, no. 6 (1980): 1178–81.

———. Committee on Nutrition. Follow-up or Weaning Formulas. *Pediatrics* 83, no. 6 (1989): 1067.

——. Committee on Nutrition. Indications for Cholesterol Testing in Children. *Pediatrics* 83, no. 1 (1989): 141–42.

——. Committee on Nutrition. Iron-fortified Infant Formulas. *Pediatrics* 84, no. 6 (1989): 1114–15.

——. Committee on Nutrition. Use of Oral Fluid Therapy and Posttreatment Feeding Following Enteritis in Children in a Developed Country. *Pediatrics* 75, no. 2 (1985): 358–61.

——. Committee on Nutrition. The Use of Whole Cow's Milk in Infancy. *Pediatrics* 89 (1992): 1105–9.

——. Committee on Nutrition. Vitamin and Mineral Supplement Needs in Normal Children in the United States. *Pediatrics* 66, no. 6 (1980): 1015–21.

Anderson, J.A. Milk, Eggs and Peanuts: Food Allergies in Children. *American Family Physician* 56 (1997): 1365–74.

Anderson, J.W., et al. Breastfeeding and Cognitive Development: A Meta-analysis. *American Journal of Clinical Nutrition* 70 (1999): 525–35.

Ares, S., et al. Iodine Content of Infant Formulas and Iodine Intake of Premature Babies: High Risk of Iodine Deficiency. *Archives of Disease in Childhood Fetal & Neonatal Edition* 71, no. 3 (1994): F184–91.

Arshad, S., et al. Effect of Allergen Avoidance on Development of Allergic Disorders in Infancy. *Lancet* 339, no. 8808 (1992): 1493–97.

Aukett, M., et al. Treatment with Iron Increases Weight Gain and Psychomotor Development. *Archives of Disease in Childhood* 61 (1986): 849–57.

Avery, M., et al. Oral Therapy for Acute Diarrhea. *New England Journal of Medicine* 323, no. 13 (1990): 891–94.

Baldassano, R., and Liacouras, C. Chronic Diarrhea. *Pediatric Clinics of North America* 38, no. 3 (1991): 667–87.

Balistreri, W., and Farrell, M. Gastroesophageal Reflux in Infants. *New England Journal of Medicine* 309, no. 13 (1983): 790–92.

Ballard, P. Breast-feeding for the Working Mother. *Issues in Comprehensive Pediatric Nursing* 6 (1983): 249–59.

Barr, R., et al. Carrying as Colic "Therapy": A Randomized Controlled Trial. *Pediatrics* 87, no. 5 (1991): 623–30.

——. Feeding and Temperament as Determinants of Early Infant Crying/Fussing Behavior. *Pediatrics* 84, no. 3 (1989): 514–21.

Bates, C., and Prentice, A. Breast Milk as a Source of Vitamins, Essential

Minerals and Trace Elements. *Pharmacology & Therapeutics* 62, nos. 1–2 (1994): 193–220.

Beaudry, M., et al. Who Breastfeeds in New Brunswick, When and Why. *Canadian Journal of Public Health* 80 (1989): 166–72.

Beck Fein, S., et al. Infant Formula Preparation, Handling and Related Practices in the United States. *Journal of the American Dietetic Association* 99 (1999): 1234–40.

Beckholt Polakoff, A. Breast Milk for Infants Who Cannot Breastfeed. *JOGNN* 19, no. 3 (1990): 216–20.

Bhowmick, S., et al. Rickets Caused by Vitamin D Deficiency in Breastfed Infants in the Southern United States. *American Journal of Disease in Childhood* 145 (1991): 127–30.

Birch, E.E. Visual Acuity and the Essentiality of Docosahexaenoic Acid and Arachidonic Acid in the Diet of Term Infants. *Pediatric Research* 44 (1998): 201–9.

Bishop, C., and Dye, A. Microwave Heating Enhances the Migration of Plasticizers out of Plastics. *Journal of Environmental Health* 44, no. 5 (1982): 231–35.

Bishop, N. Feeding the Preterm Infant. *Pediatric Nephrology* 8, no. 4 (1994): 494–98.

Bowles Carlson, B., and Williamson Prater, B. Pregnancy and Lactation Following Anorexia and Bulimia. *JOGNN* 19, no. 3 (1990): 243–48.

Brewer, M., et al. Postpartum Changes in Maternal Weight and Body Fat Depots in Lactating vs. Nonlactating Women. *American Journal of Clinical Nutrition* 49 (1989): 259–65.

Brown, K. Dietary Management of Acute Childhood Diarrhea: Optimal Timing of Feeding and Appropriate Use of Milks and Mixed Diets. *Journal of Pediatrics* 118 (1991): s92–s98.

Brown, K., et al. Use of Nonhuman Milks in the Dietary Management of Young Children with Acute Diarrhea: A Meta-analysis of Clinical Trials. *Pediatrics* 93, no. 1 (1994): 17–27.

Businco, L., et al. Allergenicity and Nutritional Adequacy of Soy Protein Formulas. *Journal of Pediatrics* 121 (1992): s21–s28.

Calvo, E., et al. Iron Status in Exclusively Breast-fed Infants. *Pediatrics* 90 (1992): 375–79.

Campbell, J. Dietary Treatment of Infant Colic: A Double-Blind Study. *Journal of the Royal College of General Practitioners* 39, no. 318 (1989): 11–14.

Canadian Institute of Child Health. *National Breastfeeding Guidelines for Health Care Providers*, 2nd ed. Ottawa: Canadian Institute of Health, 1996.

Canadian Paediatric Society. Breast-feeding: Fifteen Years of Progress. *Canadian Journal of Paediatrics* 5 (1994): 156–59.

———. Meeting the Iron Needs of Infants and Young Children: An Update. *Canadian Medical Association Journal* 144, no. 11 (1991): 1451–54.

———. Vitamin D Supplementation in Northern Native Communities. *Canadian Medical Association Journal* 138 (1988): 229–30.

———. Nutrition Committee. Megavitamin and Megamineral Therapy in Childhood. *Canadian Medical Association Journal* 143, no. 10 (1990): 1009–13.

———. Nutrient Needs and Feeding of Premature Infants. *Canadian Medical Association Journal* 152 (1995): 1765–85.

———. Oral Rehydration Therapy and Early Refeeding in the Management of Childhood Gastroenteritis. *Canadian Journal of Paediatrics* 1, no. 5 (1994): 160–64.

Canadian Paediatric Society, Dietitians of Canada, and Health Canada. *Nutrition for Healthy Term Infants*. Ottawa: Minister of Public Works and Government Services, 1998.

Carlson, S., et al. Long-term Feeding of Formulas High in Linolenic Acid and Marine Oil to Very Low Birth Weight Infants: Phospholipid Fatty Acids. *Pediatric Research* 30 (1991): 404–12.

Castres de Paulet, A., et al. Biological Effects on Premature Neonates of a Milk Formula Enriched with Alpha-linolenic Acid: A Multicenter Study. *Bulletin de l'Académie nationale de médecine* 178, no. 2 (1994): 267–73.

Chandra, R.K. Five-year Follow Up of High Risk Infants with Family History of Allergy Who Were Exclusively Breast-fed or Fed Partial Whey Hydrolysate, Soy and Conventional Cow's Milk Formulas. *Journal of Pediatric Gastroenterology and Nutrition* 24 (1997): 380–88.

Chandra, R.K., et al. Effect on Feeding Whey Hydrolysate, Soy and Conventional Cow Milk Formulas on Incidence of Atopic Disease in High Risk Infants. *Annals of Allergy* 63, no. 2 (1989): 102–6.

Chapman, D.J., et al. Identification of Risk Factors for Delayed Onset of Lactation. *Journal of the American Dietetic Association* 99 (1999): 450–55.

Clark, K., et al. Determination of the Optimal Ratio of Linoleic Acid to A-linolenic Acid in Infant Formulas. *Journal of Pediatrics* 120 (1992): s151–s158.

Covington, C., et al. Newborn Behavioral Performance in Colic and Noncolic Infants. *Nursing Research* 40, no. 5 (1991): 292–96.

Cunningham, A.S., et al. Breast-feeding and Health in the 1980s: A Global Epidemiologic Review. *Journal of Pediatrics* 118, no. 5 (1991): 659–66.

Curtis, D. Infant Nutrient Supplementation. *Journal of Pediatrics* 117 (1990): s110–s118.

Dagnelie, P., et al. Effects of Macrobiotic Diets on Linear Growth in Infants and Children until 10 Years of Age. *European Journal of Clinical Nutrition* 48, no. 1 (1994): s103–s112.

———. Increased Risk of Vitamin B_{12} and Iron Deficiency in Infants on Macrobiotic Diets. *American Journal of Clinical Nutrition* 50, no. 4 (1989): 818–24.

de Boissieu, D., et al. Allergy to Nondairy Proteins in Mother's Milk as Assessed by Intestinal Permeability Tests. *Allergy* 49 (1994): 882–84.

Deckelbaum, R. Nutrition, the Child and Atherosclerosis. *Acta Paediatrica Scandinavia* 365, suppl. 13 (1990): 7–12.

Dewey, K.G., et al. A Randomized Study of the Effects of Aerobic Exercise by Lactating Women on Breast-milk Volume and Composition. *New England Journal of Medicine* 330, no. 7 (1994): 449–53.

———. Growth of Breast-fed and Formula-fed Infants from 0 to 18 Months: The DARLING Study. *Pediatrics* 89 (1992): 1035–41.

Diaz, S., et al. Breast-feeding Duration and Growth of Fully Breast-fed Infants in a Poor Urban Chilean Population. *American Journal of Clinical Nutrition* 62 (1995): 371–76.

Dietz, W. Prevention of Childhood Obesity. *Pediatric Clinics of North America* 33, no. 4 (1986): 823–33.

Duncan, B., et al. Iron and the Exclusively Breast-fed Infant from Birth to Six Months. *Journal of Pediatric Gastroenterology and Nutrition* 4, no. 3 (1985): 421–25.

Dungy, C., et al. Effects of Discharge Samples on Duration of Breast-feeding. *Pediatrics* 90, vol. 2 (1992): 233–37.

Dunlop, M. Few Canadian Hospitals Qualify for "Baby Friendly" Designation by Promoting Breast-feeding: Survey. *Canadian Medical Association Journal* 152, no. 1 (1995): 87–89.

Dusdieker, L., et al. Is Milk Production Impaired by Dieting during Lactation? *American Journal of Clinical Nutrition* 59, no. 4 (1994): 833–40.

Esteban, M. Adverse Food Reactions in Childhood: Concept, Importance, and Present Problems. *Journal of Pediatrics* 121, no. 5, part 2 (1992): s1–s3.

Evans, R., et al. Maternal Diet and Infantile Colic in Breast-fed Infants. *Lancet* 1981: 1340–42.

Faruque, A., et al. Breast feeding and Oral Rehydration at Home during Diarrhea to Prevent Dehydration. *Archives of Disease in Childhood* 67, no. 8 (1992): 1027–29.

Filer, L. A Glimpse into the Future of Infant Nutrition. *Pediatric Annals* 21, no. 10 (1992): 633–37.

Finberg, L. The Weaning Process. *Pediatrics* 75, part 1 of 2 (1985): 214–15.

Fitzgerald, J. Constipation in Children. *Pediatrics in Review* 8, no. 10 (1987): 299–302.

Fomon, S. Bioavailability of Supplemental Iron in Commercially Prepared Dry Infant Cereals. *Journal of Pediatrics* 110 (1987): 660–61.

Fomon, S., et al. Cow Milk Feeding in Infancy: Gastrointestinal Blood Loss and Iron Nutritional Status. *Journal of Pediatrics* 98, no. 4 (1981): 540–45.

———. Iron Absorption from Infant Foods. *Pediatric Research* 26, no. 3 (1989): 250–54.

———. Skim Milk in Infant Feeding. *Acta Paediatrica Scandinavia* 66 (1977): 17–30.

Font, L., et al. Incidental Maternal Dietary Intake and Infant Refusal to Nurse: Consultants' Corner. *Journal of Human Lactation* 6, no. 1 (1990): 9–13.

Forsyth, B. Colic and the Effect of Changing Formulas: A Double-blind, Multiple-crossover Study. *Journal of Pediatrics* 115, no. 4 (1989): 521–26.

Freed, G., et al. A Practical Guide to Successful Breast-feeding Management. *American Journal of Disease in Childhood* 145 (1991): 917–21.

———. Attitudes of Expectant Fathers Regarding Breast-feeding. *Pediatrics* 89 (1992): 224–27.

Friel, J., et al. Iron Status of Very-Low-Birth-Weight Infants during the First 15 Months of Infancy. *Canadian Medical Association Journal* 143, no. 8 (1990): 733–36.

———. Evaluation of Fullterm Infants Fed an Evaporated Formula. *Acta Pediatrics* 86 (1997): 448–53.

Fuchs, G.J., et al. Effect of Dietary Fat on Cardiovascular Risk Factors in Infancy. *Pediatrics* 93, no. 5 (1994): 756–63.

———. Gastrointestinal Blood Loss in Older Infants: Impact of Cow Milk versus Formula. *Journal of Pediatric Gastroenterology and Nutrition* 16 (1993): 4–9.

Gallagher, M., et al. Obesity among Mescalero Preschool Children. *American Journal of Disease in Childhood* 145 (1991): 1262–65.

Gern, J., et al. Allergic Reactions to Milk-contaminated "Nondairy" Products. *New England Journal of Medicine* 324, no. 14 (1991): 976–79.

Gerrard, J., and Shenassa, M. Food Allergy: Two Common Types as Seen in Breast and Formula Fed Babies. *Annals of Allergy* 50, no. 6 (1983): 375–79.

Gibson, R.A., et al. Dietary Fat and Neural Development. *Lipids* 31 (1996): 51–119.

Gleghorn, E., et al. No-enema Therapy for Idiopathic Constipation and Encopresis. *Clinical Pediatrics* 30, no. 12 (1991): 669–72.

Goldman, A., et al. Immunologic Factors in Human Milk during the First Year of Lactation. *Journal of Pediatrics* 100, no. 4 (1982): 563–67.

Gortmaker, S., et al. Increasing Pediatric Obesity in the United States. *American Journal of Disease in Childhood* 141 (1987): 535–40.

Grange, D., and Finlay, J. Nutritional Vitamin B_{12} Deficiency in a Breast-fed Infant following Maternal Gastric Bypass. *Pediatric Hematology & Oncology* 11, no. 3 (1994): 308–11.

Greene-Finestone, L., et al. Infant Feeding Practices and Socio-Demographic Factors in Ottawa-Carleton. *Canadian Journal of Public Health* 80 (1989): 173–76.

Greer, F. Formulas for the Healthy Term Infant. *Pediatrics in Review* 16, no. 3 (1995): 107–12.

Greer, F., and Marshall, S. Bone Mineral Content, Serum Vitamin D Metabolite Concentrations, and Ultraviolet B Light Exposure in Infants Fed Human Milk with and without Vitamin D_2 supplements. *Journal of Pediatrics* 114 (1989): 204–12.

Hall, B. Changing Composition of Human Milk and Early Development of an Appetite Control. *Lancet* (1975): 779–81.

Hammer, L. The Development of Eating Behavior in Childhood. *Pediatric Clinics of North America* 39, no. 3 (1992): 379–95.

Hanson, L., et al. Breast feeding: Overview and Breast Milk Immunology. *Acta Paediatrica Japonica* 36, no. 5 (1994): 557–61.

Hardy, S., and Kleinman, R. Fat and Cholesterol in the Diet of Infants and Young Children: Implications for Growth, Development and Long-term Health. *Journal of Pediatrics* 125 (1994): s69–s77.

Harnack, L., et al. Soft Drink Consumption among U.S. Children and Adolescents: Nutritional Consequences. *Journal of the American Dietetic Association* 99 (1999): 436–41.

Hattevig, G., et al. The Effect of Maternal Avoidance of Eggs, Cow's Milk, and Fish during Lactation on the Development of IgG, and IgA Antibodies in Infants. *Journal of Allergy and Clinical Immunology* 85 (1990): 108–15.

Health Canada. *Nutrition Recommendations Update: Dietary Fat and Children.* Ottawa: Minister of Public and Government Serivces, 1993.

Hegsted, M. Trends in Food Consumption: Implications for Infant Feeding. *Journal of Pediatrics* 117 (1990): s80–s83.

Hendricks, K., and Badruddin, S. Weaning Recommendations: The Scientific Basis. *Nutrition Reviews* 50, no. 5 (1992): 125–33.

Hill, D., et al. Charting Infant Distress: An Aid to Defining Colic. *Journal of Pediatrics* 121 (1992): 755–58.

Hillman, L. Mineral and Vitamin D Adequacy in Infants Fed Human Milk or Formula between 6 and 12 Months of Age. *Journal of Pediatrics* 117 (1990): s134–s142.

Himes, J., et al. Maternal Supplementation and Bone Growth in Infancy. *Paediatric and Perinatal Epidemiology* 4 (1990): 436–47.

Hyams, J., and Leichtner, A. Apple Juice and Diarrhea. *American Journal of Disease in Childhood* 139 (1985): 503–5.

Hyams, J., et al. Carbohydrate Malabsorption following Fruit Juice Ingestion in Young Children. *Pediatrics* 82, no. 1 (1988): 64–67.

Iacono, G., et al. Chronic Constipation as a Symptom of Cow Milk Allergy. *Journal of Pediatrics* 126, no. 1 (1995): 34–39.

——. Intolerance of Cow's Milk and Chronic Constipation in Children. *New England Journal of Medicine* 339 (1998): 1100–4.

Innis, S. Lipids in Infant Nutrition. *Journal of Pediatrics* 120, no. 4 (1992): 551–61.

Issenman, R., et al. Are Chronic Digestive Complaints the Result of Abnormal Dietary Patterns? *American Journal of Disease in Childhood* 141 (1987): 679–82.

Jakobsson, I., and Linberg, T. Cow's Milk Proteins Cause Infantile Colic in Breast-fed Infants: A Double-blind Crossover Study. *Pediatrics* 71, no. 2 (1983): 268–71.

Johnston, D., and Roghman, K. Recommendations for Soy Infant Formula: A Review of the Literature and a Survey of Pediatric Allergists. *Pediatric*

Asthma, Allergy and Immunology 7, no. 2 (1993): 77–88.

Joseph K.S., et al. Determinants of Preterm Birth Rates in Canada from 1981–1983 and from 1992–1994. *New England Journal of Medicine* 339 (1998): 1434–39.

Kaplan, R., and Toshima, M. Does a Reduced Fat Diet Cause Retardation in Children's Growth? *Preventive Medicine* 21 (1992): 33–52.

Klesges, R., et al. A Longitudinal Analysis of Accelerated Weight Gain in Preschool Children. *Pediatrics* 1 (1995): 126–30.

Krebs, N., et al. Growth and Intakes of Energy and Zinc in Infants Fed Human Milk. *Journal of Pediatrics* 124, no. 1 (1994): 32–39.

Lanata, C., et al. Feeding during Acute Diarrhea as a Risk Factor for Persistent Diarrhea. *Acta Paediatrica Scandinavia* 81 (1992): 98–103.

Larson, K., and Ayllon, T. The Effects of Contingent Music and Differential Reinforcement on Infantile Colic. *Behaviour Research & Therapy* 28, no. 2 (1990): 119–25.

Lascari, A. "Early" Breast-feeding Jaundice: Clinical Significance. *Journal of Pediatrics* 108 (1986): 156–58.

Lauer, R. Should Children, Parents and Pediatricians Worry about Cholesterol? Commentary. *Pediatrics* 89, no. 3 (1992): 509–11.

Lawrence, P. Breast Milk: Best Source of Nutrition for Term and Preterm Infants. *Pediatric Clinics of North America* 41, no. 5 (1994): 925–41.

Lawrence, R.A. Breast-feeding. *Pediatrics in Review* 11, no. 6 (1989): 163–71.

Lebrun, J.B., et al. Vitamin D Deficiency in a Manitoba Community. *Canadian Journal of Public Health Association* 84, no. 6 (1993): 394–96.

Lee-Han, H., et al. Infant Feeding Practices in North York: Compliance with CPS Guidelines. *Journal of the Canadian Dietetic Association* 59 (1998): 24–29.

Lehmann, F., et al. Iron Deficiency Anemia in 1-year-old Children of Disadvantaged Families in Montreal. *Canadian Medical Association Journal* 146, no. 9 (1992): 1571–77.

Lehtonen, L., et al. Intestinal Microflora in Colicky and Noncolicky Infants: Bacterial Cultures and Gas-Liquid Chromatography. *Journal of Pediatric Gastroenterology & Nutrition* 19, no. 3 (1994): 310–14.

Leung, A., and Robson, L. Acute Diarrhea in Children. *Postgraduate Medicine* 86, no. 8 (1989): 161–74.

Liebman, B. Baby Formula: Missing Key Fats? *Nutrition Action Healthletter* 17 (1990): 8–9.

Lifshitz, F., et al. Role of Juice Carbohydrate Malabsorption in Chronic Nonspecific Diarrhea in Children. *Journal of Pediatrics* 120, no. 5 (1992): 825–29.

Lothe, L., et al. Cow's Milk Formula as a Cause of Infantile Colic: A Double-blind Study. *Pediatrics* 70, no. 1 (1982): 7–10.

Lovegrove, J., et al. The Immunological and Long-term Atopic Outcome of Infants Born to Women following a Milk-free Diet during Late Pregnancy and Lactation: A Pilot Study. *British Journal of Nutrition* 71, no. 2 (1994): 233–38.

Lozoff, B. Iron and Learning Potential. *Bulletin in the New York Academy of Medicine* 65, no. 10 (1989): 1050–66.

——. Long-Term Development Outcome of Infants with Iron Deficiency. *New England Journal of Medicine* 325, no. 10 (1991): 687–94.

Lozoff, B., and Zuckerman, B. Sleep Problems in Children. *Pediatrics in Review* 10, no. 1 (1988): 17–24.

Lubec, G., et al. Aminoacid Isomerisation and Microwave Exposure. *Lancet* 2, no. 8676 (1989): 1392–93.

Lucas, A., et al. Breast Milk and Subsequent Intelligence Quotient in Children Born Preterm. *The Lancet* 339 (1992): 261–64.

Lust, K.D., et al. Maternal Intake of Cruciferous Vegetables and Other Foods and Colic Symptoms in Exclusively Breast-fed Infants. *Journal of the American Dietetic Association* 96, no. 1 (1996): 46–48.

Macaulay, A., et al. Breastfeeding in the Mohawk Community of Kahnawake: Revisited and Redefined. *Canadian Journal of Public Health* 80 (1989): 177–81.

Macknin, M., et al. Infant Sleep and Bedtime Cereal. *American Journal of Disease in Childhood* 143 (1989): 1066–68.

Maclean, H. Breastfeeding in Canada: A Demographic and Experiental Perspective. *Journal of the Canadian Dietetic Association* 59 (1998): 15–23.

Maisels, J. Jaundice in the Newborn. *Pediatrics in Review* 3, no. 10 (1982): 305–19.

Makrides, M., et al. Changes in Polyunsaturated Fatty Acids of Breast Milk from Mothers in Full-term Infants over 30 Weeks of Lactation. *American Journal of Clinical Nutrition* 62 (1995): 1231–33.

Marchand, L., and Morrow, M. Infant Feeding Practices: Understanding the Decision-Making. *Family Medicine* 26, no. 5 (1994): 319–24.

Mehta, K.C., et al. Trial on Timing of Introduction to Solids and Food Type on Infant Growth. *Pediatrics* 102 (1998): 569–73.

Melnikow, J., and Bedinghaus, J. Management of Common Breast-feeding Problems. *Journal of Family Practice* 39, no. 1 (1994): 56–64.

Mennella, J.A., et al. Early Flavor Experiences: Research Update. *Nutrition Reviews* 56 (1998): 205–11.

Mannella, J., and Beauchamp G. Maternal Diet Alters the Sensory Qualities of Human Milk and Nursing's Behavior. *Pediatrics* 88, no. 4 (1991): 737–43.

——. The Transfer of Alcohol to Human Milk. *New England Journal of Medicine* 325, no. 14 (1991): 981–85.

Mes, J., and Lau, P. Distribution of Polychlorinated Biphenyl Congeners in Human Milk and Blood during Lactation. *Bulletin of Environmental Contamination and Toxicology* 31 (1983): 639–43.

Michaelsen, K., et al. The Copenhagen Cohort Study on Infant Nutrition and Growth: Breast-milk Intake, Human Milk Macronutrient Content and Influencing Factors. *American Journal of Clinical Nutrition* 59, no. 3 (1994): 600–11.

Moffat, M.E.K., et al. Prevention of Iron Deficiency and Psychomotor Decline in High Risk Infants through Use of Iron-fortified Infant Formula: A Randomized Clinical Trial. *Journal of Pediatrics* 125 (1994): 527–34.

Morse, J., et al. Patterns of Breastfeeding and Work: The Canadian Experience. *Canadian Journal of Public Health* 80 (1989): 182–88.

Morton, R., et al. Iron Status in the First Year of Life. *Journal of Pediatric Gastroenterology and Nutrition* 7, no. 5 (1988): 707–12.

Myres, A. Weaning: The Timeless Transition. *The Canadian Journal of Pediatrics* (1991): 16–24.

Nelson, S., et al. Lack of Adverse Reactions to Iron-fortified Formula. *Pediatrics* 81, no. 3 (1988): 360–64.

Nemethy, M., and Clore, E. Microwave Heating of Infant Formula and Breast Milk. *Journal of Pediatric Health Care* 4, no. 3 (1990): 131–35.

Newburg, D.S. Human Milk Glycoconjugates That Inhibit Pathogens. *Current Medical Chemistry* 6 (1999): 117–27.

Newman, J., and Wilmott, B. Breast Rejection: A Little-Appreciated Cause of Lactation Failure. *Canadian Family Physician* 36 (1990): 449–53.

Nicoll, A., et al. Supplementary Feeding and Jaundice in Newborns. *Acta Paediatrica Scandinavia* 71 (1982): 759–61.

O'Connell, J., et al. Growth of Vegetarian Children: The Farm Study. *Pediatrics* 84, no. 3 (1989): 475–81.

Orenstein, S., et al. The Infant Seat as Treatment for Gastroesophageal Reflux. *New England Journal of Medicine* 309 (1983): 760–63.

Oski, F. Hyperbilirubinemia in the Term Infant: An Unjaundiced Approach. *Contemporary Pediatrics.* 1992: 148–55.

———. Iron Supplementation and the Breast-fed Infant. *Journal of Pediatric Gastroenterology and Nutrition* 4, no. 3 (1985): 344–45.

Oski, F., and Landaw, S. Inhibition of Iron Absorption from Human Milk by Baby Food. *American Journal of Disease in Childhood* 134 (1980): 459–60.

Peipert, J., et al. Infant Obesity, Weight Reduction with Normal Increase in Linear Growth and Fat-free Body Mass. *Pediatrics* 89, no. 1 (1992): 143–45.

Pelchat, M.L., and Pliner, P. Antecedents and Correlates of Feeding Problems in Young Children. *Journal of Nutrition Education* 18, no. 1 (1986): 23–29.

Pinyerd, B. Strategies for Consoling the Infant with Colic: Fact or Fiction? *Journal of Pediatric Nursing* 7, no. 6 (1992): 403–11.

Pizarro, F., et al. Iron Status with Different Infant Feeding Regimens: Relevance to Screening and Prevention of Iron Deficiency. *Journal of Pediatrics* 118 (1991): 687–92.

Potter, S., et al. Does Infant Feeding Method Influence Maternal Post-partum Weight Loss? *Journal of the American Dietetic Association* 91 (1991): 441–46.

Prentice, A., et al. The Effect of Water Abstention on Milk Synthesis in Lactating Women. *Clinical Science* 66 (1984): 291–98.

Pugliese, M., et al. Parental Health Beliefs as a Cause of Nonorganic Failure to Thrive. *Pediatrics* 80, no. 2 (1987): 175–81.

Rappaport, L., and Levine, M. The Prevention of Constipation and Encopresis: A Developmental Model and Approach. *Pediatric Clinics of North America* 33, no. 4 (1986): 859–68.

Rees, J., et al. Iron Fortification of Infant Foods. *Clinical Pediatrics* 24, no. 12 (1985): 707–10.

Roberts, S.B., et al. Energy Expenditure and Intake in Infants Born to Lean and Overweight Mothers. *New England Journal of Medicine* 318 (1988): 461–66.

Rogan, W.J., and Gladen, B.C. Breast-feeding and Cognitive Development. *Early Human Development* 31 (1993): 181–93.

Ryan, A.S., and Martinez, G.A. Breast-feeding and the Working Mother: A Profile. *Pediatrics* 83, no. 4 (1989): 524–31.

Sabharwal, H., et al. A Prospective Cohort Study on Breast-feeding and Otitis Media in Swedish Infants. *Pediatric Infectious Disease Journal* 13, no. 3 (1994): 183–88.

Sampselle, C.M., et al. Physical Activity and Postpartum Well-Being. *Journal of Obstetrics, Gynecology and Neonatal Nursing* 28 (1999): 41–49.

Sampson, H., et al. Fatal and Near-fatal Anaphylactic Reactions to Food in Children and Adolescents. *New England Journal of Medicine* 327 (1992): 380–84.

Sanders, T., and Reddy, S. The Influence of a Vegetarian Diet on the Fatty Acid Composition of Human Milk and the Essential Fatty Acid Status of the Infant. *Journal of Pediatrics* 120 (1992): s71–s77.

——. Vegetarian Diets and Children. *American Journal of Clinical Nutrition* 59 (1994): s1176–s1181.

Shea, S., et al. Failure of Family History to Predict High Blood Cholesterol among Hispanic Preschool Children. *Preventive Medicine* 19 (1990): 443–55.

——. Is There a Relationship between Dietary Fat and Stature or Growth in Children Three to Five Years of Age? *Pediatrics* 92, no. 4 (1993): 579–86.

——. Relationships of Dietary Fat Consumption to Serum Total and Low-Density Lipoprotein Cholesterol in Hispanic Preschool Children. *Preventive Medicine* 20 (1991): 237–49.

——. Variability and Self-regulation of Energy Intake in Young Children in Their Every Day Environment. *Pediatrics* 90, no. 4 (1992): 542–45.

Sigman-Grant, M., et al. Microwave Heating of Infant Formula: A Dilemma Resolved. *Pediatrics* 90, no. 3 (1992): 412–15.

Sigurs, N., et al. Maternal Avoidance of Eggs, Cow's Milk and Fish during Lactation: Effect on Allergic Manifestations, Skin-prick Test, and Specific IgE Antibodies in Children at Age 4 years. *Pediatrics* 89, no. 4 (1992): 735–38.

Smith, M., et al. Carbohydrate Absorption from Fruit Juice in Young Children. *Pediatrics* 95, no. 3 (1995): 340–44.

Smith, M., and Lifshitz, F. Excess Fruit Juice Consumption as a Contributing Factor in Nonorganic Failure to Thrive. *Pediatrics* 93, no. 3 (1994): 438–43.

Snyder, J., et al. Home-based Therapy for Diarrhea. *Journal of Pediatric Gastroenterology and Nutrition* 11 (1990): 438–47.

Société canadienne de pédiatrie, Section d'allergie. Réaction anaphylactiques alimentaires mortelles chez les enfants. *Canadian Medical Association Journal* 150, no. 3 (1994): 339–42.

Sorva, R., et al. Beta-lactoglobulin Secretion in Human Milk Varies Widely after Cow's Milk Ingestion in Mothers of Infants with Cow's Milk Allergy. *Journal of Allergy and Clinical Immunology* 93, no. 4 (1994): 787–92.

Specker, B., Do North American Women Need Supplemental Vitamin D during Pregnancy or Lactation? *Americal Journal of Clinical Nutrition* 59 (1994): s484–s491.

Specker, B., et al. Sunshine Exposure and 6 Serum 25 Hydroxyvitamin D Concentrations in Exclusively Breast-fed Infants. *Journal of Pediatrics* 107, no. 3 (1985): 372–76.

——. Vitamin B_{12}: Low Milk Concentrations Are Related to Low Serum Concentrations in Vegetarian Women and to Methyl-malonic Aciduria in Their Infants. *American Journal of Clinical Nutrition* 52, no. 6 (1990): 1073–76.

Stender, S., et al. The Influence of Trans Fatty Acids on Health: A Report from the Danish Nutrition Council. *Clinical Science* 88 (1995): 375–92.

Sullivan, S., and Birch, L. Infant Dietary Experience and Acceptance of Solid Foods. *Pediatrics* 93, no. 2 (1994): 271–77.

Taubman, B. Clinical Trial of the Treatment of Colic by Modification of Parent-Infant Interaction. *Pediatrics* 74, no. 6 (1984): 998–1003.

——. Parental Counseling Compared with Elimination of Cow's Milk or Soy Milk Protein for the Treatment of Infant Colic Syndrome: A Randomized Trial. *Pediatrics* 81, no. 6 (1988): 756–61.

Taylor, J., and Bergman, A. Iron-fortified Formulas: Pediatricians Prescribing Practices. *Clinical Pediatrics* 28, no. 2 (1989): 73–75.

Tiwary, C., and Holguin, H. Prevalence of Obesity among Children of Military Dependents at Two Major Medical Centers. *American Journal of Public Health* 82, no. 3 (1992): 354–57.

Touhami, M., et al. Clinical Consequences of Replacing Milk with Yogurt in Persistent Infantile Diarrhea. *Annales de pédiatrie* 39, no. 2 (1992): 79–86.

Treem, W. Chronic Nonspecific Diarrhea of Childhood. *Clinical Pediatrics* (1992): 413–19.

——. Infant Colic: A Pediatric Gastroenterologist's Perspective. *Pediatric Clinics of North America* 41, no. 5 (1994): 1121–38.

Tunnessen, W., and Oski, F. Consequences of Starting Whole Cow Milk at 6 Months of Age. *Journal of Pediatrics* 111 (1987): 813–16.

Tyson, J., et al. Adaptation of Feeding to a Low-Fat Yield in Breast Milk. *Pediatrics* 89, no. 2 (1992): 215–20.

Unger, R., et al. Childhood Obesity. *Clinical Pediatrics* 29, no. 7 (1990): 368–73.

Vandenplas, Y. Myths and Facts about Breastfeeding: Does It Prevent Later Atopic Disease? *Acta Paediatrics* 86 (1997): 1283–87.

Ventura, A., et al. Diet and Atopic Eczema in Children. *Allergy* 44 (1989): 159–64.

Weaver, L. Bowel Habit from Birth to Old Age. *Journal of Pediatric Gastroenterology and Nutrition* 7 (1988): 637–40.

Weaver, L., et al. The Bowel Habit of Milk-fed Infants. *Journal of Pediatric Gastroenterology and Nutrition* 7 (1988): 568–71.

Weizman, Z., et al. Efficacy of Herbal Tea Preparation in Infantile Colic. *Journal of Pediatrics* 122, no. 4 (1993): 650–52.

Whitehead, R. The Human Weaning Process. *Pediatrics* 75, suppl. (1985): 189–93.

Willatts, P., et al. Effect of Long-Chain Polyunsaturated Fatty Acids in Infant Formula on Problem Solving at 10 Months of Age. *Lancet* 352 (1998): 688–91.

Woolridge, M., and Fisher, C. Colic, "Overfeeding," and Symptoms of Lactose Malabsorption in the Breast-fed Baby: A Possible Artifact of Feed Management? *Lancet* (1988): 382–84.

Writing Group for the DISC Collaborative Research Group, The. Efficacy and Safety of Lowering Dietary Intake of Fat and Cholesterol in Children with Elevated Low-density Lipoprotein Cholesterol. *Journal of the American Medical Association* 273 (1995): 1429–35.

Yamauchi, Y., and Yamanouchi, I. Breast-feeding Frequency during the First 24 Hours after Birth in Full-term Neonates. *Pediatrics* 86, no. 2 (1990): 171–75.

Zavaleta, N., et al. Effect of Acute Maternal Infection on Quantity and Composition of Breast Milk. *American Journal of Clinical Nutrition* 62 (1995): 559–63.

Ziegler, E., et al. Cow Milk Feeding in Infancy: Further Observations on Blood Loss from the Gastrointestinal Tract. *Journal of Pediatrics* 116, no. 11 (1990): 11–18.

Zlotkin, S. Nutrition in Infants during the Second Six Months of Life. *Canadian Journal of Pediatrics* (1993): 310–17.

Index

fruit juice. *See also* baby foods
  citrus, 132, 197
  and diarrhea, 190
  introducing into diet, 132, 197
  recipes using, 77, 188, 260
  for toddlers, 230
Fruit Juice and Yogourt Yop, 77
Fruit Kebabs, 258

galactose, 18
galactosemia, 26, 90
gastrointestinal problems, 4, 187,
    190–91. *See also* colic; constipa
    tion; diarrhea
  and iron, 108
  role of breast milk in preventing,
    22, 23
glucose, in formulas, 90
gluten intolerance, 143
glycoconjugates, 19, 23
Green Bean Puree, 171
Green Pea Puree, 172
grocery shopping
  with children, 262–64
  and meal planning, 67–69

halibut oil, 59
HIV, 26
hospitals, Baby-Friendly, 39–40
hunger mechanism, development of,
    9–10
hydrolysate formulas, 91, 189,
    196–97, 230

immunoglobulins, in breast milk, 23
immunological system. *See* infections
infants. *See also* cereals, infant
  food choices of, 2
  supplements for, 114 (table) (*see
    also* essential fatty acids;

  minerals; vitamins)
infections. *See also* mastitis
  and food restrictions, 4
  role of breast milk in reducing, 3, 22
intolerance. *See* allergies, food
iron, 106–9, 219
  in breast milk, 20, 107
  in cereals, 140–41, 145 (table)
  food sources of, 69, 109, 219
  in formulas, 88, 107–8, 112
  in other milks, 97, 112
  recommended amounts, 108 (table),
    114–15 (tables)
  side effects of, 108
  stores in body, 106–7
  supplements, 93, 107–9, 112, 143
  toxicity of, 114
iron deficiency. *See* anaemia

jaundice, in newborns, 33–34, 42
Jellied Fruit Dessert, 257

kidneys, and solid foods, 126–27

lactation consultant, 33
lactoferrin, 23
lactose. *See also* allergies, food;
    galactose
  in breast milk, 17, 18, 25
  and colic, 50, 188–89
  in formulas, 88, 90
  and tooth decay, 111
lactose intolerance, 190
lactoserum, 87
La Leche League International, 27, 81
leeks, recipe using, 246
Legume Puree, 175
legumes, 229
  recipes using, 175, 252, 253
lentils, 175, 253

Lentils, Brown Rice, and Vegetables,
253
letdown reflex, 16, 43–44, 57
linoleic acid, 19–20, 88
liver, recipes using, 184, 247
L-methionine, 90
long-chain fatty acids, 19–20

macaroni, 254
magnesium, 220
mastitis, 49
meat. *See also* baby foods
    preparing for toddlers, 229
    recipes using, 182, 184, 244–47
    reducing pollutants from, 59
medications
    caffeine content of, 65 (table)
    use of while breastfeeding, 35, 36, 61
menu planning
    after delivery, 53–54
    and grocery shopping, 67–69
menu plans
    for infants, 129, 133, 134–35
    for mothers, 63–64, 70–76
    for toddlers, 234–40
milk
    compared to solid foods, 124–25
    goat's, 86, 92–93, 97, 98
    introducing into diet, 100 (table)
    recipes using, 77, 185, 241, 248,
        249, 259
    skim, 4, 98–99
    supplementing with solid foods, 144
    supplements required for, 112
    transition, 17
milk, cow's, 3, 86, 97–98
    allergies to, 91–92, 196–97, 230
    compared to breast milk, 18, 20
    and constipation, 191
    introducing into diet, 97–98, 197

nutrients in, 20, 97
    protein in, 18, 24, 97
milk, evaporated, 86
    diluting, 93, 101 (table)
    as formula replacement, 92–93
milk-based infant formulas, 87–89
milk fever, 120
milk products
    and allergies, 50–51, 61, 189, 190
    eliminating from diet, 62, 64
    introducing into diet, 136
    substitutes for (*see* formulas, infant;
        soy beverages)
    for toddlers, 230
minerals. *See also specific minerals*
    in breast milk, 20–21, 25
    foods rich in, 68
    in formulas, 88, 91
    supplements, 62, 115 (table)
Mystery Liver and Beef Loaf, 247

niacin. *See* vitamin B3
nipples
    conditioning, 39
    inverted, 27–28
    sore, 47–48
nutrition. *See specific nutrients*

obesity in children, 3–4, 199–201
oligosaccharides, 23
omega fatty acids, 19–20, 205
organic foods, 60
otitis. *See* ear infections
overfeeding
    and colic, 50, 188
    and spitting up, 187

pain medication. *See* medications
pasta, 254
PCBs